Introductory Guide to NHS Finance in the UK

Contents

Foreword

Welcome to the ninth edition of the HFMA's *Introductory Guide to NHS Finance in the UK*. This version retains the same format as its 2006 predecessor but has been extensively updated to take account of the many developments and challenges that the NHS has faced over the past two years. In particular it reflects key changes to the financial regime since the last version including the end of the RAB regime for NHS trusts, the replacement of brokerage with a more transparent system of repayable, interest bearing loans and the introduction of a new capital regime in England. Key policy areas, such as payment by results and practice based commissioning, are also fully updated, while in terms of structure, the guide reflects the post-*Commissioning a patient-led NHS* configuration.

The chapters have been written by practitioners who have a working knowledge of finance in the NHS and wherever possible they have included practical examples to help explain often complicated financing rules and regulations. Although the guide focuses on the policy and organisational framework for the NHS in England, it includes chapters that highlight the key differences in Scotland, Wales and Northern Ireland.

The *Introductory Guide* is designed to give readers a solid grounding in – and practical understanding of – all key aspects of NHS finance. It also provides some contextual background that helps explain why the NHS is as it is today and gets to grips with the jargon that has built up around NHS finance over the years.

As well as appealing to its traditional audience, which ranges from executive and non-executive directors to accounts assistants and budget holders, this guide is an excellent accompaniment for anyone embarking on the HFMA's e-learning programme.

As always, the *Guide* is written in simple, straightforward and accessible language and includes extensive references at the end of each chapter so that readers can delve into subjects in more detail if they wish. There is also a handy glossary and a list of abbreviations.

The HFMA is committed to improving the awareness of finance and financial management across the NHS and beyond and we trust that this *Guide* will further this objective. Above all we hope that you will find it useful, informative and that it is a 'good read'.

Keith Wood,
Chair, HFMA Financial Management and Research Committee

Acknowledgements

The production of the *Introductory Guide to NHS Finance in the UK* involves a large number of people who contribute their time and expertise to the production of one or more chapters. It has been prepared primarily by members of the HFMA's Financial Management and Research Committee. The main contributors to this edition – either as chapter authors or 'quality assurors' – are:

Tony Bettridge
Phil Bradley
Steve Brown
Andy Colledge
Nigel Davies
Steve Elliot
Clive Field
Vicky Flanagan
Nick Gerrard
Anna Green
Andy Goor
Emma Knowles
Colin Langford
Carla Moody
Janet Perry
Sheenagh Powell
Chris Reid
Neil Robson
Karen Ross
Dave Self
Pat Shroff
Karl Simkins
Michael Vicars
Robert White
Keith Wood
Janet Wood
Alex Young

Editorial work was undertaken by Steve Brown and Anna Green.

The HFMA is grateful for the contributions of all those listed above, who give their time free of charge, often in addition to the long hours routinely worked by most senior members of NHS finance.

1. Introduction

Purpose

For twenty years, the *Introductory Guide to NHS Finance* has been providing easy to read, accessible guidance on the unique workings and language of NHS finance to practitioners and observers. The guide is produced by The Healthcare Financial Management Association (HFMA), a charity established to support those working within the NHS finance function. By improving financial literacy both within and outside NHS finance, the HFMA hopes it can inform and improve the debate on healthcare financial issues.

The guide is designed to provide a wide variety of readers with a single, self-contained source of advice and guidance that will also help demystify the mass of jargon that has developed. There are many aspects of NHS finance that are unique to the service. Even the most experienced and able staff transferring from the private sector can find themselves bewildered or bemused by unfamiliar arrangements, targets, language and acronyms, which fellow 'NHS seasoned' practitioners will quote intuitively. The guide aims to provide advice to all levels of finance staff from finance directors (who often use the guide as an aide memoir to more recent changes) to accounts assistants, non-executive and executive directors (who may not be finance specialists but still have shared corporate responsibility for understanding and managing the financial position), budget holders and service managers, and people who need an understanding of NHS finance for academic study purposes. The list is not exhaustive – the guide has been spotted on bookshelves and coffee tables in the least likely of locations.

Over the years the guide has grown in size to the substantial document that you now hold – however, it remains as its title suggests an introductory guide; a basic description of the structures and processes of the varying health economies of England, Northern Ireland, Scotland and Wales.

This version of the *Introductory Guide* is produced in the aftermath of a period of substantial structural change within the NHS. Change and refinements to the finance regime will continue. However, essentially it seems that the NHS is entering a period of evolution, rather than revolution, with consolidation the key.

Contents

To make it easier to get to grips with a particular aspect of NHS finance, each chapter of the guide treats its topic in a largely self-contained way. Cross-references are included where they are helpful and sources of further advice and technical guidance are listed at the end of each chapter.

The greater part of the guide concentrates on the financial arrangements for the NHS in England. There are also chapters highlighting key differences in Northern Ireland, Scotland and Wales. Separate sister introductory guides covering NHS finance in Scotland and in foundation trusts have also been produced and one is planned for Wales.

The guide ends with a data file of key facts and figures and a glossary of terms and abbreviations. Data for the tables has been obtained primarily from the Department of Health's

Departmental Report 2007 and sets out the most up-to-date information available at the time of publication. Website references are included so that readers can access updated information as it is released.

The Authors

The Introductory Guide is produced by the HFMA's Financial Management and Research Committee. Members of the committee are finance staff from across the NHS who give up their time voluntarily to help improve financial management standards and control in the NHS, and to promote an understanding of NHS finance both inside and outside the finance department.

The Introductory Guide as a Training Tool

The copyright for the guide is held exclusively by the HFMA. Further copies can be obtained directly from the HFMA or via the website at www.hfma.org.uk

The guide is designed as both a reference source and a training tool. Although normal copyright restrictions apply, in recognition of the guide's training role, the HFMA allows the reproduction of diagrams, statistics and quotes.

2. Background to the NHS

Introduction

The NHS is a large and complex organisation employing over a million staff. Since its formation in 1948, the NHS has been reorganised, reformed and modernised. To an observer, changes can appear in many cases to be cyclical so understanding a little more about the history of the NHS and why it has got to where it is today is useful and instructive. It is also invaluable for individual members of staff – both those who spend their entire careers working within the NHS and those that bring in skills from other industries and graft on NHS experience.

This chapter aims to provide a brief outline history of key policy developments in the NHS over the last 10 years or so – it follows a broadly chronological approach so that readers can see how and why the NHS has grown in the way it has. The chapter then goes on to highlight some of the main underlying financial issues and recent/upcoming developments that are of particular relevance to NHS finance.

NHS Finance in Context – Key Policy Developments

The internal market

Perhaps the most significant change in health economics was the decision taken initially in the late 1980s to reconfigure the NHS along purchaser and provider lines. This required the NHS to operate a 'quasi-market', known as the internal market. The key feature of this approach was the separation of the provision of hospital/community services from the commissioning or purchasing function – the so-called 'purchaser/provider split'. Hospitals were encouraged to apply for self-governing trust status, creating organisations quite separate from the health authorities from which they were devolved. To achieve trust status, and formally separate from the health authorities, provider organisations had to follow an application process that assessed viability and robustness – this has parallels with the current foundation trust application process.

There was also an optional scheme to give general practitioners (GPs) the ability to hold budgets for the purchase of hospital services for their patients (GP fund holding). At the same time, trusts were encouraged to invest in and develop services and to compete with each other to win patient service contracts with purchasers.

There were a number of criticisms associated with the internal market. In particular, competition between providers led to winners and losers, which in turn led to overall increases in administration costs to the NHS as 'losing' organisations had to be sustained to ensure that other services could be maintained.

In 1997, a change of government resulted in plans to scrap the internal market.

The New NHS – Modern, Dependable

The current reform of the NHS started with the issue of the 1997 White Paper *The New NHS – Modern, Dependable*. These proposals became law with the *1999 Health Act* and the focus shifted away from a purchaser provider split to a collaborative model, where NHS organisations worked together and with local authorities to refocus healthcare on the patient. By removing the competitive nature of the internal market the changes in policy sought to ensure the seamless delivery of services.

Key changes were an end to GP fund holding and the introduction of new organisations for primary care. Primary care organisations (either groups or trusts) were formed from groups of local GP practices, or 'natural communities'. Boundaries were encouraged to coincide where possible with local authority borders to simplify the integration of health and social care. In their initial stages these groups were sub-committees of health authorities, used to inform the commissioning process. As these new organisations found their feet, they were able to apply for trust status, creating bodies independent from the health authority and managing increasingly significant portions of former health authority budgets.

The *1999 Health Act* also established the Commission for Health Improvement (to be succeeded by the Commission for Healthcare Audit and Inspection – CHAI – and now known as the Healthcare Commission) and the National Institute for Health and Clinical Excellence (NICE) as special health authorities.

There was also a renewed emphasis on cutting management costs, a challenging objective given the increase in the number of NHS organisations, and greater involvement of management at a local level. Although the cap on management costs has since been lifted, pressures to contain these costs remain. The shared services initiative was, at least to an extent, an attempt to mitigate this pressure by reducing the cost of providing support services. National shared service centre pilots were established and there are now three shared business services centres in Leeds, Bristol and Hampshire run as a joint venture between the Department of Health and Xansa. Alongside these national centres, there are many other shared service arrangements within local health communities that aim to provide efficient, cost-effective services.

The purchaser/provider split created by the internal market has been retained. Initially health authorities remained and continued to purchase healthcare using service and financial framework agreements (SaFFs). These health authorities have now been abolished but the division between commissioning and provision continues with primary care trusts (PCTs) taking over responsibility for commissioning hospital services. PCTs also have a provider role for community services.

The 1997 White Paper also heralded a move towards longer planning time frames, promising the replacement of annual contract negotiations with three-year resource announcements. This has been delivered successfully at a Department of Health level, with the budget announcement now including levels of funding for the next three years (the 2002 Budget in fact provided a five-year settlement). Three-year allocations to PCTs were introduced from 2003/04 to help improve the service planning process. In 2003/04 most organisations committed to three-year local development plans (LDPs), although the level of detail incorporated in years two and three was limited.

The NHS is now encouraged to form partnerships with both private and public sector partners, including local authority social services. The *1999 Health Act* (now superseded by the *NHS Act*

2006) broadened the scope for pooling of health and social services budgets. Partnership working with the private sector was formalised in a so-called 'concordat' agreement, which highlighted scope for partnerships in elective, critical and intermediate care. New independently run diagnosis and treatment centres or independent sector treatment centres (ISTCs) were established so extending the role of the private sector in the NHS.

The NHS Plan

In July 2000 the NHS Plan was presented to Parliament. The plan consisted of a vision of the NHS first outlined in the 1997 White Paper – modernised, structurally reformed, efficient and properly funded. Much of the document is dedicated to identifying new targets and milestones on wide ranging issues (from waiting lists to implementation of electronic patient records) and measures that need to be taken to facilitate the achievement of those targets.

The Health Act 2002

In April 2002 a further tranche of changes came into effect. At the end of March 2002, the 95 health authorities in England were abolished and replaced by 28 strategic health authorities (SHAs). At the same time the eight regional offices were dissolved and replaced by four directorates of health and social care (DHSCs).[1] The changes, first outlined in April 2001 in the policy paper Shifting the Balance of Power, were designed to transfer management resource and control closer to the locality, and hence to the patient.

The establishment of PCTs was also completed in 2002 – a key change here was the fact that PCTs were allowed to directly provide services other than those traditionally provided by GPs. This prompted a growth in GPs with special interests and in services provided in the community by PCTs where previously they had been provided in an acute hospital setting.

Many of the monitoring and planning processes were devolved from the old regional offices to the new SHAs, while commissioning functions were transferred to PCTs. Individual chapters in this guide look at the current state of affairs for each type of organisation.

The structure that was introduced in 2002 for the NHS in England is shown over the page.

Comprehensive spending reviews and budgets

The government has committed to increasing NHS funding to a level that would bring the UK's health spending in line with the average for the rest of Europe. The first step toward this target was taken in the 2000 budget, with a further significant increase in 2001. However, it was the 2002 budget that gave the first indication of the substantial and long-term increases required if that promise was to be delivered (or exceeded). Funding for these increases was achieved by the introduction of employer and employee national insurance surcharges at a rate of 1%, and from the release of funds from other sources, enabled by the government's comprehensive

---

[1] DHSCs were dissolved in 2003.

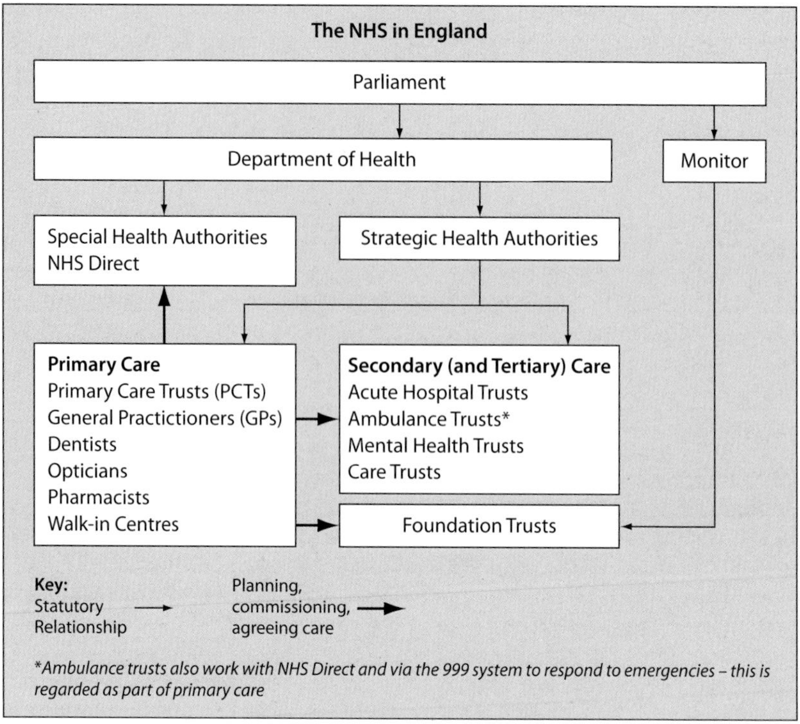
The NHS in England
Parliament
Department of Health
Monitor
Special Health Authorities
NHS Direct
Strategic Health Authorities
Primary Care
Primary Care Trusts (PCTs)
General Practictioners (GPs)
Dentists
Opticians
Pharmacists
Walk-in Centres
Secondary (and Tertiary) Care
Acute Hospital Trusts
Ambulance Trusts*
Mental Health Trusts
Care Trusts
Foundation Trusts
Key:
Statutory Relationship
Planning, commissioning, agreeing care
*Ambulance trusts also work with NHS Direct and via the 999 system to respond to emergencies – this is regarded as part of primary care

spending review (CSR). The three-year CSR process is designed to assess critically the spending of government departments in the light of changing government priorities.

Successive budgets have maintained the commitment to longer-term budgeting. The most recent CSR process resulted in funding announcements in October 2007, covering the three year period from 2008/09. The increases over this period are more modest than for the preceding period, averaging 4% growth in real terms, compared with 7.5% for the previous CSR period.

Payment by results

A key element of the government's modernisation plans is reforming the financial framework and the way funding flows around the NHS. The proposal for bringing about this change was set out in *Delivering the NHS Plan* and involves the introduction of a system of payment by results (PbR). This is intended to ensure that money will flow with patients as:

- PCTs commission from a plurality of providers on the basis of a standard national tariff, which reflects the complexities of the cases commissioned (the 'casemix')
- Instead of block contracts, hospitals (and other providers) are paid for the actual activity they undertake.

The main driver behind this initiative is patient choice – by introducing standard tariffs, the need for local negotiation on price is removed and instead the focus is on quality and responsiveness, the things that are important to the patient. The combination of patient choice and PbR is expected to drive an increase in healthcare capacity and deliver shorter patient waiting times.

Both patient choice and the new financial framework have been phased in over a period of years. Key milestones in the development of patient choice have included the need to provide patients waiting for elective surgery for over six months the choice of an alternative provider by summer 2004; by the end of December 2005, patients requiring a routine elective referral had to be offered a choice of four or five providers (including one private sector provider) at the point of referral (i.e. at their GP). From April 2008, choice has been extended still further with patients effectively having a 'free choice' in relation to hospital-based services.

The first steps to introduce the new financial framework were taken in the 2003/04 contracting process. Cost and volume contracts were required in six surgical specialties and the new tariff was introduced for growth activity in 15 surgical procedures. The scope has been extended progressively over the years that have followed. Most secondary sector acute activity is now commissioned on the basis of tariff, although notably ambulance and mental health trusts are not yet covered.

PbR is undoubtedly one of the key challenges for finance in the NHS – as the project rolls out and commissioning arrangements are changed in response to patient choice, provider capacity and service quality, the requirement for robust financial systems to underpin PbR is critical. Chapter 13 looks in detail at PbR.

Commissioning a Patient-led NHS (CPLNHS)

In December 2005 a consultation process for the reconfiguration of SHAs, PCTs and ambulance trusts was launched by the Department of Health. Its implementation has resulted in a significant reduction in their numbers. The aim is that the reconfiguration of organisations will reduce management overheads and generate cost savings that can be re-invested in the provision of healthcare.

The reduction in PCT numbers is consistent with the simplification of the commissioning process inherent in the patient choice and PbR initiatives. Increasingly patients will be able to select their preferred healthcare provider, thereby refocusing the commissioning role on assessing overall supply levels, negotiating provider standards, and managing demand.

Implementation of CPLNHS resulted in a reduction in the number of SHAs from 28 to 10. The structure of SHAs is based on the assumption that, by reflecting the geographical span of the government offices for the regions, working with other public sector partners will be easier – chapter 5 looks more closely at SHAs.

Ambulance trust merger was designed to achieve purchasing and management economies of scale and to allow them to develop greater resilience than was possible with smaller scale operations. The aim was for all ambulance trusts to be coterminous with SHAs. This has almost been achieved – following the merger of Staffordshire Ambulance Service with West Midlands Ambulance Service NHS Trust in October 2007, only the Avon, Gloucester and Wiltshire ambulance service does not match SHA boundaries.

Underlying Financial Issues

Although government policy on the NHS changes constantly, many features have remained unchanged since its inception in 1948 – for example:

- The principle of the service remaining free at the point of delivery
- The fact that the NHS is funded through taxation – the Wanless report, published in April 2002, concluded that funding the NHS through taxation is both fair and efficient. Although less formally reviewed in 2007 the government re-committed itself this principle in the run-up to the CSR
- The need to manage within overall resource limits determined by the government each year
- The need to match finite resources to what is essentially infinite demand for health services
- The expectation that continued efficiency savings can be made, often as a result of structural or technological advances
- Intense public and media interest in, and scrutiny of, the NHS.

New or Changing Financial Issues

Although many of the fundamental principles that underpin the NHS remain the same, recent structural and policy developments will continue to have an impact. This section summarises those changes and challenges that are likely to affect finance in the NHS over the months and years to come:

- The CSR 2007. The CSR suggests a significant reduction in the real rate of funding growth in the NHS from about 7.5% per annum (for the three year period to 2007/08) to just under 4.0%. In addition the CSR announced the expectation that trusts will deliver 3% efficiency savings in each of the three years of the review period. The reduction in the rate of funding growth in a period of population growth and ageing will present significant challenges to NHS organisations (see chapter 3)
- Practice based commissioning. PCTs are required to devolve 'indicative' commissioning budgets to GP practices as a means of bringing greater accountability and control to commissioned healthcare expenditure. Unlike GP fund holding, which was a feature of the original purchaser/provider split of the 1990s, commissioning extends to emergency services as well elective activity. PCTs are required to develop processes to devolve budgets and incentivise effective budgetary management by GPs (see chapter 11 for more on commissioning)
- The growth in numbers of NHS foundation trusts (FTs) in line with the government's expectation that all acute and mental health activity will be provided by foundation organisations by around 2011 (see chapter 8 for more about FTs)

- The effective delivery of corporate and clinical governance targets. Structural changes within the NHS, combined with measures to curb management costs have placed great pressure on NHS financial resources. The Healthcare Commission's role in testing the way in which these resources are used provides further challenges
- Clinical negligence – the costs of medical litigation continue to rise
- *Agenda for Change* – to simplify pay arrangements and in response to a growing number of equal pay claims, the NHS modernised its pay structures. The basic principle of *Agenda for Change* is that all posts can be assessed against a single set of criteria, and then against a single pay scale. The evaluation of so many diverse jobs represented a huge challenge to organisations and a significant financial risk. Although implemented in October 2005, many claims and disputes remain unresolved either nationally or locally, which means there is a risk of incurring significant additional costs
- Revised GP contracts. Allied to changes taking place for other professions under *Agenda for Change*, GPs have revised terms of employment (the so-called GMS2 or nGMS). This includes the ability of GPs to withdraw from providing out of hours services. Across the country a variety of models have been adopted to ensure that such services are still available. These involve ambulance trusts, GP co-operatives and private sector providers. More recently, out of hours services have been the subject of criticism following external scrutiny – as a result the right to opt out may be subject to review
- A new consultant contract has been implemented across the UK. Although the contract does not introduce a ban on private work, it does give the NHS first call on consultants' time for a session of four hours before they can undertake private work. The contract resulted in a substantial pay rise for consultants
- Connecting for Health (also known as National Programme for IT or NPfIT). The reform of the NHS includes massive investment in supporting information technology – the ten-year programme is the world's largest IT investment project. Although elements of NPfIT are now in place (including digital radio and chose and book), there are some complex governance issues relating to the sharing of information – for example, the national electronic patient record project. Harnessing the benefits of these changes and planning for the remainder of the Connecting for Health project are proving to be a major challenge
- The Gershon Review and the development of shared service centres. The Gershon review looked at the efficiency of public service administrative functions and set targets for reductions in these 'non-productive' costs. To an extent these can be achieved by reductions in the numbers of healthcare organisations. The drive to reduce finance costs has also re-invigorated a shared service initiative with the Department of Health setting up a joint venture with shared service specialist Xansa. Although the capability of the shared service centres is limited to financial services and payroll, the impact of Gershon is likely over time to lead to the inclusion of other administrative functions such as human resources and information and communications technology support
- The Darzi Review. In July 2007, the government asked health minister Lord Darzi to carry out a wide ranging review of the NHS. An interim report was issued in October 2007 and recommended a number of changes to the provision of healthcare services within the primary/secondary sector, including the development of 'poly-clinics' where appropriate – a primary healthcare equivalent of the 'one-stop shop'. The final report is expected in June 2008 – in time for the 60th anniversary of the NHS on 5th July 2008.

References and Further Reading

The New NHS: Modern, Dependable (1997 White Paper): www.archive.official-documents.co.uk/document/doh/newnhs/forward.htm

Healthcare Commission: www.healthcarecommission.org.uk

NICE: www.nice.org.uk

NHS Shared Business Services: www.sbs.nhs.uk/

HM Treasury – Comprehensive Spending Reviews and Budget Reports: www.hm-treasury.gov.uk

NHS Act 2006: www.opsi.gov.uk/Acts/acts2006/pdf/ukpga_20060041_en.pdf

Management Costs, Department of Health: www.dh.gov.uk/en/Managingyourorganisation/Financeandplanning/NHSmanagementcosts/DH_4000338

The NHS Plan: a plan for investment, a plan for reform, Department of Health, 2000: www.dh.gov.uk/en/Publicationsandstatistics/Publications/PublicationsPolicyAndGuidance/DH_4002960

Shifting the Balance of Power – see the publications, policy and guidance pages of the Department of Health's website: www.dh.gov.uk/PublicationsAndStatistics/Publications/PublicationsPolicyAndGuidance/fs/en

Creating a Patient-led NHS: Delivering the NHS Improvement Plan: www.dh.gov.uk/en/Publicationsandstatistics/Publications/PublicationsPolicyAndGuidance/DH_4106506

Payment by Results: www.dh.gov.uk/PolicyAndGuidance/OrganisationPolicy/FinanceAndPlanning/NHSFinancialReforms/fs/en

Commissioning a Patient-led NHS, Department of Health, 2005: www.dh.gov.uk/en/Publicationsandstatistics/Publications/PublicationsPolicyAndGuidance/DH_4116716

Patient Choice: www.dh.gov.uk/PolicyAndGuidance/PatientChoice/fs/en

The Wanless Report: www.hm-treasury.gov.uk/consultations_and_legislation/wanless/consult_wanless_final.cfm

Practice Based Commissioning: www.dh.gov.uk/en/Managingyourorganisation/Commissioning/Practice-basedcommissioning/index.htm

NHS Foundation Trusts: www.dh.gov.uk/en/Healthcare/Secondarycare/NHSfoundationtrust/index.htm

Monitor (the Independent Regulator of NHS Foundation Trusts): www.monitor-nhsft.gov.uk

Agenda for Change: www.dh.gov.uk/PolicyAndGuidance/HumanResourcesAndTraining/ModernisingPay/AgendaForChange/fs/en

Consultant contract: www.dh.gov.uk/en/Managingyourorganisation/Humanresourcesandtraining/Modernisingpay/Consultantcontract/index.htm

Primary care contracting (including the GP contract): www.dh.gov.uk/en/Healthcare/Primarycare/Primarycarecontracting/index.htm

NHS Connecting for Health: www.connectingforhealth.nhs.uk/

Releasing Resources for the Frontline: Independent Review of Public Sector Efficiency (the Gershon Review): www.hm-treasury.gov.uk/spending_review/spend_sr04/associated_documents/spending_sr04_efficiency.cfm

Our NHS Our Future: NHS Next Stage Review (the Darzi review), 2007: www.dh.gov.uk/en/Publicationsandstatistics/Publications/PublicationsPolicyAndGuidance/DH_079077

3. Funding the NHS

Introduction

Health spending has always been a topic of political and public interest and in the last decade spending on health has increased at a significantly higher rate than many other government spending programmes. This chapter looks at how resources are allocated nationally for health, and then how they are divided up amongst the different areas of health spending.

To give an idea of the scale of spending on health, the World Health Organisation's 2007 report shows that in the UK in 2004 health expenditure as a percentage of gross domestic product (GDP – the total value of goods and services produced by the nation) had reached 8.1% compared with 7.6% in 2001. By way of comparison, over the same period health expenditure as a percentage of GDP in Australia rose from 8.9% to 9.6%, in Sweden from 8.7% to 9.1% and in the USA from 13.9% to 15.4%. It is also interesting to note that, in 2004, over 86% of total spending on health in the UK came from general government expenditure (i.e. from the public purse).

The Role of the Treasury

The responsibility for allocating and managing the finances of national government lies with the Chancellor of the Exchequer, who heads up the Treasury. The Treasury also draws up public service agreements (PSAs), which define the key improvements that the public can expect to see from these resources.

To promote better planning of public spending the Treasury has in recent years undertaken periodic spending reviews to set firm and fixed three-year 'departmental expenditure limits' for each government department. In fact following on from the first comprehensive spending review in 1998, spending reviews have taken place every two years, meaning there is one year of overlap. Each subsequent spending review confirms, or occasionally revises the figures for the first year and then announces new figures for the following two years. A special case was made for health in 2002 when a five-year settlement was announced. This followed on from a major review of funding needs for the UK health system undertaken by former NatWest chief executive Derek Wanless (see later in this chapter) and was intended to put the NHS on a sustainable, long-term financial footing.

There have been five spending reviews since they were first introduced in 1998. These spending reviews are reviewed twice a year – in the budget and the pre-budget report, where the government sets out how it will finance its spending commitments and makes any necessary or technical adjustments to its spending plans. The most recent spending review took place in October 2007 and set out departmental spending plans for the three years from 2008/09 to 2010/2011.

The 2007 review is the first **comprehensive** spending review (CSR) since 1998 and takes a more 'bottom up' approach to spending rather than the incremental method used for the reviews of 2000, 2002 and 2004.

Public expenditure falls into one of two categories:

- Departmental expenditure limit (DEL) spending, which is planned and controlled on a three year basis in spending reviews
- Annually managed expenditure (AME), which is expenditure that cannot reasonably be subject to firm, multi-year limits in the same way as DEL. Examples of such spending would be social security benefits which are subject to fluctuation depending on the level of unemployment.

Together, DEL plus AME sum to total managed expenditure (TME).

A key issue for any government is the relative level of public spending compared to national wealth. The following graph shows how the percentage of public spending compared to GDP has fluctuated over the years. Relative to GDP, spending since 1970/71 has varied from a maximum of 49.9% in 1975/76 to a minimum of 37.4% in 1999/00. The predicted position for 2007/08 is 42.3% of GDP spent in the public sector.

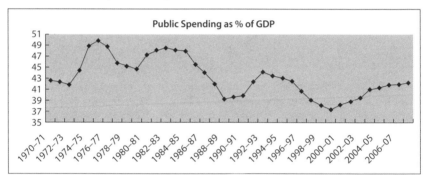

The Treasury's 2007 CSR resulted in the following pattern of allocations to government departments:

Total Department Expenditure Limits (resource and net capital)

	2007/08 £bn	2008/09 £bn	2009/10 £bn	2010/11 £bn
NHS (England)	90.4	96.4	102.9	109.8
Other Health	1.4	1.5	1.5	1.6
Children, Schools and Families	50.1	52.9	55.6	59.5
Local Government	34.2	36.1	37.5	38.6
Defence	32.6	34.1	35.4	36.9
Home Office, Justice and Law	19.4	20.1	20.3	20.7
Innovation, Universities and Skills	18.0	18.7	19.7	20.8
Transport	12.6	13.4	13.8	14.5
Scotland	26.1	27.2	28.4	29.8
Wales	13.6	14.3	15.0	15.8
Northern Ireland	9.6	10.0	10.4	10.8
Other Departments and Reserve	36.6	36.4	37.0	38.1
TOTAL DEL	**344.6**	**361.1**	**377.5**	**396.9**

Source: 2007 Pre-budget Report and CSR, HM Treasury.

Of the DELs, the amount allocated to the NHS is greater than any other spending area. However, growth in health funding from 2008 is lower than that experienced in the previous 5 years (i.e. the 5 years ending 2007/08) when there was annual real terms growth of 7%. In fact, the 2007 CSR marks a return to more traditional levels of resource growth – 3.9% real terms average annual growth. The drop is in part explained by the fact that expenditure levels are now closer to European levels of investment in health services.

Funding for health services in other UK nations is included in the separate Scottish, Welsh and Northern Ireland block grants. Any changes in planned spending in the NHS in England are matched by relative increases within these block grants. However, the individual administrations may spend less or more than these amounts on health services depending on their own priorities.

Adequacy of Funding and Wanless

The adequacy of NHS funding has been the subject of heated political debate since the NHS was formed in 1948. At that time it was believed that once the initial backlog of ill health had been treated NHS funding levels could reduce. Clearly this has never been the case for a variety of reasons.

In 2001 former chief executive of NatWest Bank, Derek Wanless was commissioned to undertake a review of the funding mechanisms for the NHS and to establish the levels of investment required to meet the objectives of the *NHS Plan* and the government's election manifesto commitments.

Securing Our Future Health: Taking a Long-Term View (the Wanless report) was published in April 2002 and concluded that public funding was a 'fair and efficient' way to provide a comprehensive, high quality service based on need, not the ability to pay. In addition it set out a number of major influences on the resources needed to provide such a service. These included:

- The commitments already made in relation to the improvements expected in the NHS including the *NHS Plan* itself and the various national service frameworks setting standards in key service areas
- Rising patient and public expectations
- Improvements in medical technologies and pharmaceuticals – particularly the potential expansion in genetics
- The demands of an ageing population that is living longer.

The report set out a number of scenarios which made different assumptions about the take-up of services and the extent to which the public assisted or otherwise in their own health improvement. Wanless concluded that, assuming that private health expenditure remained constant at around 1.2% of gross domestic product, total UK health spending would need to rise to between 10.6% and 12.5% of national income in 20 years time. The report anticipated that the growth in manpower required could be managed if 20% of GPs' and junior doctors' work could be carried out by nurse practitioners and 12.5% of nurse workload could shift to healthcare assistants.

At the time of the Wanless report the government was projecting that investment in health would reach 9.4% by 2007/08 – as shown below:

UK Health Spending as a Proportion of GDP						
	Per cent of GDP					
	2002/03	2003/04	2004/05	2005/06	2006/07	2007/08
Total UK health spending	7.7	8.0	8.3	8.7	9.0	9.4
of which						
Gross UK NHS spending	6.6	6.9	7.2	7.5	7.8	8.2
Non-NHS health spending	1.2	1.2	1.2	1.2	1.2	1.2
The figures above include an estimated 1.1% of GDP linked to private healthcare expenditure.						

Source: 2002 Spending Review, HM Treasury.

The government accepted the conclusions of the Wanless report and in its April 2002 budget matched the funding levels that it called for over the next five years.

The Role of the Department of Health

The Department of Health is responsible in England for the NHS, personal social services and the Food Standards Agency. Health and social services in Scotland, Northern Ireland and Wales is the responsibility of devolved administrations (see chapters 18, 19 and 20).

The Treasury allocates DELs for revenue and capital spending. Revenue spending is for day-to-day items such as salaries and running costs, while capital spending is for buying larger items such as buildings and equipment, which have a usable life of over one year.

Spending split

Most of the NHS settlement is spent on hospital, community and family health services (HCFHS) – this includes general medical services (GMS) expenditure through the new GP contract and (since April 2006) general dental services. There are also much smaller budgets for:

- Non-discretionary (i.e. demand-led) family health services (FHS) such as ophthalmic services and dispensing remuneration
- Central health and miscellaneous services (CHMS), covering some centrally administered services including some public health functions and support to the voluntary sector
- The Department's own running costs.

The Department of Health's *Departmental Report 2007* shows that in 2006/07, HCFHS accounted for 96.9% of net NHS expenditure; FHS for 1.2%; CHMS for 1.5% and the Department's running costs for 0.4%.

NHS funding allocated by the Department of Health

The vast majority of NHS funding is channelled into the HCFHS programme with some 80% of overall NHS funding allocated directly by the Department of Health to the commissioners of healthcare – primary care trusts (PCTs). This is looked at in more detail later in this chapter. In line with the three year spending review settlement, the Department has been making three year allocations to assist the service in its medium term planning and investment requirements.

The diagram over the page shows how NHS resources were allocated in 2007/08. It shows that PCTs control over 80% of the total NHS revenue budget.

Centrally funded initiatives, services and special allocations (CFISSA)

In addition to direct allocations to PCTs there are a number of centrally held budgets that are sometimes referred to as CFISSA. CFISSA provides budgets for initiatives where the Department of Health specifically allocates the resources to statutory bodies, education, training and research activities – for example:

- Common services – a range of services and projects managed centrally for the benefit of the NHS, for instance clinical negligence, consultants' distinction awards and the purchase of supra-regionally designated services
- A range of statutory and other bodies funded centrally including the NHS Business Services Authority, the Healthcare Commission and the Information Centre for Health and Social Care
- Modernisation and other special funding – increasingly used by the Department of Health to target policy initiatives and act as agents for change
- Non-medical education and training (NMET) – used to purchase pre- and post-registration education and training for nurses, midwives, or allied health professionals (AHPs) and other staff, mainly from higher education institutions
- Medical and dental education levy (MADEL) – to pay for postgraduate education and training for doctors and dentists. The service increment for teaching (SIFT) levy is also managed by the Department of Health
- Research and development.

Primary Care Trusts

Allocations to PCTs

Recurrent revenue allocations to PCTs cover hospital and community health services (HCHS), GP prescribing (the drugs bill), 'primary medical services' (i.e. general and personal medical services – see chapter 6 for more details) and HIV/AIDS. Resources are allocated to each individual PCT by the Department of Health on the basis of:

- The historic level of recurrent funding
- A minimum distribution of cash resources to account for inflation, cost pressures and a minimal development addition
- An assessment of whether the PCT already receives more or less than its fair share of the resources available through the use of a 'fair shares formula'.

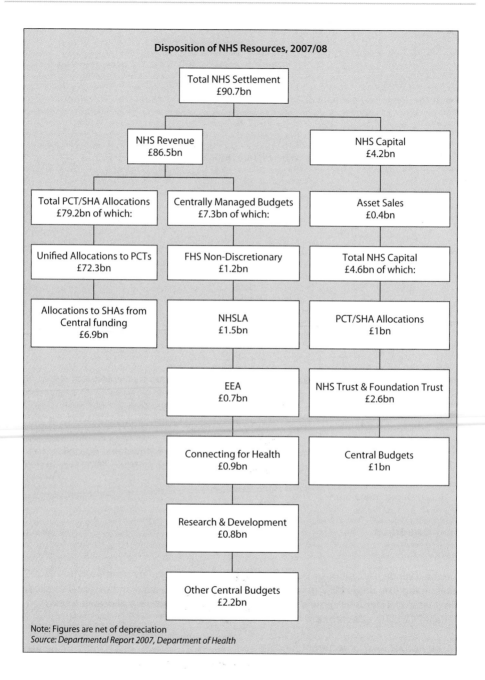

Disposition of NHS Resources, 2007/08

Total NHS Settlement
£90.7bn

NHS Revenue
£86.5bn

NHS Capital
£4.2bn

Total PCT/SHA Allocations
£79.2bn of which:

Centrally Managed Budgets
£7.3bn of which:

Asset Sales
£0.4bn

Unified Allocations to PCTs
£72.3bn

FHS Non-Discretionary
£1.2bn

Total NHS Capital
£4.6bn of which:

Allocations to SHAs from
Central funding
£6.9bn

NHSLA
£1.5bn

PCT/SHA Allocations
£1bn

EEA
£0.7bn

NHS Trust & Foundation Trust
£2.6bn

Connecting for Health
£0.9bn

Central Budgets
£1bn

Research & Development
£0.8bn

Other Central Budgets
£2.2bn

Note: Figures are net of depreciation
Source: Departmental Report 2007, Department of Health

Funding is split between PCTs on the basis of the relative needs of their populations. A 'weighted capitation formula' is used to determine PCTs' target shares of available resources to enable them to commission similar levels of healthcare for populations with similar healthcare needs (see below). The weighted capitation formula is used to set targets which then inform allocations. There is also a 'pace of change policy' that determines actual allocations – this dictates how quickly PCTs are moved from their historic funding level to their target allocation through the distribution of additional funds (see below).

The four elements used to set PCTs' actual allocations are shown below:

Elements of Resource Allocation

(a) **Weighted capitation targets** – set according to the national weighted capitation formula which calculates PCTs' target shares of available resources based on the age distribution of the population, additional need and unavoidable geographical variations in the cost of providing services

(b) **Recurrent baselines** – represent the actual current allocation that PCTs receive. For each allocation year the recurrent baseline is the previous year's actual allocation, plus any adjustments made within the financial year

(c) **Distance from target (DFT)** – this is the difference between (a) and (b) above. If (a) is greater than (b), a PCT is said to be under target. If (a) is smaller than (b), a PCT is said to be over target

(d) **Pace of change policy** – this determines the level of increase which all PCTs get to deliver on national and local priorities and the level of extra resources to under target PCTs to move them closer to their weighted capitation targets. The pace of change policy is decided by ministers for each allocations round.

The weighted capitation formula

Healthcare is for people and the primary determinant of need must be the size of the population for which a PCT is responsible. Population is therefore the basic divisor used to distribute available resources to PCTs. A simple capitation formula would provide the same level of funding for every person in the population (i.e. per capita). However, this would not reflect the fact that the healthcare needs of an individual depend on a range of factors including age and needs. The make up of each PCT's population will also vary as a result. The population for a PCT therefore needs to be 'weighted' (or adjusted) for:

- Age related need – recognising that levels of demand for health services vary according to the age structure of the population
- Additional need – reflecting relative need for healthcare over and above that accounted for by age
- Unavoidable costs – taking account of unavoidable geographical variations in the cost of providing services.

PCTs are responsible for funding the healthcare provision of all patients registered with GPs in practices forming part of the PCT. This means that patients registered with a GP in one PCT area who are resident in a neighbouring or other PCT area remain the responsibility of the PCT with which their GP of registration is associated. PCTs are also responsible for residents within their geographical boundaries who are not registered with a GP. The population for which the PCT is responsible is referred to as the 'relevant population'.

To ensure that the sum of individual PCT populations add up to the total population for England, a 'scaling factor' is applied to give a 'normalised population' for each PCT. This involves scaling GP registered populations to the resident populations from the Office for National Statistics (ONS) Census.

Components of the formula

The weighted capitation formula considers relative need in four separate areas with each component given a relative weighting to reflect the make up of overall health spending. The four components and their relative weights (all rounded) are:

- Hospital and community health services (HCHS) (77.4%)
- Prescribing (13.2%)
- Primary medical services (8.8%)
- HIV/AIDS (0.6%).

A similar approach is followed for each component – each PCT's relevant population is weighted for age related need, additional need and unavoidable cost. Unavoidable costs are assessed using two indices – the market forces factor (MFF) and the emergency ambulance cost adjustment (EACA).

The weighted capitation formula is currently under review and the intention is that a revised formula will be used to make allocations to PCTs from 2009/10 onwards.

A worked example

The following tables show how the formula was used to calculate a PCT's allocation for 2006/07. Please note that roundings are used. Also, the HCHS and HIV/AIDS components include (and the PMS and prescribing components exclude) prisoners and armed forces from the relevant population figures – hence the two different relevant population figures.

To calculate the normalised weighted population of 198,555 a number of steps are taken – first a normalised population is calculated for each of the four components by adjusting the relevant population for age, need and unavoidable costs. These are then multiplied by their relative weightings to produce the final weighted population. The Aids/HIV formula is too complex for simple exposition here but only accounts for 0.59% of the overall figure.

Example Calculation of Weighted Population using 2006/07 figures					
% of formula	77.36%	13.23%	8.81%	0.59%	
	HCHS	Prescribing	Primary medical services	HIV/Aids	TOTAL
Relevant population	238,853	237,811	237,811	238,853	
Age index	0.9780	0.9862	0.9824		
Need index	0.8312	0.8997	0.8794		
MFF	1.0052		0.9896		
EACA	0.9968				
Weighted population	194,537	211,004	203,323		
Normalised weighted population	196,292	212,692	204,958	83,302	198,555
English population					50,476,231
Proportion of English weighted population					0.3934%

This weighted proportion of the England population was then applied to the total resources allocated to PCTs (before the growth monies) to determine a DFT. This PCT was deemed to be below its target allocation by 0.9% or £2m – as shown below:

Calculation of the Target Allocation 2006/07		
	£000	£000
Resources to be allocated – England	58,783,993	
Fair shares based on weighted population		231,235
Small adjustments for growth area and English language difficulty		18
2006/07 target allocation		**231,253**
Baseline allocation 2006/07		229,241
Distance from target (DFT)		−2,012
Percentage under target		−0.9%

This PCT was deemed to be close to or at its target allocation and received an average uplift of growth monies of 8.9% – see below:

Allocation of Growth 2006/07		
	England £000	Example PCT £000
Baseline allocation	58,783,993	229,241
Growth monies	5,207,525	20,290
Revised Allocation	**63,991,518**	**249,531**
% increase	8.9%	8.9%

A PCT deemed to be spending significantly above its 'fair shares' level would have received less than the 8.9% uplift (there is usually a minimum percentage allocation). Conversely PCTs significantly below target would receive a higher than average growth increase.

Resource accounting and budgeting (RAB)

A major development in recent years was the introduction from 2001/02 of resource accounting and budgeting (RAB) for all government departments including health. This means that resource limits rather than cash limits are now allocated. RAB introduced accruals accounting to government, which had previously voted cash limits to spending departments. Accruals accounting – where resources earned and consumed in a year are measured rather than cash received and paid out – is not new to the NHS: it has been managing the hybrid of balancing both cash limits and income/expenditure positions since 1991. However resource allocations rather than cash limits are now made to commissioners. A resource allocation effectively specifies the resources that must be spent within the year for which they are allocated. This prevents commissioners from spending more than their annual income, whilst still being able to meet their cash limits – for example, by managing the timing of payments to suppliers at the year-end.

Flow of funds from PCTs

Once a PCT has been notified of its resource position for the forthcoming year, it will plan how best to improve the health of its patients with that resource level. For example, the pattern of spending for one PCT in 2006/07 was:

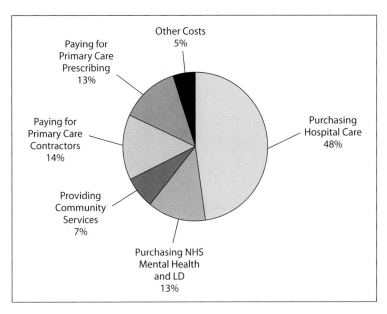

Nearly half of the available resources were used to commission hospital services on behalf of the PCT's patients, whilst over a quarter of costs were spent on primary care contractors or on primary care prescribing.

Resources are allocated differently depending on the area of spend – but the objective remains to improve the health of the local population in the most cost effective manner.

Practice based commissioning

Practice based commissioning (PBC) is part of a suite of measures aimed at making the NHS more patient centred through the use of choice in elective care, and by empowering primary care professionals to commission more specifically on behalf of patients.

Essentially, GPs can elect to take on the commissioning and financial responsibility for large parts of the PCT budget, and to change the traditional ways of providing care. In conjunction with the payment by results (PbR) regime (see chapter 13) any savings made through more effective commissioning are available to invest locally to improve patient care. See chapter 11 for more on commissioning.

Foundation and NHS Trusts

Funding secondary care

The majority of acute, specialist and mental health care in England is provided by either NHS trusts (see chapter 7), or NHS foundation trusts (see chapter 8).

Trusts meet the costs of providing healthcare (salaries are the biggest part of this cost) and then get their income from PCTs via contracts or service level agreements that specify the quantity, quality and price of services to be provided (for activity covered by PbR the unit price is the nationally set tariff). The financial objective of a trust is to balance the cost of provision against the income received. Each patient registered with a GP is allocated to a PCT – which determines who pays for which patient. PCTs pay for treatment undertaken for their patients. Trusts carry out the treatment and get paid. It is in PCTs' interests to ensure that only those patients who need treatment are treated and that they are treated in the most clinically and cost effective way.

Additional sources of funding

Trusts also get a small element of income from other sources such as private patient income, car park receipts and leasing of buildings.

In addition some trusts get substantial sums from the monies earmarked in the CFISSA outlined earlier in this chapter. In particular teaching trusts receive significant sums to offset the cost of teaching and research.

Many trusts also have charitable funds. However these can be used only for the purpose for which they were given (see chapter 17).

Community Services

The majority of community services (for example, district nursing, health visitors and allied health professionals such as speech therapists and community physiotherapists) are currently provided by PCTs. PCTs retain an element of their resource limit for these services but are required to be equitable in their treatment between these services and those they commission – for example, through the use of a common inflationary uplift and savings targets.

Primary Care

The majority of primary care services are provided by independent contractors such as general medical practitioners (GPs) or general dental practitioners (GDPs). Whilst they are an integral part of the NHS, these contractors actually operate as small businesses that contract with the NHS to provide primary care services. The nature of the contract with GPs and GDPs has changed dramatically over the past few years to one that rewards the quality of treatment rather than just a piece-work based approach to treatment.

PCTs reimburse GPs and GDPs according to a nationally negotiated contract – although extensions to the basic contract are negotiated locally. For example, under the new practice based contract to GPs, practices receive a global sum to cover the provision of core services to their registered practice list and additional 'quality' payments for achieving goals set out in the quality and outcomes framework (QOF). However, if practices overachieve this can create a significant cost pressure for PCTs.

The interface between primary and secondary care is not always a clear one and GPs with specialist interests are increasingly playing a significant part in managing patients outside of the traditional hospital routes.

Where does the Money go?

So that it is easier to see how the billions invested in the NHS are spent, an initiative known as programme budgeting was introduced as part of the 2003/04 annual accounts process and has since been developed further. The idea is to capture in a consistent manner the areas in which NHS resources are being spent. Traditionally classifications of spending have been difficult and inconsistent – programme budgeting has introduced a more structured framework to answer the question 'what are you spending our money on?'

The programme budgeting results for 2005/06 are summarised below:

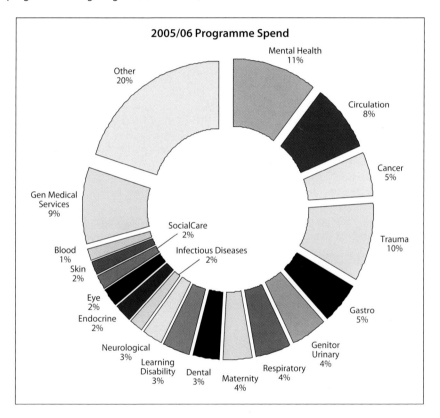

2005/06 Programme Spend

Mental Health 11%
Circulation 8%
Cancer 5%
Trauma 10%
Gastro 5%
Genitor Urinary 4%
Respiratory 4%
Maternity 4%
Dental 3%
Learning Disability 3%
Neurological 3%
Endocrine 2%
Eye 2%
Skin 2%
Blood 1%
Gen Medical Services 9%
Infectious Diseases 2%
SocialCare 2%
Other 20%

Of the programme areas identified, spending on mental health accounts for the largest single proportion of NHS spending at 11% of the total.

References and Further Reading

World Health Statistics 2007, World Health Organisation: www.who.int/whosis/whostat2007/en/index.htmlCom

HM Treasury Spending Reviews: www.hm-treasury.gov.uk/spending_review/spend_index.cfm

2007 Pre-budget Report and Comprehensive Spending Review, HM Treasury:
www.hm-treasury.gov.uk/pbr_csr/report/pbr_csr07_repindex.cfm

Securing Our Future Health: Taking a Long-Term View (the Wanless Report):
www.hm-treasury.gov.uk/consultations_and_legislation/wanless/consult_wanless_final.cfm

2002 Spending Review, HM Treasury:
www.hm-treasury.gov.uk/Spending_Review/spend_sr02/report/spend_sr02_repchap07.cfm

Departmental Report, Department of Health, 2007:
www.dh.gov.uk/en/Publicationsandstatistics/Publications/AnnualReports/DH_074767

NHS Allocations (including the weighted capitation formula), Department of Health:
www.dh.gov.uk/en/Policyandguidance/Organisationpolicy/Financeandplanning/Allocations/
index.htm

Office for National Statistics: www.statistics.gov.uk/

Resource Accounting and Budgeting:
www.hm-treasury.gov.uk./about/resourceaccounts/resourceaccounts_index.cfm

Primary care contracting (including the GP contract):
www.dh.gov.uk/en/Healthcare/Primarycare/Primarycarecontracting/index.htm

National Programme Budget Project, Department of Health: www.dh.gov.uk/en/
Policyandguidance/Organisationpolicy/Financeandplanning/Programmebudgeting/index.htm

4. The Department of Health

Introduction

The Department of Health's aim is to improve the health and well-being of the people of England. It sets policy on all health and social care issues and is also responsible for protecting and promoting the health of the public, ranging from preparations for a flu pandemic to preventing childhood obesity. The Department of Health website, www.dh.gov.uk can be used to obtain further information.

Background

The NHS was established under the *National Health Service Act of 1946*. This and other subsequent Acts of Parliament relating to the NHS set out the duty of the Secretary of State for Health to provide a comprehensive health service in England. Parliament holds the health secretary to account for the functioning of the NHS and the use of resources. Parliamentary accountability and scrutiny require that managers in the NHS provide information to ministers to enable MPs' queries to be answered.

The Secretary of State and Ministers

The Department of Health has six ministers, including the Secretary of State who is a Cabinet minister. The ministers are appointed by the government and are either MPs elected by the public, or members of the House of Lords.

The Secretary of State for Health has overall responsibility for the work of the Department of Health, and works closely with the five junior ministers for health, the permanent secretary, the NHS chief executive and the chief medical officer.

The five junior ministers each have individual responsibility for different aspects of the Department of Health's work. The portfolios attached to the ministerial posts often change, depending on the priorities at that point in time and the personal interests of the individuals. Further information on ministerial portfolios is available on the Department's website.

Parliamentary Scrutiny

The work of the Department of Health is examined by the House of Commons Health Committee on behalf of the House of Commons. This is one of 16 cross-party committees overseeing individual government departments. These committees conduct inquiries and have the power to require the submission of written evidence and documents and to send for and examine witnesses. The members of these committees are appointed by the House.

The Health Committee is appointed by the House of Commons to examine the expenditure, administration and policy of the Department of Health and its associated bodies. Its constitution and powers are set out in *House of Commons Standing Order No. 152*.

The committee has a maximum of eleven members and the quorum for any formal proceedings is three. The members of the committee are appointed by the House and, unless discharged, remain on the committee until the next dissolution of Parliament.

Within its remit, the committee has complete discretion to decide which areas to investigate. The committee's oral evidence sessions are usually open to the public and are often televised. Deliberative meetings are held in private.

When an inquiry ends, a report is agreed by the committee and then published by the Stationery Office. The report is usually published in two volumes: the findings of the committee and the background (memoranda and oral) evidence. The government is committed to responding to such reports within two months of publication.

The committee is supported in its work by a team of staff and by part-time specialists, usually experts in the field of academia or professions relevant to the committee's inquiries.

Two other Parliamentary committees scrutinise the Department of Health and the health service:

- The Public Accounts Committee (PAC)
- The Public Administration Select Committee (PASC).

The PAC keeps a check on all public expenditure including money spent on health. Its remit takes it far wider than a view on the annual accounts with the results of National Audit Office value for money studies usually being considered by the committee. In these instances, the committee takes evidence on health issues, usually questioning the NHS chief executive, before publishing its own report and making recommendations.

The PASC examines the reports of the Parliamentary and Health Service Ombudsmen and considers matters relating to the quality and standards of civil service administration.

Other select committees may from time to time conduct inquiries into government policies that impact upon the Department of Health.

The Department of Health

The Department of Health supports the Secretary of State and ministers in carrying out their ministerial responsibilities for health and social care services.

The Department of Health sets policy on all health and social care issues, including public health matters. The Department is responsible for ensuring provision of a comprehensive health service through the NHS. It also leads on action to address major health and lifestyle problems (such as obesity, smoking, drug misuse, physical inactivity and high blood pressure) that impact on people's health and on future risk of chronic illness and premature death, and to tackle related health inequalities. The Department's work on health protection includes planning for future risks such as pandemic flu and the threat of a bioterrorist attack.

The Department sets national standards, policy and priorities for the NHS and manages the performance of the ten strategic health authorities (SHAs) through the NHS chief executive.

The Department of Health operates through a number of arm's length bodies, such as the Healthcare Commission, the Commission for Social Care Inspection and the National Institute for Health and Clinical Excellence (NICE). These organisations regulate the health and social care system, improve standards, protect public welfare and support local services.

In 2008, the Department is entering the final year of a three-year rationalisation programme to reduce the number of arm's length bodies from 38 to 19. As part of this programme, the government has introduced legislation to create a single health and social care regulator, the Care Quality Commission, to replace the Healthcare Commission, Commission for Social Care Inspection, and Mental Health Act Commission. The expectation is that the new Commission will be established in October 2008 and take over the regulation of health and social care from April 2009.

The Department of Health employs around 2,300 people, with headquarters staff based in Leeds and London. Public health teams are co-located within each of the government offices in the English regions, headed by a Regional Director of Public Health, who is also Director of Public Health in the relevant SHA.

The Department of Health's Role, Aims, and Objectives

The Department of Health has three distinct but inter-related roles:

- The effective national HQ of the NHS
- The lead Department of State for a broad and complex range of governmental activity
- Setting policy on public health, adult social care and a swathe of related topics extending from genetics to international work.

The Department of Health's overall aim is to improve the health and well-being of the people of England, through the resources available, by:

- Developing strategy and direction for the health and social care system
- Providing the legislative framework
- Building capacity and capability
- Setting some standards and ensuring others are met
- Securing and allocating resources, and ensuring that their usage provides value for money
- Ensuring accountability to the public and Parliament.

The Department's medium term targets are defined by its public service agreements (PSAs) with the Treasury. The seven strategic objectives as set out in the Department's *2007/08 Business Plan* are to:

- Improve and protect the health of the people of England – with special attention to the needs of disadvantaged groups and areas

- Enhance the quality and safety of services for patients and users, giving them faster access to services and more choice and control
- Deliver a better experience for patients and users, including those with long term conditions
- Improve the capacity, capability and efficiency of the health and social care systems
- Ensure system reform, service modernisation, IT investment and new staff contracts deliver improved value for money and higher quality
- Improve the service it provides as a Department of State to – and on behalf of – ministers and the public, nationally and internationally
- Become more capable and efficient in the Department, and cement its reputation as an organisation that is both a good place to do business with, and a good place to work.

These objectives translate into a number of deliverables for the NHS. While the emphasis is increasingly moving towards the establishment of locally-appropriate priorities, the context and direction of travel are set out each year in the *NHS Operating Framework*. This is available on the Department's website.

Financial Role of the Department of Health

Negotiations with the Treasury

The Treasury sets the Department of Health's budget every two years for a three-year period, with one year's overlap. This budgetary exercise is known as the spending review and takes place across government. The Department submits evidence to the Treasury setting its proposals for expenditure plans covering the three-year period, in line with the PSA objectives. The plans are discussed and challenged over several months before being finalised. The outcome of the spending review is announced via a White Paper. The most recent spending review was SR2007 which took place in October 2007 and covers the years 2008/09 to 2010/11.

Allocating resources

Once the Treasury has set the overall budget total, the Department determines how this should be allocated. The vast majority of funding is allocated to primary care trusts (PCTs) via the revenue allocations but some is retained in central budgets.

The 2008/09 revenue allocations represent a £74.2 billion investment in the NHS and as a result of the SR2007, every PCT received an above inflation cash increase of 5.5% in its allocation for 2008/09. The Department is currently working on revenue allocations for future years and the aim is to announce the allocations for 2009/10 and 2010/11 in the summer of 2008.

Pace of change policy

Funding is allocated to PCTs on the basis of the relative needs of their populations using the weighted capitation formula (see chapter 3). This formula determines PCTs' target shares of available resources to enable them to commission similar levels of healthcare for populations with similar healthcare needs.

The weighted capitation formula is used to set targets, which then inform allocations. It is the pace of change policy that determines actual allocations, as it dictates how quickly PCTs are brought nearer to target through the distribution of additional funds. The aim of the pace of change policy is to ensure stability of funding for PCTs and allow them to make progress nationally and in local priority areas – it is considered by ministers at each allocations round.

The pace of change policy considers the average growth available from the spending review settlement and commits to ensuring a minimal level of growth for the period. This is likely to be less than the average rate to ensure that there is a balance of funding available to accelerate the move of those PCTs furthest from target, closer to target.

Payment by results – uplifting the tariff

The NHS is continuing to work through a number of financial reforms in support of the overall aim of creating a patient-led NHS. Payment by results (PbR) has allowed the Department to:

- Reimburse NHS trusts and other providers fairly and transparently for the services they deliver, while managing demand and risk
- Reward efficiency and quality in providing services
- Refocus discussion from disputes over costs to the volume and mix of services that meet the population's need and reflect appropriate pathways and packages of care for patients
- Enable patients to choose their hospital and ensure that payment follows the patient.

The tariff has been introduced on a phased basis with 2007/08 being the final year that transitional adjustments were made. For 2007/08 the tariff was based on reference costs for 2004/05. The three year uplift to the tariff that is applied takes account of pay and price pressures, investment in quality improvements, technical changes and other cost pressures as well as making assumptions for efficiency savings between the year of the underpinning costs (for 2007/08 this is 2004/05) and the year the tariff is put into operation.

The principles underpinning the tariff calculation methodology and the more robust quality assurance processes are in response to the 2006 *Lawlor Review* (an independent review of tariff setting). Amongst the recommendations was the suggestion that more time be built into the timetable for quality assuring the tariff.

For 2008/09 the tariff was road tested by the NHS during October/November 2007 and has been updated for 2005/06 activity and cost data.

Monitoring the NHS

Once resources have been allocated, the Department of Health has an on-going responsibility to ensure that the NHS lives within its resources, and that its objectives are achieved as efficiently as possible. PCTs and NHS trusts are accountable to their SHAs for their performance, which includes activity and financial data. On a monthly basis, financial monitoring information is collected from NHS bodies on the financial information management system (FIMS).

NHS foundation trusts are regulated by Monitor, a non-departmental public body that is directly accountable to Parliament. This information is shared between Monitor and the Department of Health so that the Department has a comprehensive understanding of the overall financial position of the NHS.

Arm's Length Bodies

Arm's length bodies (ALBs) are stand alone national organisations sponsored by the Department of Health to undertake executive functions to facilitate the delivery of its agenda. They range in size but tend to have boards, employ staff and publish accounts. Executive agencies are accountable to the Department of Health. Executive non-departmental public bodies are created by primary legislation and are accountable directly to Parliament. Uniquely, the Department of Health has a third class of ALB – special health authorities – that are created by secondary legislation.

In 2004, there was a review of ALBs. This took place as part of the government's commitment to public sector efficiency and minimising bureaucracy, and represents an overhaul of the way in which the Department of Health works with all stakeholders in health and social care.

The review concluded with a commitment to restructure the existing bodies and achieve the following efficiencies:

- Reduce the number of ALBs from 38 to 19 by 2008/09
- Reduce the number of posts by 25% within the ALB sector by 2008/09
- Redistribute £500m to front-line services by 2008, comprising £250m savings on ALB operating costs and £250m from procurement savings
- Move 1,000 posts out of London and the South East, in accordance with the Lyons agenda.

As a result of the restructuring, the ALBs will be more clearly categorised by function as follows:

Regulation and inspection – carrying out inspection of health and social care provision, regulation and specialist functions:

- Commission for Social Care Inspection (to become part of the Care Quality Commission in 2008)
- Mental Health Act Commission (to become part of the Care Quality Commission in 2008)
- Healthcare Commission (to become part of the Care Quality Commission in 2008)
- Council for Healthcare Regulatory Excellence
- General Social Care Council
- Human Fertilisation and Embryology Authority (to become part of the Regulatory Authority for Tissue and Embryos – RATE – in 2009)
- Human Tissue Authority (to become part of RATE in 2009)
- Medicines and Healthcare Products Regulatory Agency
- Monitor

- National Institute for Health and Clinical Excellence (NICE)
- Postgraduate Medical Education and Training.

Central services – providing services for the NHS and social care organisations ranging from the reimbursement of dentists to the supply of blood and transplant organisations:

- NHS Appointments Commission
- NHS Business Services Authority
- Health and Social Care Information Centre
- NHS Blood and Transplant
- NHS Connecting for Health
- NHS Institute for Innovation and Improvement
- NHS Litigation
- NHS Purchasing and Supply Agency
- NHS Professionals (to leave the ALB sector in 2009).

Public welfare and standards – including crucial health protection functions and guidance for the NHS about the cost effectiveness of new treatments:

- Alcohol Education Research Council
- Health Protection Agency
- National Patient Safety Agency
- National Treatment Agency for Substance Misuse.

References and Further Reading

Department of Health website: www.dh.gov.uk

Select Committees: www.parliament.uk/parliamentary_committees/parliamentary_committees16.cfm

House of Commons Standing Orders:
www.publications.parliament.uk/pa/cm200102/cmstords/27501.htm

Office of Public Sector Information (for details of legislation including Health Acts):
www.opsi.gov.uk/legislation/about_legislation.htm

Healthcare Commission: www.healthcarecommission.org.uk

NICE: www.nice.org.uk/

Commission for Social Care Inspection: www.csci.org.uk/

Department of Health Business Plan 2007/08: www.dh.gov.uk/en/Publicationsandstatistics/Publications/PublicationsPolicyAndGuidance/DH_073546

Public services agreements, spending reviews and budgets – details available from the treasury's website: www.hm-treasury.gov.uk/spending_review/spend_index.cfm

The NHS in England: the operating framework for 2008/09, Department of Health, 2007:
www.dh.gov.uk/en/Publicationsandstatistics/Publications/PublicationsPolicyAndGuidance/
DH_081094

NHS allocations:
www.dh.gov.uk/en/Managingyourorganisation/Financeandplanning/Allocations/index.htm

Payment by Results (including details of tariff uplifts etc): www.dh.gov.uk/en/
Managingyourorganisation/Financeandplanning/NHSFinancialReforms/index.htm

Independent Review of the Tariff Setting Process for 2006/07 (the Lawlor review):
www.dh.gov.uk/en/Policyandguidance/Organisationpolicy/Financeandplanning/
NHSFinancialReforms/DH_4137253

Department of Health Arm's Length Bodies:
www.dh.gov.uk/en/Aboutus/OrganisationsthatworkwithDH/Armslengthbodies/index.htm

Care Quality Commission (includes consultation paper), Department of Health, 2007:
www.dh.gov.uk/en/Publicationsandstatistics/Legislation/Actsandbills/HealthandSocialCareBill/
DH_080438

Lyons Review – Independent Review of Public Sector Relocation: www.hm-treasury.gov.uk/
consultations_and_legislation/lyons

5. Strategic Health Authorities

Introduction

Strategic health authorities (SHAs) were introduced in 2002 to manage the local NHS on behalf of the Secretary of State for Health. Originally, there were 28 SHAs but in March 2005, proposals to reduce them in number were included in the consultation paper, *Creating a Patient-Led NHS*. The overall aim of this document was to move from a service that does things to and for its patients to one where the service works with patients to support them with their healthcare needs (i.e. patient led).

Following consultation, the number of SHAs dropped to ten covering the following geographical areas:

- East Midlands
- East of England
- London
- North East
- North West
- South Central
- South East Coast
- South West
- West Midlands
- Yorkshire and the Humber.

The rationale for this restructuring was that 'fewer, more strategic organisations will deliver stronger commissioning functions, leading to improved services for patients and better value for money for the taxpayer'.

Role and Functions

The ten new SHAs came into being in July 2006 and their three main tasks as stated on the Department of Health's website are:

- 'to develop a strategic framework for the health and social care community, which clarifies priorities for action in the short, medium and long term
- to manage and improve performance, establishing performance agreements with all local NHS organisations and working to redesign care processes with a very strong focus on patient pathways
- to build capacity and capability in terms of people, facilities and buildings within and across organisations.'

SHAs are accountable to the Secretary of State through the NHS chief executive. In effect, they are the local headquarters of the NHS and a key link between the Department of Health and the NHS. Although they do not themselves provide services, SHAs do give leadership, coordination and support to NHS organisations across their geographical area and are accountable to their local populations. The performance of SHAs is monitored by the

Department of Health against targets set out in the *NHS Plan* and annual *Operating Frameworks*.

SHAs detailed responsibilities are set out in the Department of Health's annual *Operating Framework*. For 2008/09 this states that 'SHAs will:

- sign off PCT strategic plans and ensure that the priorities reflect local health needs, informed by the 'vital signs[2]' for each PCT
- work in partnership with the Department of Health's team in each region's government office to encourage PCTs to develop new LAAs [local area agreements[3]] that reflect those vital signs for health and social care, against which local performance is in the lower quartile nationally, is poor compared to other PCTs in the cluster, or can be stretched to demonstrate exceptional strong outcomes
- assess and sign off PCT operational plans with a more risk-based approach, looking at 'best', 'worst' and 'likely' scenarios for the year, particularly around hospital activity and care and resource utilisation. Clear, quantifiable contingency measures need to be identified before the commencement of the year to deal with 'worst-case' scenarios
- reconcile plans across health communities, so that the different expectations of money and activity held by commissioners and providers are known to all parties and unrealistic expectations are moderated
- be able to describe the regional position on expenditure, staffing, service improvement and health improvement in the same way as the Department does nationally
- profile expenditure, workforce and cost-reduction programmes on a month-by-month basis and report it through their boards
- performance-manage PCTs and NHS trusts on behalf of the Department
- develop a talent and leadership plan
- locally manage the national assurance system for world-class commissioning, ensuring that their PCTs are held to account for, and supported in, their development towards becoming world-class commissioners[4].'

The *Operating Framework* goes on to say: 'SHAs are expected to play a supporting role, providing visible leadership to local leaders in developing approaches to responding to patients and reforming services, whilst enabling local creativity and innovation. SHAs will only intervene where it is necessary in the interests of patients or the taxpayer. When SHAs do intervene, they will act quickly and decisively.'

Creating a Coherent Strategic Framework

One area where SHAs play a key role is in creating a coherent strategic framework for the development of services across the full range of local NHS organisations. SHAs carry out this role in consultation with stakeholders, balancing the needs and concerns of local people.

---

[2] See chapter 6 for more about 'vital signs'.
[3] See chapter 9 for more on working with local authorities and LAAs.
[4] See chapter 11 for more on commissioning.

Working in this way is an important step towards developing a genuine partnership between the NHS and the people who use it.

As part of creating this strategic framework, SHAs are responsible for ensuring strong and coherent professional leadership and the involvement of all relevant professional groups.

SHAs also develop and support the delivery of cohesive strategies for:

- Capital investment
- Information management
- Workforce development.

Performance Management

Another key function is the performance management of local non foundation NHS trusts and PCTs. SHAs manage their performance across organisational boundaries and networks to secure the best possible improvements for patients. SHAs lead on the creation and development of public health networks and help ensure sound clinical performance and that adequate arrangements for patient safety are in place.

Where conflicts occur between local NHS bodies or problems arise that threaten the delivery of objectives, the SHAs intervene and broker solutions as necessary.

Many targets require NHS bodies to work in close partnership and, recognising this, some SHAs have accountability agreements with local health systems (including social care) that specify the contribution of each partner toward achieving the targets. The accountability agreements are the foundation of the performance management processes between the SHA and NHS bodies. Where in place, accountability agreements cover:

- The achievement of key *NHS Plan* targets (and the annual milestones toward delivery of those targets, such as the gradual reduction of maximum waiting times)
- Improvements to health and health services
- Financial balance
- Organisational development needs.

SHAs have no direct responsibility for foundation trust (FT) performance as FTs report to Monitor – see chapter 8 for details.

During the year SHAs hold NHS trusts and PCTs to account for their performance against *NHS Plan* targets and their use of public funds. The SHA ensures that the service delivery and financial position of these NHS bodies is fairly and accurately reported to government throughout the year. Where it sees that performance differs from plan, the SHA ensures that the NHS locally takes appropriate remedial action.

The financial performance management of NHS bodies covers a number of elements. In particular, SHAs seek to establish how NHS bodies are performing against the various financial and operational targets. Where performance varies from targets, SHAs will look for recovery plans to be in place, and assess the ability of those plans to deliver results. Interim reviews may also be held with chief executives on a quarterly or half-yearly basis through the year.

SHAs also monitor other financial performance indicators, including capital expenditure compared to plan, external financing requirements (performance against the external financing limit or EFL) and how promptly NHS bodies are paying bills (the target is to pay 95% within 30 days) under the *Better Payment Practice Code* (see chapter 14 for more on financial reporting and performance).

Supporting Improvement and Modernisation

SHAs support the improvement of the NHS by working with local PCTs and NHS trusts to enhance the involvement of patients, the public and health and social care professionals in developing services. SHAs also support the implementation of clinical governance programmes to improve the quality and consistency of care through the development of clinical networks across organisations.

SHAs work with the Healthcare Commission, the National Clinical Assessment Authority and other bodies to ensure local PCTs and NHS trusts are equipped to meet national standards and improve performance.

SHA Budgets

SHAs hold budgets for two purposes:

- Their own management – to cover staffing, accommodation, office expenses and some development support for NHS organisations within their boundaries
- Workforce development (see later in this chapter).

Financial Duties

Like all NHS bodies, SHAs are required to meet a number of financial duties and targets. They must:

- Contain expenditure, measured on an accruals basis, within revenue resource limits. The revenue resource limit (RRL) is set by the Department of Health for accrued revenue expenditure. SHAs are required to stay within this limit when measuring gross revenue expenditure less miscellaneous income
- Contain expenditure, measured on an accruals basis, within capital resource limits (CRLs). The CRL is set by the Department of Health for accrued capital expenditure in year. SHAs are required to stay within this limit when measuring gross capital expenditure less the book value of assets disposed of during the year
- Remain within cash limits. There is a combined cash limit for both revenue and capital.

SHAs must also apply the *Better Payment Practice Code* and achieve a public sector payment standard of valid invoices paid within 30 days of the receipt of the invoice. A target is set at the start of the year by the Department of Health for the value and volume of invoices that must be paid within 30 days (currently the target is 95%).

Setting a Strategic Financial Framework

Revenue

In spite of their limited budgets, SHAs have enormous managerial influence, typically overseeing in excess of £5bn spent in their local health communities. Their influence is exercised through their responsibilities for ensuring coherent services and financial plans, robust business processes, and the performance management of NHS bodies in meeting their service targets and financial duties.

For example, although PCTs are required to produce operational plans (previously known as a local delivery plans or LDPs) showing how they will deliver targets and priorities within available resources, it is the SHA that reconciles these plans across the local health community. The SHA then submits them to the Department of Health so that plans for national priorities, activity plans and financial plans can be reviewed before the start of the financial year.

Capital

Between 2003/04 and 2006/07, the Department of Health distributed capital allocations for strategic (discretionary) capital to SHAs, which in turn allocated amounts to NHS trusts and PCTs for approved schemes.

From 2007/08 a new regime was introduced for NHS trusts. This involves each trust being set an annual prudential borrowing limit and is similar to the approach used by FTs (see chapter 16 for more about capital investment). The approach to capital for PCTs is also changing – from 2008/09 PCTs will develop three year rolling capital expenditure plans that SHAs will sign off. Funding for these plans will be provided by the Department of Health subject to affordability within a national total.

SHAs remain responsible for assessing, approving and monitoring individual capital schemes that have been funded from strategic capital, and for managing the CRL. This involves a number of activities:

- Advising NHS bodies on the development of business cases and project management
- Advising on the selection of the most appropriate procurement process (using the private finance initiative, a public-private partnership or public capital – see chapter 10) and the provision of support in the procurement process
- Formally appraising business cases, focusing on value for money and technical robustness
- Performance managing and monitoring the implementation of schemes
- Maintaining a knowledge of future capital investment needs across the SHA area in order to prioritise the deployment of capital funds
- Liaising with the Department of Health's private finance unit and capital branch on scheme development and final approvals for schemes in excess of SHA delegated limits (currently £35m)
- Managing the CRL, EFL and capital cash limit within the SHA area.

SHAs also approve outline and full business cases for investment from PCTs and NHS trusts, where the scheme value is above trusts' delegated limits. These limits are based on trusts' most recent performance ratings (as assessed by the Healthcare Commission) and turnover. The current limits are set out in Department of Health's 2007 guidance – *Delegated limits for capital investment*. In summary:

- SHAs can approve trust and PCT business cases up to £35m
- Best performing trusts have delegated limits of between £8m and £12m
- Medium performing trusts have delegated limits of between £6m and £8m
- Lowest performing trusts have a basic delegated limit of £3m.

Financial Performance

The SHA reports to the Department of Health on the overall financial position of the organisations within its area. Where an organisation flags a deviation from its agreed financial plan, then the SHA may request a financial recovery plan from that organisation that will demonstrate how a return to financial balance will be achieved. The SHA will then closely monitor delivery of the financial recovery plan and meet regularly with the organisation to provide advice and support in relation to the achievement of financial balance.

Since April 2006, SHAs have operated a bank system whereby PCTs are required to hold reserves at levels agreed with the SHA. These reserves are 'banked' with the SHA to ensure that the overall financial control totals can be met. *The Operating Framework 2008/09* makes clear that SHAs 'have the flexibility to determine, within their economies, the level of contingency necessary to ensure delivery of their financial plans, and where this contingency is best held. There will be no central determination of the level of contingency necessary'.

Workforce Development

SHAs are charged with leading on the planning and development of the healthcare workforce and have a key role in delivering government workforce targets.

There are five workforce development key priorities against which SHAs monitor performance:

- Reconfigure the workforce to meet *NHS Improvement Plan* commitments and service delivery targets
- Implement national policies and make the NHS a model employer
- Modernise processes and roles and the development of skill-mix to increase productivity and capacity
- Modernise learning and personal development to facilitate skill-mix and support the skills escalator
- Develop human resources (HR) management capacity and capability – reversing the trend of concentrating on managing immediate operational problems at the expense of considered and strategic HR change management programmes.

In addition, there is a separate workforce development business plan agreement with the postgraduate deanery, which sets down those functions to be undertaken by the deanery on behalf of the SHA. SHAs are responsible for the management of the multi-professional education and training (MPET) budget, which encompasses the non-medical education and training (NMET) levy, the service increment for teaching (SIFT) and the medical and dental education and training levy (MADEL). In addition, funds are managed in relation to specific areas such as workforce modernisation.

Other Functions

SHAs are required to perform a range of other supporting functions. These include:

- Case work in support of parliamentary questions and parliamentary business
- External communications, media handling and public relations
- Complaints, appeals and dispute resolution for delayed discharges, continuing care funding and similar matters
- Ad hoc investigations into serious incidents or providing support/information for national investigations
- Dispute resolution between commissioners and providers.

References and Further Reading

How the Department of Health works – Managing the System:
www.dh.gov.uk/en/Aboutus/HowDHworks/DH_074634

Creating a Patient-Led NHS: Delivering the NHS Improvement Plan:
www.dh.gov.uk/PublicationsAndStatistics/Publications/PublicationsPolicyAndGuidance/fs/en

The NHS Plan: a plan for investment, a plan for reform, Department of Health, 2000:
www.dh.gov.uk/en/Publicationsandstatistics/Publications/PublicationsPolicyAndGuidance/DH_4002960

The Operating Framework for the NHS in England 2008/09: www.dh.gov.uk/en/Publicationsandstatistics/Publications/PublicationsPolicyAndGuidance/DH_081094

Operational Plans 2008/09–2010/11, Department of Health, 2008: www.dh.gov.uk:80/en/Publicationsandstatistics/Publications/PublicationsPolicyAndGuidance/DH_082542

Better Payment Practice Code: www.payontime.co.uk/

Delegated limits for capital investment, Department of Health, 2007: www.dh.gov.uk/en/Publicationsandstatistics/Publications/PublicationsPolicyAndGuidance/DH_080864

6. Primary Care Trusts

Introduction

There are 152 primary care trusts (PCTs) in England responsible for managing around 80% of the national NHS budget. PCTs are key to all aspects of the NHS as they contract for services from independent primary care practitioners such as GPs, dentists, and pharmacists; commission acute and non-acute services from secondary care hospital providers both in the NHS and independent sector; and provide other hospital care (for example, in community hospitals) and out of hospital community services via community nurses and health visitors. A small number of PCTs are also providers of mental health services both in hospitals and in the community.

PCTs are expected to ensure that decisions about local services are made at a local level by those best placed to make them, and that they reflect the needs and views of their population.

Recent Policy Developments

Commissioning a Patient-led NHS

As well as reducing the number of PCTs (from 303 to 152 from October 2006), the Department of Health strategy paper – *Commissioning a Patient-led NHS* – strengthened the focus on the way health services are commissioned. These changes complement the policies of patient choice, payment by results and the government's expectation that all acute and mental health activity will be provided through foundation organisations by around 2011.

PCTs are expected to develop their role to:

- Better engage with local clinicians in the design of services
- Implement the universal roll out of practice based commissioning (PBC)
- Manage performance via contracts with all providers.

Strategic health authorities (SHAs) were also reduced in number (from July 2006 there have been ten) and their role strengthened to support and 'performance manage' commissioning and contracting. See chapter 5 for more about SHAs.

PCTs as service providers

There has been some discussion as to whether or not PCTs should provide as well as commission health services – in its *Operating Framework 2008/09* the Department of Health states that 'during 2008/09 PCTs should review their requirements for community services and use this process to consider all options for models of provision'. The *Framework* goes on to add that whilst this review is going on 'all PCTs should create an internal separation of their operational provider services, and agree service level agreements for these, based on the same business and financial rules as applied to all other providers'.

Primary care and 'care closer to home' services

Our Health, Our Care, Our Say – A New Direction for Community Services (2006)

National policy, reflected in commissioning intentions, is to encourage the transfer of services to the community from hospital settings wherever this improves patient care and is practical. The success of this initiative will, in large part, be determined by the provision of sufficient numbers of trained, highly skilled community-based staff to support clients in their own homes or other community accommodation.

The new GP contract also offers incentives to GPs to develop enhanced services from their practices, which may provide assistance in the long term monitoring and clinical management of patients within the community.

Our NHS Our Future: NHS Next Stage Review – (the Darzi Review, October 2007)

In July 2007, the government asked health minister Lord Darzi to carry out a wide ranging review of the NHS. An interim report was issued in October 2007 and set out his emerging vision to develop a universally world-class NHS delivering effective, higher quality services that are safe, personalised to individual needs, and equally available to all. To achieve this, greater influence must be placed in the hands of local NHS staff and others working in partnership across the service, based on the best available evidence, using the latest technological innovations and responding to the needs of local communities.

The report recommended a number of changes to the provision of healthcare services within the primary/secondary sector, including the development of 'poly-clinics' where appropriate – a primary healthcare equivalent of the 'one-stop shop'. The final report is expected in June 2008 (in time for the 60th anniversary of the NHS on 5th July 2008).

Roles and Functions

PCTs are responsible for the planning and securing of health services and improving the health of their local population. The precise population size covered by each PCT varies, but ranges from around 250,000 to 1,000,000. PCTs must make sure that there are enough GPs to meet the needs of their population and that they are accessible to patients. PCTs must also ensure the provision of other health services including hospitals, dentists, mental healthcare, walk-in centres, NHS Direct, patient transport, population screening, pharmacies and opticians. In addition, they are responsible for integrating health and social care so that the two systems work together for patients.

PCT objectives can be summarised as being to:

- Improve health/reduce inequalities
- Commission health services (see chapter 11 for more on commissioning)
- Develop primary care and community services
- Provide community services
- Promote partnership working (see chapter 9 for more on working with local authorities).

Governance and Accountability

PCTs provide and manage services delivered within the primary and community care sector as well as commission acute and other services. Policy developments have been aimed at putting primary care professionals 'in the driving seat'.

A PCT board can have up to seven non-executives and seven executive directors plus a chair. The executive members must include the chief executive, the finance director, the public health director and the chair of the professional executive committee (PEC).

The PEC provides clinical leadership to the PCT and is made up of a variety of clinical professionals. As far as the PEC's roles and responsibilities are concerned, PCTs are required to follow guidance set out on the Department of Health's March 2007 guide *Primary Care Trust Professional Executive Committees – Fit for the Future*. Although PCTs have the freedom to determine how PECs operate in line with local circumstances, the guiding principles for all PECs are that they need to:

- Be patient focussed and promote the health and well-being of communities as well as addressing health inequalities
- Be drivers of strong clinical leadership and enablers of clinical empowerment
- Be decision making and firmly part of the governance and accountability framework of the PCT
- Reflect a range of clinical professions and the wealth of experience this brings.

Although PECs work differently in different PCTs they are always a key part of the organisation's governance and accountability framework.

PCTs are financially accountable to the Department of Health and the public and are performance managed by their SHA. The mechanisms for delivering and demonstrating this accountability are set out in the table below:

Accountability for	Public	Strategic Health Authority	Local Health Economy
Planning	Board report/service plan	Operational (local delivery) plans	Local strategic partnership (LSP)
Monitoring progress	Board meetings/ reports	Monitoring returns	Local arrangements
Confirming outturn	Annual report and accounts	Annual return forms	

Planning

PCTs are required to produce three-year 'operational plans' (known as local delivery plans – LDPs – before the 2008/09 planning round) outlining how they intend to meet NHS plan targets and local priorities within the three-year financial allocations. The Department's

Operating Framework for the NHS in England 2008/09 and *Operational Plans 2008/09 – 2010/11* make clear that PCTs will be performance managed against an agreed set of indicators referred to as 'vital signs'. These comprise a variety of national and locally agreed indicators and targets. Every year PCTs prepare new three-year rolling plans which involves firming up service developments and resources at the beginning of each year. PCTs must also make an annual service plan available to the public.

Generally, PCTs receive three-year resource allocations. However, for 2008/09 allocations were made to cover just one year – this was to allow additional time for work on revising the allocation formula. Allocations for 2009/10 and 20010/11 (based on the revised formula) are expected in summer 2008. PCTs are also expected to set out a clear medium term 'commissioning strategy' which reflects public health needs and expectations, and a current year 'commissioning prospectus'. These documents are supported by underpinning delivery strategies including a medium term financial strategy, procurement strategy and manpower strategy.

Monitoring

All PCTs must hold board meetings in public at which regular financial reports on progress towards achieving financial targets are presented. Most PCTs provide the following information in these reports:

- Operating cost statement
- Balance sheet
- Cash flow
- Manpower information
- Forecast performance against statutory duties
- Commentary highlighting any significant issues.

All PCTs are subject to monthly financial monitoring by their SHA. In addition PCTs report to the Department of Health on a regular basis throughout the year through their SHAs.

Annual Report and Accounts

PCTs must prepare annual reports and accounts to be presented at the annual public meeting of the PCT and made available to any member of the public. The annual report is similar to a commercial annual report and gives an account of the PCT's operations over the last financial year. The annual accounts comprise:

- Foreword to the accounts
- Directors' statement of responsibilities
- External auditors' report
- Statement on internal control
- The four primary statements (operating cost statement, balance sheet, cash flow statement, statement of recognised gains and losses)
- Notes to the accounts.

The accounts give a financial picture of the PCT over the year and are expected to meet generally accepted accounting practice (GAAP) which includes the requirements of financial reporting standards (FRSs) – see chapter 14 for more details. The *Manual for Accounts* issued by the Department of Health sets out the full set of accounting statements to be completed by PCTs. The HFMA has also produced (in conjunction with the Audit Commission) *PCT accounts: a Guide for Non-executives*. From 2009/10, international financial reporting standards (IFRS) will be followed for the preparation of accounts.

PCTs are required to submit a set of accounting statements for external audit in the prescribed format in accordance with the Department of Health's timetable. Failure to do so will result in audit criticism and will form part of the SHA performance assessment.

Auditors' Local Evaluation (ALE)

Since 2005/06, external auditors have been using an assessment approach called Auditors' Local Evaluation (ALE). Using ALE, auditors assess how well PCTs (and NHS trusts) manage and use their financial resources. ALE has been developed to enable auditors to make scored judgements on five key themes:

- Financial reporting
- Financial management
- Financial standing
- Internal control
- Value for money.

The auditors award NHS organisations a score of between one (inadequate performance) and four (performing strongly) for each of the five areas. These scores are then combined using a set of rules to calculate an overall score for each organisation, which is passed on to the Healthcare Commission to be used as the 'use of resources' assessment. From 2008/09 the Audit Commission will be using a new approach for the assessment of PCTs as part of the development of 'comprehensive area assessments' – a more generic approach that will apply across a range of public sector bodies.

Chapter 15 looks in more detail at the Healthcare Commission's assessment approach.

PCT Funding

PCTs receive funding in two forms – revenue and capital. Revenue funding covers general, day-to-day running costs for the commissioning of health services in primary and secondary care settings and other areas of expenditure.

Capital, which is relatively small for the pure primary care arm of the PCT and larger for the provider arm component of the PCT, provides for expenditure on items with a useful life expectancy in excess of one year (such as land and buildings) and equipment assets with a value greater than £5,000.

Chapter 3 looks in detail at how the NHS is funded but the key elements relating to PCTs are summarised below.

Revenue

PCTs receive various types of funding to enable them to provide and manage primary care and community services and commission acute and mental health services.

The main source of funding for PCTs is their revenue resource limit (RRL) which essentially is a 'unified allocation' which includes allocations for hospital and community health services (HCHS), the GP contract and prescribing. These unified allocations are determined by the Department of Health using an allocation process based on a weighted capitation formula – this formula is currently under review.

There are four elements of resource allocation which affect the level of funding received by PCTs in their unified allocations:

- Recurrent baselines (a) – for each year the recurrent baseline is the prior year's allocation adjusted as necessary
- Weighted capitation targets (b) – targets are set according to the national weighted capitation formula, which calculates PCT 'fair shares' of available resources based on the health needs of their populations. These targets are recalculated regularly prior to the allocation of resources to take account of changes such as the latest census data. Changes in the targets do not immediately lead to changes in actual allocations
- Distance from target (DFT) – this is the difference between (a) and (b); if (b) is greater than (a) a PCT is said to be under target; if (b) is less than (a) it is said to be over target. These are expressed in monetary and percentage terms
- Pace of change – this is the speed at which PCTs are moved closer to target (or 'levelled up') and is a policy that has been operating for some years. Levelling up is achieved through the distribution of extra resources – a process known as differential growth, where all PCTs receive some growth funds, but higher levels of growth are targeted at PCTs most under target.

PCTs may also receive funding from NHS central budgets or the 'central bundle' – essentially these are funds allocated to SHAs or resources held centrally by the Department of Health for specific development initiatives. The level of funds held centrally has significantly reduced over the last few years with more resources being included in unified allocation baselines.

Since 2006/07, PCTs have also received allocations for funding dental services in accordance with the national contract for dentists. There is also currently a small amount of non-discretionary/non cash-limited funding where the costs are essentially charged back to the Department of Health at the level incurred – for example, for optical payments. It is likely that these payments will be phased out in full in the near future and consolidated into the baseline resource limits. The way in which different primary care practitioners are paid is discussed later in this chapter.

PCTs can also seek funding from non-NHS sources such as the European Community and charitable trusts in order to meet their overall objectives.

For more details about the resource allocation process (including the weighted capitation formula), see chapter 3.

Capital

Until 2007/2008, PCTs received a capital allocation through what was denoted as 'operational capital funding' based on a formula that took into account their current asset depreciation and total turnover. For larger projects PCTs were also able to bid for funds held by their SHA. From 2008/2009 this approach will change and PCTs will have to bid each year for the capital they require through their SHAs based on three year rolling capital plans that are robust and affordable (i.e. sustainable from a revenue consequences perspective). Funding for these plans will be provided by the Department of Health subject to affordability within a national total.

PCTs can also access:

- Private finance through the private finance initiative (PFI)
- Funding for improved premises through the NHS local improvement finance trust (LIFT) scheme if they are in a LIFT health economy. LIFT was launched in 2001 and is a form of public private partnership designed to help develop and improve primary care premises. LIFT companies build and refurbish healthcare premises, retain ownership and lease them to providers, such as GPs, pharmacists, dentists, PCTs and NHS trusts. LIFT developments are also used by PCTs to co-locate related services to form multi purpose primary care centres – for example, combining social services, community care services, dentistry, pharmacy and ophthalmology.

For more about PFI and LIFT see chapter 10.

Providing and Commissioning Health Services

PCTs use their resources to ensure that a full range of primary and secondary care services are available for their populations. These are discussed in turn below.

Primary care services

Payments for primary care services are funded almost entirely through the unified allocation to PCTs. Primary care includes a wide range of services provided principally by independent contractors – see below for more details.

GP services

There are two main contract types for GP services – General Medical Services (GMS) or Personal Medical Services (PMS). About 60% of GP practices have a GMS contract. Both GMS and PMS are funded from the unified allocations that PCTs receive.

GMS

The new GMS contract, also known as the GP contract, came into effect in April 2004. The practice-based contract (the 'old' GMS was with the individual GP) provides practices with three main income streams, all of which are funded from the unified allocation:

- A global sum to cover running costs and the provision of essential and additional services

- Enhanced service payments for practices which expand the services they provide
- The Quality and Outcomes Framework (QOF) to reward improved standards in both clinical and non clinical areas.

The global sum is calculated through a resource allocation formula based on the age/sex of the practice's population, additional needs, list turnover, nursing home patients and rurality. In addition to general running costs, this global sum covers the provision of essential and additional services. Essential services, which have to be provided by every practice, cover the care of patients during an episode of illness, the general management of chronic disease and care for the terminally ill. Additional services, such as contraceptive services, child health surveillance and out of hours services are voluntary. Practices that opt out of additional services have their global sum reduced by a nationally agreed percentage rate.

Practices and other providers are able to apply to PCTs for additional funding to meet the costs of specialised or enhanced services commissioned by the PCT (for example, extended minor surgery and childhood immunisations). These are usually paid to practices on an activity basis at locally set rates. PCTs also have to commission a number of 'directed enhanced services' that are agreed at a national level and which usually reflect national policy – for example covering access or 'choose and book' initiatives and targets. These are subject to annual review and change. PCT unified allocations have also contained a guaranteed minimum expenditure level for the development of these enhanced services.

A significant proportion of money is available to reward practices for providing higher quality services. This is achieved via the QOF which sets out a range of clinical and organisational standards. Practices are awarded points for achieving these standards, set out in some 150 indicators, and receive a set payment per point. PCTs initially make 'aspiration payments' to practices throughout the year based upon 60% of their previous year's QOF achievement levels. Full QOF payments are made once it is known how successful a practice has been in delivering the QOF. Final achievement payments are made in the first quarter of the following financial year.

Practices that might have lost out under the resource allocation formula are protected by a minimum practice income guarantee (MPIG). This guarantees a practice's level of income based on rates achieved prior to the implementation of the new GMS contract in April 2004.

There are also separate funding streams for:

- Premises: under the terms of the new contract PCTs reimburse practices for their premises costs. This includes rent and rates charges incurred. A notional rent payment is made to practices that own their premises
- Seniority pay: this is paid at nationally agreed rates and is dependent upon the number of years a GP has worked in the NHS
- Locum cover: PCTs may also make a contribution to practices towards the costs of them employing a locum to cover maternity, paternity and sickness of a partner
- Information communications and technology (ICT): funding the purchase, maintenance, future upgrades and running costs of ICT within primary care is the responsibility of PCTs, rather than practices.

PMS

Under PMS GPs are paid contract sums to deliver a defined service to give PCTs and providers freedom to develop innovative options for meeting primary care needs. This forms part of a PCT's normal primary care commissioning budget

PMS continues side-by-side with the new GMS contract and PMS practices are also able to receive quality payments and are eligible for enhanced services (if these are not already in their PMS contract) plus the premises, ICT and seniority pay. PMS practices can opt to switch into the new GMS contract.

Prescribing

The costs of drugs prescribed by GP practices are calculated by the Prescription Pricing Authority (PPA) and charged to the cash-limited budget held by the relevant PCT. PCTs fund prescribing expenditure from their unified allocations.

The rising cost of primary care prescribing is a significant cost pressure for PCTs with estimated drug inflation of 7% for 2008/09. Prescribing costs have always risen faster than general inflation as new, more effective and more expensive drugs become available. However, this has become even more pronounced in recent years with the introduction of national service frameworks (NSFs) which have led to increased prescribing in areas such as coronary heart disease. Guidance from the National Institute for Health and Clinical Excellence (NICE), which assesses the clinical and cost-effectiveness of new drugs and technologies, is also driving both prescription volume and cost.

Dental services

General dental services

From April 2006 a new general dental services (nGDS) contract came into force. Under this contract, dentists are paid a set contract value for an agreed number of units of dental activity (UDAs). A reform of patients' charges also came into place in April 2006 with the introduction of three bands depending on the type of treatment received.

PCTs also have responsibility for dental public health and commissioning suitable 'high street' specialised dental services to meet local health needs.

Personal dental services

Some practices have a personal dental services (PDS) contract. These practices were paid a set contract value in return for having an agreed number of patients on their list. The contract was designed to give a 10% decrease in working time to allow dentists to use 5% for PCT access slots for unregistered patients to be seen urgently, and 5% to take them off the 'treadmill' of items of service payments.

From April 2006 these contracts converted to new PDS or nPDS contracts which, as with nGDS, see the agreed list size replaced by an agreed level of UDAs per annum.

Under the new GDS and PDS contracts, PCTs are required to gain the budgeted level of patients' charge revenue via the dentists. If national estimates are above actual patient charges collected by dentists from patients, PCTs suffer a shortfall in income.

Pharmacy services

Under the *NHS (Pharmaceutical) Regulations 1992*, payments are made to pharmacists and some doctors for supplying and dispensing certain drugs (net of prescription charges collected) and for items such as rota services, the supply and maintenance of oxygen concentrators and providing services to residential homes. In sparsely populated country areas, essential small pharmacy allowances may also be payable. Normally payments are made monthly by PCTs. The payments do not come out of PCTs' unified budgets.

For the supply and dispensing of drugs, payments are made according to calculations by the PPA. The PPA receives details of all prescriptions dispensed in England, and then calculates the amounts payable, allowing for the drug and container cost and a service fee.

New pharmacy contract

In April 2005, a new pharmacy contract came into effect. This enables community pharmacies to provide services in four main areas:

- Self care
- Management of long term conditions
- Public health
- Improving access to services.

These roles are split into the following services:

- Essential services – such as: dispensing; disposal of unwanted medicines; promoting healthy lifestyles; signposting; support for self care; support for people with disabilities; and clinical governance
- Enhanced/local services – commissioned by PCTs to meet local needs, including: out-of-hours service; minor ailments schemes; anticoagulant monitoring; stop smoking schemes
- Advanced services – accreditation of pharmacy required to allow medicine use reviews (MURs) and prescription intervention.

There is also a move to electronic transmission of prescriptions (ETP) between prescriber, dispenser and the PPA.

The contract is partly funded by a global sum (held centrally) and money released from price reductions in generic drug reimbursement which causes a reduction in the PCT's GP prescribing expenditure.

Ophthalmic services

Payments are made to ophthalmic medical practitioners, dispensing opticians and ophthalmic opticians for NHS tests (where a fee or reduced fee is payable by the recipient of the test) and similarly for the supply, repair or replacement of spectacles. Sometimes a fee is paid for home visits. These payments are normally made monthly by the PCT but the payments are not cash-limited and do not form part of the unified budget. The possibility of these payments being devolved to PCTs as part of unified allocations is being considered.

Hospital and community health services

PCTs assess the needs of their populations and commission hospital services from local and national providers. They also provide and commission a range of community services. A new national contract has been drawn up by the Department of Health for use from the 2008/09 contracting round which is to be entered into by all PCTs and their provider acute trusts including foundations trusts (FTs) (see chapter 11 for more on the national contract).

NHS trusts are paid for activity undertaken commissioned by PCTs in a number of ways. Acute trusts receive the bulk of their income through payments for a spell of activity according to a nationally set tariff rate, meaning that variations in activity are generally paid for at full cost either by the PCT for 'over performance' or repaid by the trust as 'under performance'. This system is called payment by results (PbR) and provides tariffs for groups of treatments/ procedures known as healthcare resource groups (HRGs).

PbR means that money moves with the patient and allows patients to choose in which hospital they receive their treatment. The PCT pays a set national tariff to all providers so that they do not compete on price but quality. As the system of PbR has been rolled out, more services have been covered by tariff. The focus initially has been on hospital-based services but the intention is that PbR will eventually apply to mental health, community services, ambulance services and an increasing range of specialist services.

Payments are also made by PCTs for services provided on a non-tariff basis at local negotiated prices.

For more information about PbR see chapter 13.

Practice Based Commissioning

All GP practices are encouraged to operate practice based commissioning (PBC) and hold indicative budgets for all services commissioned (and provided) by the PCT. This initiative is designed to engage clinicians in making decisions about the most appropriate and cost effective treatment for their patients.

Just as PbR is designed to incentivise hospitals to use capacity productively and efficiently, so PBC is seen as incentivising GPs and local clinicians to manage demand for hospital care and therefore balance the system. Savings made by GP practices from operating their indicative budgets can be used for investment in other services provided by the practices with the agreement of the PCT. The PCT remains accountable for the overall budget and entering into contracts with providers, as well as meeting the operational targets set down by the Department of Health. For more on PBC see chapter 11.

Financial Duties and Targets

Like SHAs and NHS Trusts, PCTs are required to follow UK GAAP except where departures are allowed under the *NHS Manuals for Accounts*.

PCTs have a range of financial duties:

- Contain expenditure, measured on an accruals basis, within the revenue resource limits set by the Department of Health for accrued revenue expenditure. PCTs are required to stay within this limit when measuring gross revenue expenditure less miscellaneous income
- Contain expenditure, measured on an accruals basis, within a capital resource limit. The CRL is set by the Department of Health for accrued capital expenditure in year. PCTs are required to stay within this limit when measuring gross capital expenditure less the book value of assets disposed of during the year
- Cash limit – a statutory duty not to spend more than the cash allocated to them. PCTs have a combined cash limit for both revenue and capital
- A duty to recover the full cost of provider activities. In other words, provider activities must not be subsidised by commissioning funds
- PCTs have flexibility to transfer any amount of resource limit from revenue to capital but transfers from capital to revenue (to allow for 'capital grant' payments to non-NHS organisations) are subject to SHA control totals
- A requirement to pay capital charges on their assets. These include a depreciation charge to reflect the use of fixed assets (other than land) and a 3.5% cost of capital charge on net relevant assets (see chapter 16)
- Apply the *Better Payment Practice Code*. PCTs have to achieve a public sector payment standard of valid invoices paid within 30 days of the receipt of the invoice. A target (currently 95%) is set at the start of the year by the Department of Health for the value and volume of invoices that must be paid within 30 days.

See chapter 14 for more about financial reporting and performance.

Partnership Working

PCTs have a general responsibility to maximise partnership working for the benefit of patients. In recent years flexibilities have been introduced to allow pooling of budgets so that, for example, a PCT and its local social services department can pool their resources for mental health and social care services. This enables PCTs to commission and provide services through a joint pool so that services may be delivered more flexibly. In the future children's trusts will also promote much closer working between health and local authorities. Chapter 9 looks in more detail at partnership working with local authorities.

References and Further Reading

Guidance relating to PCTs is available on the Department of Health's website: www.dh.gov.uk/en/Healthcare/Primarycare/Primarycaretrusts/index.htm

Commissioning a Patient-led NHS, Department of Health, 2005: www.dh.gov.uk/en/Publicationsandstatistics/Publications/PublicationsPolicyAndGuidance/DH_4116716

Department of Health commissioning web pages:
www.dh.gov.uk/en/Managingyourorganisation/Commissioning/index.htm

Our Health, Our care, Our Say: a new direction for Community Services, Department of Health, 2006: www.dh.gov.uk/en/Healthcare/Ourhealthourcareoursay/index.htm

Our NHS Our Future: NHS Next Stage Review (the Darzi review), 2007: www.dh.gov.uk/en/ Publicationsandstatistics/Publications/PublicationsPolicyAndGuidance/DH_079077

PCT Professional Executive Committees – Fit for the Future, Department of Health, 2007: www.dh.gov.uk/en/Healthcare/Primarycare/Primarycaretrusts/DH_4125193

The NHS in England: the Operating Framework for 2008/09, Department of Health, 2007: www.dh.gov.uk/en/Publicationsandstatistics/Publications/PublicationsPolicyAndGuidance/ DH_081094

Operational Plans 2008/09–2010/11, Department of Health, 2008: www.dh.gov.uk:80/en/ Publicationsandstatistics/Publications/PublicationsPolicyAndGuidance/DH_082542

NHS allocations (including the weighted capitation formula):
www.dh.gov.uk/policyandguidance/organisationpolicy/financeandplanning/allocations/fs/en

Patient Choice:
www.dh.gov.uk/en/Healthcare/PatientChoice/index.htm

The NHS Plan: a plan for investment, a plan for reform, Department of Health, 2000: www.dh.gov.uk/en/Publicationsandstatistics/Publications/PublicationsPolicyAndGuidance/ DH_4002960

Manual for Accounts, Department of Health: www.info.doh.gov.uk/doh/finman.nsf

Primary Care Trust Accounts: a Guide for Non-executives, HFMA/Audit Commission: www.hfma.org.uk or www.audit-commission.gov.uk

Private Finance Initiative: www.dh.gov.uk/en/Procurementandproposals/ Publicprivatepartnership/Privatefinanceinitiative/index.htm

NHS LIFT: www.dh.gov.uk/ProcurementAndProposals/PublicPrivatePartnership/NHSLIFT/fs/en

New GMS contract: www.dh.gov.uk/PolicyAndGuidance/OrganisationPolicy/PrimaryCare/ PrimaryCareContracting/GMS/fs/en

Quality and Outcomes Framework: www.dh.gov.uk/PolicyAndGuidance/OrganisationPolicy/ PrimaryCare/PrimaryCareContracting/QOF/fs/en

Prescription Pricing Authority: www.ppa.org.uk

National Service Frameworks:
www.dh.gov.uk/en/Healthcare/NationalServiceFrameworks/index.htm

National Institute for Health and Clinical Excellence: www.nice.org.uk/

Dental Contract – details available via the Chief Dental Officer's website:
www.dh.gov.uk/AboutUs/HeadsOfProfession/ChiefDentalOfficer/fs/en

The Standard NHS Contract for Acute Hospital Services and Supporting Guidance:
www.dh.gov.uk/en/Publicationsandstatistics/Publications/PublicationsPolicyAndGuidance/
DH_081100

Pharmacy Contract: www.dh.gov.uk/PolicyAndGuidance/MedicinesPharmacyAndIndustry/
CommunityPharmacyContractualFramework/fs/en

Payment by Results: www.dh.gov.uk/en/Managingyourorganisation/Financeandplanning/
NHSFinancialReforms/index.htm

Practice Based Commissioning: www.dh.gov.uk/en/Managingyourorganisation/Commissioning/
Practice-basedcommissioning/index.htm

7. NHS Trusts

Introduction

NHS trusts were formed from 1991 onwards under the *NHS and Community Care Act 1990*. All NHS hospitals in England providing acute and mental health services form part of an NHS trust and in some areas they also host community services. However, most community hospitals are currently run by primary care trusts (PCTs). NHS trusts provide mainly, but not exclusively, hospital-based (secondary care) services in England and Wales.

Although managerially independent, all NHS trusts are statutory bodies and as such are accountable to the Secretary of State for Health through the Department of Health via strategic health authorities (SHAs).

Types of NHS Trust

There is a wide range of NHS trusts covering the population's different health needs:

- District acute general hospital trusts
- Specialist hospitals that provide regional or national services – for example, Great Ormond Street Hospital for Children NHS Trust
- Combined teaching, specialist and district general hospitals, for example, Leeds Teaching Hospitals NHS Trust
- Mental health and learning disability services, for example, Derbyshire Mental Health Services NHS Trust
- Care trusts – organisations that work in both health and social services, for example, Sandwell Mental Health NHS and Social Care Trust. Care trusts may carry out a range of services including social care, mental health services, learning disability and primary care services (see chapter 9 for more about working in partnership with local authorities)
- Ambulance services, including paramedical and patient transport services – for example, London Ambulance Service NHS Trust.

There are also a number of NHS foundation trusts (FTs) which first came into being in April 2004. Although they are part of the NHS, FTs operate under different governance and financial arrangements – see chapter 8 for more details. Over time, the expectation is that all NHS trusts will move towards FT status.

Across the country there are a variety of models of service delivery based on locally determined best practice. Since 1999 there have also been many trust reconfigurations. This has included mergers of trusts, usually to form larger acute or mental health service trusts, with disaggregation of community services into PCTs. Again, the key determining factor is local needs and priorities, although a desire to 'unlock' management savings and efficiencies has also been a consideration.

This process of reconfiguration has continued following the publication by the Department of Health in February 2006 of *Our Health, Our Care, Our Say: A New Direction for Community Services*. This looked at options for providing out-of-hospital care.

Governance Arrangements

Primary legislation under *The NHS Trusts (Membership and Procedure) Regulations* stipulates the make up of NHS trust boards but does give some flexibility over the number of non-executives.

The maximum number of directors of an NHS trust was originally set at 11. However, since 1998, each board can have a maximum number of 12 directors excluding the chairman – up to seven non-executive members (although the majority have five) and no more than five executive directors.

Within the executive director team, each trust must have:

- A chief officer
- A chief financial officer
- A medical or dental practitioner and registered nurse or midwife (except in the case of ambulance trusts).

In 2000, the board structure of mental health trusts was set at a maximum of 14, excluding the chairman, to include no more than seven non-executive directors (NEDs) and seven executive directors. This structure was extended to care trusts in 2001.

Other executive directors may attend board meetings but do not hold the full range of responsibilities – for example, they do not have the right to vote on board decisions. While the medical and nursing professions must be represented at board level, this could be through a chief executive with a medical or nursing background.

The Role of Boards and NEDs

An NHS trust board is collectively responsible for promoting the success of the organisation by directing and supervising its affairs. This involves:

- Setting the organisation's values and standards and ensuring that its obligations to patients, the local community and the Secretary of State are understood and met
- Providing active leadership of the organisation within a framework of prudent and effective controls which enable risk to be assessed and managed
- Setting the organisation's strategic aims
- Ensuring that the necessary financial and human resources are in place for the organisation to meet its objectives
- Reviewing management performance.

Over recent years, increased emphasis has been placed on the board's role in improving financial management and on the part played by NEDs. In particular, the Audit Commission and NHS Confederation briefing *Good Governance: Good Financial Management* recommends that all board members 'need to have the necessary knowledge, skills and approach to discharge their financial management responsibilities effectively' and that NEDs should take a lead role on finance in the board and on the audit committee.

Accountability and Responsibilities

NHS trusts are accountable to the Secretary of State through the Department of Health via SHAs. There are five main accountability tools:

- The planning process
- The annual report on the previous year's performance
- The annual accounts
- Performance monitoring through monitoring returns against trust financial duties
- The Healthcare Commission's 'annual health check'.

Since 2002 trusts have been 'performance managed' by the relevant SHA. The SHA collates and acts upon the monitoring returns (both financial and non-financial) to assess trusts' performance and evaluates progress against key national and local targets. In addition trusts' performance is assessed by the Healthcare Commission for certain aspects of performance (see chapter 14 for more details).

Ongoing improvements in trusts' efficiency is expected, particularly in terms of achieving further activity related targets and improvements in the quality of care delivered to patients.

Planning Process

The planning process is designed to:

- Ensure efficient and effective delivery of services
- Demonstrate public accountability
- Ensure congruence with national and local commissioning plans and targets.

Plans must be consistent with the level of resources negotiated in PCTs' 'operational plans' (known as local delivery plans or LDPs before the 2008/09 planning round). These operational plans are three-year plans designed to show a clear commissioned plan for community wide strategies that will address health inequalities, improve health outcomes and improve the targeting of healthcare provision in accordance with national targets, local service frameworks and PCT commissioning strategies. Prior to the commencement of the 2005/06 financial year PCTs were given resource allocations covering the three financial years to 2007/08 so that they were able to work with providers to plan and commission more effectively. For 2008/09 allocations were made to cover just one year – this was to allow additional time for work revising the resource allocation formula. Allocations for 2009/10 and 2010/11, based on the revised formula, are expected in the summer of 2008.

The PCT leads the planning process which requires health communities to submit 'refreshed' plans each year to demonstrate that the direction of travel is being maintained and that national targets etc are being planned for and achieved in terms of the required commissioned capacity.

Plans are reviewed regularly (for example at performance meetings held with the SHA) and if there are significant issues – for example if serious financial problems develop in the health economy – changes may be needed. To ensure that the health economy is performing as it should and in line with plans, targets and health improvement objectives, the SHA reviews all performance for the health community on a regular basis.

Annual Report

NHS trusts are required to produce annual reports. From 2006/07, these must be published with the full set of audited accounts as one document and presented to the trust's annual general meeting. Trusts may also produce summarised versions to aid communication with stakeholders.

The annual report is primarily a narrative document similar to the directors' report described in the *Companies Act*, but with additional information reflecting the trust's position in the community. The report gives an account of the trust's activities and performance over the last financial year.

Although the overall layout of the annual report is at each trust's discretion, there are mandatory items that must be included. These are set out in the *Manual for Accounts* which is available on the Department of Health's website. For example, in addition to the financial statements, the report must include a directors' statement of responsibilities and the auditor's report on the accounts. Trusts also use the annual report as an opportunity to set out their achievements in the year and highlight the challenges ahead.

From 2005/06, it has been best practice to prepare an operating and financial review (OFR) as part of the annual report. The OFR focuses on matters that are of interest to the public and gives a comprehensive picture of the trust's business incorporating future plans and aspirations as well as past performance. Guidance on preparing an OFR is available from the HFMA's website.

The annual report must be approved by the trust's board of directors before presentation at a public meeting. This meeting must be held before 30 September following the end of the relevant financial year.

Annual Accounts

The annual accounts must comprise:

- A foreword and notes to the accounts
- The four primary statements (income and expenditure account, balance sheet, cash flow statement and statement of total recognised gains and losses)
- Directors' statements of responsibilities
- The statement on internal control
- Independent auditors' report, giving an opinion on the accounts.

The accounts give a financial picture of the trust over the year and are expected to meet generally accepted accounting practice (GAAP) which includes the requirements of financial reporting standards (FRSs). The *Manual for Accounts* gives details of the full set of accounting statements to be completed by NHS trusts, including trust financial monitoring and accounting forms (TRUs), together with detailed guidance for their completion.

Trusts are required to submit a set of accounting statements for external audit in the prescribed format in accordance with the Department of Health's timetable. Failure to do so will result in audit criticism and will form part of the SHA performance assessment.

In its *Budget 2008*, the Treasury announced that international financial reporting standards (IFRS) will be followed for the preparation of accounts from 2009/10.

Monthly Performance Monitoring Returns

All NHS trusts are subject to financial performance monitoring against plan on a minimum quarterly basis. This is undertaken by the SHA. Current practice is for these returns to be collected on a monthly basis. The returns as a minimum include:

- Income and expenditure – both capital and revenue covering year to date and forecast outturn
- Balance sheet
- Cash flow
- Current period and forecast outturn run rate (variance between income and expenditure)
- Update on delivery of cost improvement (savings) plans
- Performance against the *Better Payment Practice Code*
- Break-even duty
- Performance against the capital cost absorption duty and external financing limit duty
- Provisions for liabilities and charges
- A commentary on variances against plan and previous expenditure levels
- A written narrative summary of the financial position.

Trusts are also subject to monthly workforce monitoring which includes analysis of pay expenditure.

Trusts' financial duties and targets are discussed in more detail later in this chapter.

Healthcare Commission – Annual Health Check

The Healthcare Commission is responsible for reviewing the performance of each NHS trust and awarding an annual rating. This 'annual health check' is designed to provide a full picture of the performance of an NHS body and assesses four elements:

- Performance against 'core standards' which set out the minimum level of service patients and service users have a right to expect
- Performance against existing national targets
- Performance against new national targets
- The use of resources.

The annual performance ratings are derived from these assessments – for each trust there is a two part rating:

- Quality of services based on performance against core standards, existing and new national targets (and the results of any improvement reviews)
- The use of resources.

The ratings use a four point scale – excellent; good; fair or weak.

The Healthcare Commission's approach is looked at in more detail in chapter 15.

In October 2008, it is expected that the Healthcare Commission will be merged with the Commission for Social Care Inspection and the Mental Health Act Commission to form a single regulatory body for health and social care called the Care Quality Commission – see the Department of Health's website for details.

Auditors' Local Evaluation (ALE)

Since 2005/06, external auditors have been using an assessment approach called Auditors' Local Evaluation (ALE). Using ALE, auditors assess how well PCTs and NHS trusts manage and use their financial resources. ALE has been developed to enable auditors to make scored judgements on five key themes:

- Financial reporting
- Financial management
- Financial standing
- Internal control
- Value for money.

The auditors award NHS organisations a score of between one (inadequate performance) and four (performing strongly) for each of the five areas. These scores are then combined using a set of rules to calculate an overall score for each organisation, which is passed on to the Healthcare Commission to be used as the 'use of resources' assessment. See chapter 14 for more details.

Financing of NHS Trusts

NHS trusts are financed in two main ways:

- Revenue financing for their day to day running
- Capital financing to fund the purchase of new and replacement assets (buildings and equipment).

Revenue financing

NHS trusts receive revenue income from five main sources:

- Through the commissioning process with PCTs and other NHS trusts. This usually represents 75% to 90% of total income
- Specific funding to NHS trusts providing nursing, medical and non-medical staff education and training services (generally based on numbers in training)
- Through research and development allocations to trusts undertaking agreed research and development
- Charges to staff, visitors or patients for services provided, such as catering or the provision of private patient facilities
- Grants from other government bodies or charitable organisations.

Capital financing

From 2007/08, a new capital regime has been introduced for NHS trusts to provide funding for new capital expenditure. This replaces the old method of an annual operational capital allocation calculated by the SHA and provided via the issue of new 'public dividend capital' (PDC – see below), and brings trusts into line with the approach followed by FTs. The implementation of this new approach is designed to ease the transition to FT status and is consistent with the drivers and incentives that support payment by results and patient choice.

Under this new regime, NHS trusts need to generate sufficient surplus cash flow to finance capital investment. Trusts can retain cash generated through non-cash charges to the income and expenditure account (principally depreciation), income and expenditure account surpluses and the proceeds of asset sales for capital re-investment. They can also borrow further sums (from a Department of Health lending facility), subject to a prudential borrowing limit (PBL).

The PBL is not an annual limit, but reflects the maximum cumulative borrowing that a trust may have. Using a system that mirrors arrangements for FTs, this maximum borrowing is calculated by applying a series of financial ratios to calculate an overall financial risk rating for each trust. This risk rating corresponds to a maximum borrowing limit. PBLs are reviewed at least annually when the latest accounts data becomes available.

Borrowing within the limit set by the PBL is in the form of interest-bearing loans from the Department of Health. The period over which the loan will be repaid is subject to the discretion of the SHA, and is related to the type of assets being acquired. The loan should not exceed the life of the asset. All loans attract interest at a rate equivalent to the National Loans Fund rate. The loan principal is repaid in equal instalments, at half-yearly intervals, over the loan term. The expectation is that loan principal will be repaid out of surpluses made by the trust. Interest payments are also made bi-annually and are a revenue expense that is recorded in the income and expenditure account.

The SHA has a key role in NHS trust capital investment plans before the start of each financial year. The plans must show detailed schemes and sources of funding. The SHA needs to be satisfied that the plans are consistent with the strategic plans of each trust and the wider SHA region. If a trust requires loans to finance part of its capital plan, the SHA needs to be assured that they are within the trust's current PBL. Exceptionally, loans may be approved where not supported by a trust's PBL if the trust has a very low level of net assets, which would prevent it from passing the gearing test, or where the capital investment itself will lead to future income streams that will enable repayment of the loan.

This new regime applies to NHS trusts only. For details of PCT capital funding see chapter 6.

As well as capital financing under the new regime, trusts have access to a number of other forms of capital:

- Originating capital – under the *NHS and Community Care Act 1990*, NHS trusts had transferred to them 'such of the property, rights and liabilities as are needed for their functions'. The value of the net assets (assets less liabilities) transferred was matched by public dividend capital (PDC). This is a form of long-term government finance on which the NHS trust pays dividends to the Exchequer. It carries an expected return of 3.5% – this percentage figure is generally regarded as the long-term cost of capital in the public sector

- New PDC may be issued in the following exceptional circumstances:
  - for ongoing capital schemes where the contract was let on or before 1st September 2006 and the trust's PBL does not support the issuing of loans
  - for centrally funded capital initiatives – for example, the picture archiving and communications system
  - for the funding of asset transfers between NHS trusts in excess of £100,000. These arrangements will continue as the increase in PDC in the purchasing trust is off-set by a reduction in PDC in the selling trust; therefore there is no net outflow of cash from the Department of Health
  - for very large publicly-funded schemes which would not be possible under a trust's PBL
- Charitable donations
- For very large schemes, trusts may consider financing via a private finance initiative (PFI) contract with the private sector. The SHA will closely scrutinise any such planned financing and will want be assured that the trust can generate cash in future years to fund the substantial interest payments.

FTs have different capital funding opportunities – see chapter 8 for more details.

Elements of previous capital planning requirements remain in that NHS trusts are expected to have clear related strategic plans for clinical service development, particularly in areas where performance review has highlighted deficiencies. These should feature in operational plans (formerly known as local delivery plans or LDPs) and be supported by PCTs. NHS trusts are also required to submit annual financial plans to the SHA to demonstrate achievement of key financial targets, including cash-generation to service loans.

Financial Duties and Targets

NHS trusts have a number of statutory financial duties – i.e. duties that are a formal requirement of trusts as laid down in statute through Parliament. The principal financial duty is to achieve a break-even position on income and expenditure taking one year with another. In the NHS this has been interpreted as meaning over a three-year rolling period (see break-even duty below).

Secondary duties are to:

- Manage within a preset external financing limit (EFL)
- Meet the capital resource limit (CRL) – in other words manage capital expenditure within a preset limit
- Achieve a capital cost absorption rate of 3.5%
- Comply with the *Better Payment Practice Code*
- Produce a set of annual accounting statements in the prescribed format.

NHS trusts are normally expected to plan to meet their statutory break-even duty (measured over three rolling years) by achieving a balanced position on their income and expenditure accounts each and every year. This 'annual' break-even requirement is sometimes referred to as an 'administrative duty'. This is monitored by the SHA. An administrative duty is not the same as a statutory duty – rather it is an additional rule and regulation set down by the Department of Health that clarifies or specifies how a trust will operate. With trusts now required to plan for making a surplus, break-even is taken to mean break-even or better.

Until 2007, trusts were also subject to the resource accounting and budgeting (RAB) regime. Under RAB NHS trusts faced a deduction from their income equal to any deficit incurred in the prior year. However, in March 2007, the Department of Health announced that this would no longer be the case. This move followed recommendations made in the Audit Commission's *Review of the NHS Financial Management and Accounting Regime*.

Break-even duty

Section 10(1) of the *NHS and Community Care Act 1990* requires trusts to achieve break-even. This means that a trust must ensure that its revenue is not less than sufficient, taking one financial year with another, to meet outgoings properly charged to the income and expenditure account. 'Taking one financial year with another' has been interpreted to mean that over a three (or exceptionally a five) year period, trusts are required to achieve break-even position in their income and expenditure account. This is to allow some flexibility where exceptional costs are incurred and when managing the financial recovery of a trust with serious financial difficulties.

The statutory break-even duty currently has a materiality test, which is interpreted as 0.5% of turnover. Application of the materiality concept by an NHS trust should be with the prior agreement of the relevant host SHA.

Given its importance, break-even (and related issues) is discussed in more detail below:

Break-even, Deficits and Working Capital Loans

Break-even

Trusts' statutory duty to break-even taking one year with another has been interpreted within the NHS as meaning breaking even over three rolling years, allowing trusts to make deficits in one year as long as they are recovered within the next two years. In the past, trusts' real financial position was not always completely clear as break-even was at times achieved through the use of brokerage (financial support from other trusts, sometimes treated as income rather than a loan). However changes have now been made to improve transparency and from 2006/07 a new regime of working capital loans has been introduced to allow trusts to manage cash shortfalls caused by income and expenditure account deficits. These loans are shown in the accounts and trusts pay interest on the borrowing. This means that any deficit would be clearly shown on the income and expenditure account, with the cash consequences of that deficit dealt with through a working capital loan, reported on the balance sheet.

In-year financial performance

This is the outcome of income compared with expenditure in any one year.

Underlying or 'normalised' financial position

This is in effect the financial position a trust would be in if one-off sources of income and/or non-recurrent expenditure are discounted. A trust could break-even in-year, for instance by taking a number of one-off measures such as leaving vacancies unfilled or delaying initiatives, but still have an underlying deficit that needs to be addressed if it is to continue to deliver a balanced position in future years.

Projected financial position

A trust may start the year planning, or 'projecting', to break-even. Throughout the year it will re-analyse its original plans and estimates on the basis of the actual activity and expenditure that is occurring. At various points throughout the year, it will review and revise its projected year-end position. A trust that is projecting a year-end deficit mid-year will not necessarily end the year in deficit. The projection may simply be highlighting the need to take action to avoid ending the year in deficit – for example, by identifying further cost savings or 'stalling' planned service developments.

Working capital loans

In the final quarter of 2006/07, the informal and 'un-transparent' system of cash brokerage that had previously operated across the NHS in order to assist trusts with temporary cash flow difficulties was replaced by a formal system of interest bearing loans and deposits. This is consistent with moving trusts to a system similar to that operated by FTs, which need to borrow for working capital needs. Trusts requiring cash to manage temporary cash flow problems will take out interest-bearing loans from the Department of Health, which will be disclosed in the balance sheet (unlike the cash brokerage system where brokerage received was treated as income and the income and expenditure balance was distorted as a result).

An affordable repayment strategy must be identified, agreed and formally approved by the host SHA before a working capital loan to a trust can be sanctioned by the Department of Health. In order to repay the loan the trust must generate sufficient income and expenditure surplus to cover the capital repayments over the duration of the loan term – therefore the request for a loan must form part of the trust's overall recovery plan. Loan repayments must be managed in this way and must not be funded through retained depreciation, cash from asset sales or extending payment terms to creditors. Interest is charged at a rate equivalent to the National Loans Fund rate and is a charge to the income and expenditure account. Loan repayments and interest payments are currently made on a bi-annual basis.

External financing limit

The external financing limit (EFL) can be defined as the difference between what a trust plans to spend on capital in a year and what it can generate internally from its operations. The EFL is therefore a cash limit on net external financing. This is an absolute financial duty, with a maximum tolerance of only 0.5% of turnover under the agreed limit. There is no tolerance above the EFL target without prior notification and agreement. The purpose of the EFL is to control the cash expenditure of the NHS as a whole to the level agreed by Parliament in the public expenditure control totals.

The EFL can be either positive or negative. A positive EFL arises when a trust is required to draw down additional government funding above what it can generate internally to support its capital expenditure plans. A negative EFL arises where the trust is required to repay PDC or save cash. The target EFL will be set at the start of the financial year by the Department of Health and the trust will be expected to manage its resources to ensure it achieves the target.

Now that new arrangements are in place for interest-bearing loans for both capital and working capital purposes, EFL adjustments will be reduced in number as additional PDC and brokerage payments are no longer necessary. For most trusts the EFL statement in the monthly monitoring returns will cover capital allocations from central funding and loan repayments.

If a trust under or over shoots its EFL at the end of a financial year adjustments (reversals) are made in the next financial year.

Capital resource limit

NHS trusts must control capital expenditure to meet their capital resource limit (CRL). The CRL is set by the Department of Health and is the total of the following:

- SHA-agreed amounts brought-forward from the previous year
- Depreciation as charged to the income and expenditure account
- Proceeds from asset sales
- Capital loans
- Funding from central funds (provided as PDC).

The charge against the CRL is calculated as follows:

> Gross capital expenditure less: book value of assets disposed
> Plus: loss on disposal of donated assets
> Less: capital grants and donations.

Capital cost absorption duty

The financial regime of NHS trusts recognises that there is a cost associated with the maintenance of the capital of the organisation. NHS trusts are required to absorb the cost of capital (effectively the dividend paid on PDC) at a rate of 3.5% of average net relevant assets (the average of the asset values held at the beginning and end of the year). See chapter 16 of this guide and the *NHS Capital Accounting Manual* for more details.

The target rate of return is set annually and is currently 3.5%. The duty is regarded as met if the trust achieves a rate between 3.0% and 4.0%.

The PDC dividend paid by trusts for a particular year is calculated based on estimates, made by the trust in the previous year, of the trust's opening and closing asset values. The capital cost absorption calculation is in effect a way of checking at the end of the year, using the **actual** opening and closing asset values, that the dividend paid equates to the 3.5% target return.

Better Payment Practice Code

NHS trusts must comply with the *Better Payment Practice Code*. The target is set at the start of each year by the Department of Health for the value and volume of invoices that must be paid within 30 days of receipt. The target is currently 95%. Trusts may be unable to meet the target if they have inefficient internal systems or have short-term cash problems.

Other Issues

NHS trusts need to be aware of a number of other issues, including:

- Clinical litigation. The costs to the NHS of clinical litigation are rising rapidly as result of changes in court procedures and increased awards made by courts. There is also some evidence of an increased willingness by patients to resort to litigation. NHS trusts join a central scheme, the Clinical Negligence Scheme for Trusts (CNST), aimed at 'smoothing' the cash flow implications of unpredictable claims over a period. Through this process, trusts contribute to a 'risk pool', which is managed by a special health authority, the NHS Litigation Authority (NHSLA). Since April 2002 all cases have been managed by, and have become the financial responsibility of, the NHSLA. Individual trusts pay an annual premium (which they build into their costs and prices), but trusts do not need to include a provision for the expected settlement liability in their accounts above the excess. The extent to which an NHS trust has implemented best practice in risk management is assessed and discounts awarded for achieving certain pre-determined risk management levels
- Management costs. Staff and other costs included in management costs are tightly defined in guidance to trusts and auditors – details are available on the Department of Health's website
- Reference costs. NHS trusts are required to produce reference costs each year. The information is used for cost comparison purposes and to calculate the national tariff, which is used in payment by results (see chapters 12 and 13).

References and Further Reading

Our Health, Our Care, Our Say: A New Direction for Community Services: www.dh.gov.uk/PolicyAndGuidance/OrganisationPolicy/Modernisation/OurHealthOurCareOurSay/fs/en

The NHS Trusts (Membership and Procedure) Regulations, 1990:
www.opsi.gov.uk/SI/si1990/Uksi_19902024_en_1.htm

Good Governance: Good Financial Management, Audit Commission and NHS Confederation Briefing, June 2004: www.audit-comission.gov.uk

Operational Plans 2009/09 to 2010/11, Department of Health, 2008: www.dh.gov.uk/en/ Publicationsandstatistics/Publications/PublicationsPolicyAndGuidance/DH_082542

Manuals for Accounts, Capital Accounting Manual and Guide to Resource Accounting and Budgeting: www.info.doh.gov.uk/doh/finman.nsf

A Guide to Good Practice on the Annual Report/ Review incorporating requirements under Reporting Standard 1 (RS 1) for NHS Organisations including the Operating and Financial Review (OFR) – available from the HFMA: www.hfma.org.uk

Budget 2008: Stability and Opportunity: Building a Strong, Sustainable Future, HM Treasury, 2008: www.hm-treasury.gov.uk./budget/budget_08/report/bud_bud08_repindex.cfm

Annual Health Check, Healthcare Commission:
www.healthcarecommission.org.uk/Homepage/fs/en

Care Quality Commission (includes consultation paper), Department of Health, 2007:
www.dh.gov.uk/en/Publicationsandstatistics/Legislation/Actsandbills/HealthandSocialCareBill/ DH_080438

Auditors' Local Evaluation (ALE) – details available form the health pages of the Audit Commission's website: www.audit-commission.gov.uk

Review of the NHS Financial Management and Accounting Regime, Audit Commission, 2006:
www.audit-commission.gov.uk/reports/

NHS and Community Care Act 1990: www.opsi.gov.uk/ACTS/acts1990/ukpga_19900019_en_1

HSC 1999/146 Guidance to Health Authorities and NHS Trusts on Break-Even Duty; Provisions and Accumulated Deficits. Available via the HSC pages of the Department of Health's website: www.dh.gov.uk/PublicationsAndStatistics/LettersAndCirculars/HealthServiceCirculars/fs/en

Better Payment Practice Code: www.payontime.co.uk

NHS Litigation Authority: www.nhsla.com

Management costs: www.dh.gov.uk/PolicyAndGuidance/OrganisationPolicy/ FinanceAndPlanning/NHSManagementCosts/fs/en

Reference costs: www.dh.gov.uk/en/Policyandguidance/Organisationpolicy/ Financeandplanning/NHScostingmanual/index.htm

8. Foundation Trusts

Introduction

NHS foundation trusts (FTs) were created as new legal entities in the form of public benefit corporations by the *Health and Social Care (Community Health and Standards) Act 2003* – now consolidated in the *NHS Act 2006*. They were introduced to help implement the government's 10-year *NHS Plan* which set out a vision for the NHS in England that is responsive, effective and of high quality. By creating a new form of NHS trust that had greater freedoms and more extensive powers, the government hoped to liberate the talents of frontline staff and improve services more quickly. Alongside FTs, the government placed a renewed emphasis on increases in clinical staffing, use of technology, new therapies and an expansion in capacity. The government's aim is that together these initiatives will combine to provide significantly enhanced access through reduced waiting times for primary, secondary and tertiary care.

Initially, applications for foundation status were restricted to a number of 'three-star' trusts with the first wave of FTs coming into being in April 2004. Existing NHS trusts are free to register an interest in becoming an FT. The government's expectation is that all acute and mental health activity will be provided through foundation organisations by around 2011.

How FTs differ from other NHS Trusts

The FT structure represents a model of local management where central government involvement is reduced. FTs are managed by boards of directors and governors and have new freedoms to develop in line with local priorities and raise funds directly from the private sector. In practice, this means that in many ways FTs operate on a similar basis to commercial organisations.

FTs possess three key characteristics that distinguish them from NHS trusts:

- Freedom to decide locally how to meet their obligations – they can tailor their governance arrangements to the individual circumstances of their community and health economy, whilst reflecting the range of diverse relationships with patients, the local community and other stakeholders
- Accountability to local people, who can become members and governors
- Authorisation and ongoing regulation by the Independent Regulator of NHS Foundation Trusts – Monitor. Monitor also has powers to intervene if an FT fails to comply with its authorisation.

Another key difference is that FTs have a duty to engage with local communities and encourage local people to become members of the organisation. This duty is central to the mutual model on which the constitution of FTs is based.

In spite of these differences, it is important to remember that FTs remain part of the NHS with the primary purpose of providing NHS services to NHS patients according to NHS principles and standards. In particular, the public continues to receive healthcare according to core NHS principles – free care, based on need and not ability to pay.

To ensure that NHS patients do not lose out as a result of the introduction of FTs, there are statutory provisions set out in the *NHS Act 2006*, which place a 'lock' on the purpose of any FT. In particular 'mandatory goods and services' are specified in an FT's terms of authorisation – these are those goods and services that an FT must provide unless a variation is agreed first with commissioners and then with Monitor. Two other safeguards or restrictions stand out – as discussed below.

Protected assets

Any proposed change in the use (including sale) of scheduled or protected fixed assets must be authorised by Monitor. Protected assets are identified at the time of application in terms of the protected services delivered from them. When authorising an FT, Monitor will take due regard of the protected assets for subsequent monitoring. Moreover, protected assets cannot be pledged as security for loans.

Private patient income cap

To ensure that the estate and future growth in services of an FT benefit NHS patients, the Act places a cap on the growth in private patient activity. Specifically, the Act makes it clear that the proportion of income from private activity as a proportion of total income must be no greater than it was for the predecessor NHS trust. In other words if private income was 3% of defined income in 2002/03 (in most circumstances the 'base financial year'), then it must not exceed 3% of defined income in 2003/04 and beyond.

The way in which FTs apply the private patient income cap is currently (March 2008) being challenged by UNISON which is concerned that FTs are 'treating increasing numbers of private patients'. In response to UNISON's challenge, Monitor's board has decided to 're-consult fully on the range of options for applying the existing legislation' relating to the cap. See Monitor's website for details.

Governance Arrangements

A significant feature of FTs is that they are released from direct Department of Health control, which is currently exercised through strategic health authorities (SHAs). Instead their functions are managed and executed through a board of directors and a board of governors.

The board of governors

The board of governors is made up of elected individuals from a wide stakeholder and community membership (including the public, patients and staff). When applying to be a member of the FT, an individual applicant can also confirm an interest in becoming a governor.

Legislation provides for each FT to decide on the size and shape of its board of governors in the light of their local circumstances, within certain minimum parameters set out in legislation:

- More than half of the members of the board of governors must be elected from the public and, where applicable, patient membership[5]
- There must be at least three staff governors elected from the staff membership, or where there are classes within the staff constituency at least one governor from each class
- There must be at least one local authority governor, one PCT governor and (where applicable) at least one university governor, all via nomination.

Monitor's *Code of Governance* also emphasises that 'the board of governors should not be so large as to be unwieldy' and recommends that its role, structure, composition and procedures be reviewed regularly.

The board of governors represents the interests of the members and partner organisations in the local health economy in the governance of the FT. It may also be responsible for sharing information about key decisions with its membership community. Individual governors are eligible to serve for a term of up to three years and to stand for re-election.

The chair of the FT is both the chair of the board of governors and the board of directors. This ensures that views from governors are considered by the directors and gives the chair a pivotal role in the organisation.

A key role of the board of governors is to work with the board of directors to ensure that the FT acts in a way that is consistent with its terms of authorisation and to help set the strategic direction.

Monitor's *Code of Governance* gives more details about the role of governors and emphasises that they 'must act in the best interests of the FT and should adhere to its values and code of conduct'. It also states that 'the roles and responsibilities of the board of governors should be set out in a written document'.

The board of directors

The board of directors consists of executive directors (which must include the chief executive and finance director) and non-executive directors (NEDs). The chair of the board must be a NED. NEDs should have particular experience or skills that help the board function well. They are appointed by the board of governors based on recommendations made by a 'nominations committee'.

The board of directors takes full responsibility for the governance of the FT and should present a balanced and understandable assessment of the FT's position and prospects. This responsibility extends to all public statements and reports to regulators and inspectors, as well as information presented under statutory requirements.

---

[5] FTs must have public and staff membership categories but can choose whether or not they have a patient membership category.

All directors have collective responsibility for every decision of the board of directors regardless of their individual skills or status.

The role of NEDs is significantly different from their traditional role in NHS trusts. This is due in part to representation of local communities on the board of governors. As members of a unitary board, NEDs must take equal responsibility and accountability for the function and success of the business.

One particularly important duty placed on the board of directors and stated in Monitor's *Code of Governance* is that it 'must notify Monitor and the board of governors without delay, and should consider whether it is in the public interest to bring to the public attention, any major new developments in the NHS foundation trust's sphere of activity which are not public knowledge which may lead, by virtue of its effect on its assets and liabilities or financial position or on the general course of its business, to a substantial change to the financial wellbeing, healthcare delivery performance or reputation and standing of the NHS foundation trust.

The board of directors must notify Monitor and the board of governors without delay and should consider whether it is in the public interest to bring to public attention all relevant information which is not public knowledge concerning a change:

- in the NHS foundation trust's financial condition
- in the performance of its business; and/or
- in the NHS foundation trust's expectations as to its performance which, if made public, would be likely to lead to a substantial change to the financial wellbeing, healthcare delivery performance or reputation and standing of the NHS foundation trust.'

Monitor's *Code of Governance* also emphasises that 'the board of directors should not be so large as to be unwieldy'.

The Role of the Independent Regulator of NHS Foundation Trusts – Monitor

Application process

External monitoring and regulation of FTs is undertaken by Monitor in accordance with the FT's terms of authorisation which sets out the basis for an FT's establishment and future operation.

There is a two-stage application process for any aspiring FT. First, trusts apply to the Secretary of State for Health and secure his/her support. This is given only after a 'development phase' when applicants must:

- Develop a five year strategic integrated business plan
- Show strong leadership and commitment to modernising services
- Demonstrate the involvement of staff and other local stakeholders for their vision for reform
- Undertake a twelve week public consultation on their strategy and governance arrangements
- Be subject to an 'historical' due diligence report by an accounting firm.

For more about the application process and the integrated business plan, guidance is available via the FT pages of the Department of Health's website.

If the application has the support and approval of the Secretary of State, the trust is recommended to Monitor. Monitor then assesses the applicant for its financial standing, governance arrangements and management capabilities. Applicants meeting the required standards are authorised by Monitor, establishing them as an FT in the legal form of a public benefit corporation. Guidance on the application process is available on Monitor's website.

Financial duties

As part of the NHS, FTs are required to exercise proper governance, probity and responsibility for public funds. PCTs and other commissioning bodies continue to provide the majority of an FT's income.

However, considerable differences between NHS trusts and FTs arise when comparing financial duties. For example, FTs are not required to fulfil the current set of financial duties applicable to NHS trusts. In particular:

- There is no statutory duty to break-even – FTs can generate and retain a surplus each year and re-invest; they can also incur a deficit, although the regulatory framework requires FTs to demonstrate financial viability over the medium term
- There is no requirement to remain within an external financing limit target, to achieve a defined capital absorption rate as set by the Treasury or to remain within a capital resource limit. However, public dividend capital (PDC) dividends must still be paid at 3.5%
- FTs do not have access to financial support from the strategic health authority (SHA) or Department of Health. However, the Department has established the FT Financing Facility (FTFF) which operates at 'arms length' from the Department (see later in this chapter)
- FTs are subject to a different accounting regime which is consistent with generally accepted accounting practice (UK GAAP) used for commercial organisations rather then resource accounting which is used in the NHS
- FTs can decide locally the capital investment they need to improve their services and increase capacity and are able to borrow in order to support this investment, subject to Monitor's guidance as set out in *Risk Evaluation for Investment Decisions by NHS Foundation Trusts* and in the *Prudential Borrowing Code for NHS Foundation Trusts*[6].

Monitor sets the financial framework within which FTs operate and issues guidance including the *NHS Foundation Trust Financial Reporting Manual*.

Regulatory approach – the compliance framework

Monitor has adopted a 'risk based' approach to regulation – this means that assessments of risk in a number of key areas are used to determine the level and depth of monitoring that an FT is subject to. The three key areas that Monitor focuses on are:

---

[6] Since 2007/08 the capital regime for non foundation trusts has been bought into line with the FT approach – see chapters 7 and 16.

- Finance
- Governance
- Mandatory services.

Full details of Monitor's regulatory approach are set out in its *Compliance Framework* which is reviewed and updated regularly. At the time of writing (March 2008), Monitor was consulting on amendments to the framework that will take effect from April 2008.

Finance risk rating

A financial scorecard is used to generate a finance risk rating (FRR) and this is split into four main criteria of the total risk rating score. For each criterion a score of 1 to 5 is awarded with 1 indicating a high risk of a significant breach of the authorisation and 5 a low risk with no financial regulatory concerns. The four areas are:

- Achievement of plan
- Underlying performance
- Financial efficiency
- Liquidity.

In practice, FTs are scored across five metrics, with financial efficiency being measured using two separate metrics. The five metrics are:

- Achievement of plan – EBITDA (earnings before interest, taxes, depreciation and amortisation) achieved (% of plan)
- Underlying performance – EBITDA margin (%)
- Financial efficiency (1) – return on assets excluding dividend (%)
- Financial efficiency (2) – income and expenditure surplus margin net of dividend (%)
- Liquidity – liquidity ratio (days). Liquidity is defined as cash plus trade debtors plus unused working capital facility minus (trade creditors plus other creditors plus accruals) and is expressed in number of days operating expenses that could be covered.

Each FT is rated from 1 to 5 in each of these metrics and then, using weightings, an overall aggregate FRR is produced. This is also a whole number from 1 to 5. A series of over-riding rules are then applied. For instance, an FT that has a 1 or a 2 in one financial criterion, can only achieve a maximum risk rating of 3.

The weightings that have been used to derive the aggregate FRR since April 2007 are:

- Achievement of plan – 10%
- Underlying performance – 25%
- Financial efficiency – 40% (20% for each of the 2 metrics)
- Liquidity – 25%.

As stated, one purpose of the FRR is to assist the regulator in determining the frequency with which he needs to monitor the organisation or intervene as appropriate. Another is to grant autonomy to high performing organisations in order that they may maximise the financial freedoms (including borrowing) and responsibilities available to FTs whilst at the same time ensuring proper risk management. The FRR has a direct impact on one of the key ratios used to derive the prudential borrowing limit (PBL). In fact, an FRR of 1 precludes any borrowing at all.

Governance risk rating

The governance risk rating focuses on the degree to which FTs are complying with their terms of authorisation. Monitor looks at seven criteria:

- Legality of constitution
- Growing a representative membership
- Appropriate board roles and structures
- Service performance
- Clinical quality
- Effective risk and performance management
- Co-operation with NHS bodies and local authorities.

The level of governance risk is assessed using a 'traffic light' approach where green indicates a low risk and red high.

Mandatory services risk rating

This applies to services that are specified as being mandatory in the application for FT status and the terms of authorisation. Again Monitor uses a traffic light system with the focus on:

- Any changes in mandatory services
- Any disposals of protected assets.

Service line reporting and management

Service line reporting (SLR) involves looking in detail at the income and costs of an FT's services in much the same way as a private sector company analyses its business units. In practice, this means that FTs look at profitability information by specialty. Monitor has issued guidance on SLR which lists the characteristics of a typical service line as being:

- Distinct patient groups
- Distinct product/services/procedures
- Designated staff
- Clearly identified profit and loss responsibilities.

The information gleaned from SLR is used to 'manage' each service line (hence 'service line management' or SLM) and develop the FT's business plans with the FT overall effectively managed as 'a portfolio of autonomous and accountable business units.'

In its guide *Getting the most out of Managing Service Lines: Organisational Change and Incentive-based Performance*, Monitor states that 'successful SLM requires the fully integrated ownership of clinical, operational and financial objectives and outcomes at sub-board level'. The guide acknowledges that SLM is a developing area that will not achieve its full potential unless FTs have in place:

- Well defined organisational structures and processes
- Coherent operational strategies
- Comprehensive annual planning processes
- Information systems
- Performance improvement policies.

SLR and SLM are regarded as best practice for FTs and Monitor's guidance is designed to help FTs develop their approaches.

Annual Accounts

All FTs have a statutory duty to produce annual accounts as set out in the *NHS Act 2006*. The form and content of the accounts is prescribed by Monitor (with the approval of the Treasury) and is largely consistent with UK GAAP. The production of the statutory annual accounts is the principal means by which FTs discharge their accountability to taxpayers and users of services for their stewardship of public money.

NHS bodies are expected to adhere to the accounting standards issued or adopted by the Accounting Standards Board (ASB). However, the government has the final say on how these standards are applied to the public sector, including NHS bodies. The Treasury has developed a *Financial Reporting Manual* setting out how accounting standards should be implemented in the public sector. For FTs, Monitor produces an annual *NHS Foundation Trust Financial Reporting Manual* which is broadly consistent with the Treasury's manual – any divergences are approved by the Treasury. The manual includes a summary of extant accounting standards and gives details of their applicability to FTs.

In its *Budget 2008*, the Treasury announced that international financial reporting standards (IFRS) will be followed for the preparation of accounts from 2009/10.

Annual Report

FTs are required to produce an annual report which must be published with the full set of audited accounts. The annual report is primarily a narrative document similar to the directors' report described in the *Companies Act*, but with additional information reflecting the FT's position in the community. The report gives an account of activities, performance and achievements over the last financial year.

Although the layout of the annual report is at each FT's discretion, there are mandatory items which must be included – these are set out in the *NHS Foundation Trust Financial Reporting Manual*.

The annual report and accounts must be approved by the board of directors prior to submission to Monitor. From 2006/07, FTs are required to lay their report and accounts (the full accounts – not summary financial statements) before Parliament themselves. This has to be done before the summer recess.

The annual report and accounts must also be presented to a meeting of the board of governors. This meeting should be convened within a reasonable timescale after the end of the financial year, but must not be before the FT has laid the annual report and accounts before Parliament.

Audit Arrangements

All FTs must have their accounts audited by independent external auditors who are appointed by an FT's board of governors.

The audited annual accounts must be laid before Parliament. The chief executive, as accounting officer, may be required to appear before the Public Accounts Committee to answer questions.

The *Audit Code for NHS Foundation Trusts*, published by Monitor, prescribes the way in which external auditors carry out their functions.

FTs are also required to have an internal audit function.

Capital Funding and the Prudential Borrowing Code

The most significant challenge posed by the financial freedoms available to FTs is the management of cash (whether for revenue or capital expenditure) and any associated borrowing. Monitor has published a *Prudential Borrowing Code* that FTs must adhere to when applying for new borrowing. The code itself takes account of generally accepted principles followed by financial institutions and focuses heavily on liquidity, meaning the strength of cash flow available to meet both dividend payments on opening and new PDC and service interest and principal repayments on new loans. The measures are largely based around 'free cash flow' (FCF) or more specifically, 'revenue available for debt service' (RAfDS), which is defined as the operating surplus before depreciation and interest.

Without ensuring adequate levels of FCF FTs could find themselves in financial difficulties. For example, the situation might arise where new borrowing is entered into for an expansion in services, which then fails to attract sufficient patient-related income because demand falls, either through a lack of partnership working or due to a failure to assess the risk properly. FTs must therefore ensure that their financial performance is monitored closely.

Monitor has powers to intervene if an FT fails financially.

The *Prudential Borrowing Code* sets out five key financial ratios that help ensure that all borrowing remains affordable. These are:

- **Maximum debt to capital ratio (<0–40%)** – this is defined as the amount of long term borrowing as a percentage of total assets (the use of total assets, as opposed to net assets or equity means that borrowing increases the borrowing limit). The measure will range from 0% (FRR 1) to no more than 40% (FRR 5), depending on the FRR achieved at the application/plan stage. This ratio is often referred to as 'gearing'

- **Minimum dividend cover** (>1×) – this ratio effectively requires that an FT has sufficient FCF to meet its annual dividend payment to the Department of Health (at least once) calculated as 3.5% of the value of its assets. The formula is: RAfDS less interest divided by annual dividend payable
- **Minimum interest cover** (>3×) – this financial constraint is the interest coverage ratio measured by the number of times that RAfDS covers interest repayments in any one year. The formula is: RAfDS divided by maximum annual interest
- **Minimum debt service cover** (>2×) – this ratio requires that RAfDS is sufficient to meet all interest and principal payments on long term borrowing, measured as RAfDS divided by maximum annual debt service
- **Maximum debt service to revenue** (<3%) – this ratio seeks to ensure that the cost of servicing debt and loans is no more than 3% of an FT's total revenue. It is measured by calculating maximum annual debt service divided by revenue.

Affordability

The amount an FT can borrow (the prudential borrowing limit or PBL) is initially determined from the service development strategy submitted as part of the FT application, and is reviewed at least annually as part of the annual plan submission.

Borrowing includes loans from the FT financing facility, commercial borrowing and on-balance sheet leases and PFI schemes. It excludes PDC and off-balance sheet arrangements.

The PBL is calculated using the plan figures and is set so as to ensure that the five financial ratios set out above continue to be met. It is important to understand that the FRR is a key factor in determining the PBL, since any significant reduction in this figure in year could lead to a reduction in PBL in-year.

The HFMA's *Introductory Guide to NHS Foundation Trust Finance and Governance* looks in detail at the practical application of the *Prudential Borrowing Code* and includes a worked example.

Sources of Borrowing

The main source of operational capital funding is from internally generated resources – retained depreciation, land sales and surpluses. Larger schemes will require an FT to borrow within its PBL.

Although some FTs have already sought funding from the commercial sector, it was envisaged initially that the market would be too immature to attract significant interest from commercial lenders and that – in the absence of an agreed insolvency regime and asset security – it may prove expensive. For this reason the Department of Health formed the FT financing facility (FTFF) – this operates at arm's length from the Department and makes loan decisions based on the ability of the FT 'to pay back the money, not on the basis of a policy judgement'[7]. Loans

---

[7] NHS Foundation Trusts Information Guide – Financial Freedoms, Department of Health, 2004.

are made available at a preferential rate (equivalent to the National Loans Fund rate) for core business (i.e. 'to fund development to essential protected services'), and at a market rate for commercial developments or 'non-protected activity'.

Another source of funding for capital projects involves working in partnership with the private sector – most commonly using the private finance initiative or PFI. The Department of Health and Monitor have issued guidance as to the relative roles in the assessment of the affordability of future PFI projects – *Roles and Responsibilities in the Approval of NHS Foundation Trust PFI Schemes.*

PDC funding

Whereas the primary source of funding for an FT is likely to be borrowing, it is still possible that schemes in existence at authorisation, and some central initiatives will continue to be funded via PDC from the Department of Health.

If an FT has agreed PDC funding with the Department, then a 'PDC Limit' is set (by the Department). This is similar to a 'cash based capital resource limit (CRL)[8]', in that an FT may only access the PDC once it has fully utilised its own internal cash generated through retained depreciation (as calculated in the annual capital charges exercise) and sale proceeds from the disposal of fixed assets.

References and Further Reading

NHS Act 2006: www.opsi.gov.uk/Acts/acts2006/ukpga_20060041_en_1

Introductory Guide: NHS Foundation Trust Finance and Governance, HFMA, 2007: www.hfma.org.uk

Health and Social Care (Community Health and Standards) Act 2003: www.opsi.gov.uk/Acts/acts2003/ukpga_20030043_en_1

The NHS Plan: a plan for investment, a plan for reform, Department of Health, 2000: www.dh.gov.uk/en/Publicationsandstatistics/Publications/PublicationsPolicyAndGuidance/DH_4002960

Private patient income cap – Monitor's statement: www.regulator-nhsft.gov.uk/news.php?id=1092

UNISON website: www.unison.org.uk:80/news/news_view.asp?did=4002

---

[8] A CRL is an expenditure limit determined by the Department of Health for each NHS organisation limiting the amount that may be expended on capital purchases, as assessed on an accruals basis (i.e. after adjusting for debtors and creditors).

The NHS Foundation Trust Code of Governance, Monitor, 2006: www.monitor-nhsft.gov.uk/publications.php

For details of the FT application process and integrated business plan see the FT pages of the Department of Health's website: www.dh.gov.uk/PolicyAndGuidance/OrganisationPolicy/ SecondaryCare/NHSFoundationTrust/fs/en

Applying for NHS Foundation Trust Status: Guide for Applicants, Monitor, 2007: www.regulator-nhsft.gov.uk/publications.php

Compliance Framework, Monitor, April 2007: www.regulator-nhsft.gov.uk/publications.php

Getting the most out of Managing Service Lines: using Service-line Reporting in the Annual Planning Process, Monitor, 2007: www.regulator-nhsft.gov.uk/publications.php

Getting the most out of Managing Service Lines: Organisational Change and Incentive-based Performance, Monitor, 2007: www.regulator-nhsft.gov.uk/publications.php

Accounting Standards Board: www.frc.org.uk/asb/

Government Financial Reporting Manual: www.financial-reporting.gov.uk/

NHS Foundation Trust Financial Reporting Manual, Monitor: www.regulator-nhsft.gov.uk/publications.php

Budget 2008: Stability and Opportunity: Building a Strong, Sustainable Future, HM Treasury, 2008: www.hm-treasury.gov.uk./budget/budget_08/report/bud_bud08_repindex.cfm

Audit Code for NHS Foundation trusts, Monitor: www.monitor-nhsft.gov.uk/publications.php

Prudential Borrowing Code for NHS Foundation Trusts, Monitor, 2005: www.regulator-nhsft.gov.uk/publications.php

NHS Foundation Trusts Information Guide – Financial Freedoms, Department of Health, 2004 (use the search function – key in 'financial freedoms'): www.dh.gov.uk

Roles and Responsibilities in the Approval of NHS Foundation Trust PFI Schemes, Monitor and the Department of Health, June 2007: www.regulator-nhsft.gov.uk/publications.php

9. Partnerships between the NHS and Local Authorities

Introduction

NHS organisations are expected to engage with their local community to improve health and well-being and reduce health inequalities. They also contribute to sustainable community development. Increasingly this means that NHS organisations (and PCTs in particular) must work in partnership with local authorities both to manage and deliver services in which both parties have an interest (for example, services for children, the elderly, the disabled, the mentally ill and people with learning disabilities) and to plan ahead for the local area.

Partnership working operates at a number of different levels and can take a variety of forms. The focus tends to be very much on either joint commissioning of services and/or integrated service provision. The overall aim is stated on the Department of Health's website as being 'to enable partners to join together to design and deliver services around the needs of users rather than worrying about the boundaries of their organisations. These arrangements should help eliminate unnecessary gaps and duplications between services'.

This chapter looks briefly at the partnerships that are most common:

- Local strategic partnerships (LSPs)
- Local area agreements (LAAs)
- Joint strategic needs assessments (JSNAs)
- Care trusts
- Pooled budgets
- Lead commissioning
- Integrated provision
- Government grants
- Grants from the NHS to local authorities
- Grants from local authorities to the NHS.

It also looks briefly at the legal, governance and financial framework that enables the partnership arrangements to work effectively; common partnership models and other areas where NHS organisations and local authorities come into close contact.

Local Strategic Partnerships

Section 82 of the *NHS Act 2006* requires NHS bodies and local authorities to co-operate with each other 'to secure and advance the health and welfare of the people of England and Wales'. In England local strategic partnerships (LSPs) help achieve this aim.

As the name suggests, LSPs operate at a strategic level. They are led by local authorities and were first introduced in 2001. LSPs are non-statutory, non-executive, multi-agency bodies that are designed to 'bring together at local level the different parts of the public sector as well as the private, business, community and voluntary sectors so that different initiatives and services support each other and work together'.

Although the legal duty to produce sustainable community strategies (a long-term, sustainable vision for an area which sets the agenda for priorities in the local area agreement or LAA) and LAAs rests with local authorities, LSPs are responsible for collectively agreeing them and overseeing their delivery.

Local NHS bodies are expected to work within the relevant LSP to help further the partnership's aims and ensure co-ordination in planning and service delivery.

Local Area Agreements

Local Area Agreements (LAAs) are at the heart of the new local performance framework first set out in the 2006 local government White Paper *Strong and Prosperous Communities*. An LAA is a three year agreement that identifies the priorities for a local area and is agreed between central government and a locality represented by a lead local authority and its key partners (via LSPs).

LAAs for each English locality are due to be signed off by June 2008. The Department of Health's *Operating Framework* for 2008/09 makes clear that PCTs and NHS trusts should work with their local LSP to agree LAA priorities that will improve health outcomes and that 'each LAA should prove itself a strong complementary ally to its PCT's operational plan'.

Joint Strategic Needs Assessments

The 2006 White Paper, *Our health, Our care, Our say: a New Direction for Community Services*, identified a need for there to be regular assessments of the health and well-being status of local populations so that meaningful objectives for local services could be established. The idea is that these 'joint strategic needs assessments' (JSNAs) will underpin the sustainable community strategy and LAAs that local authorities are required to develop.

JSNAs are designed to 'identify the current and future health and well-being needs of a local population, informing the priorities and targets set by Local Area Agreements and leading to agreed commissioning priorities that will improve outcomes and reduce health inequalities'[9]. They are a statutory requirement as set down in section 116 of the *Local Government and Public Involvement in Health Act 2007*. This duty applies to PCTs and upper tier local authorities and comes into effect from April 2008. Guidance on JSNAs recognises that in practice, they will be jointly undertaken by the Director of Public Health, Director of Adult Social Services and Director of Children's Services, working closely with the Directors of Commissioning and Finance.

As well as underpinning the sustainable community strategy, JSNAs will feed into PCTs own planning processes. In particular, they will help PCTs develop and refine their:

---

[9] Guidance on Joint Strategic Needs Assessment, Departments of Health and Communities and Local Government, 2007.

- Strategic direction
- Priorities and targets for improving health and social care outcomes and health inequalities
- Operational/local delivery plans
- Service and financial plans.

Care Trusts

Care trusts were announced in 2000 in the *NHS Plan* and section 45 of the *Health and Social Care Act 2001* legislated for their introduction. A care trust is a statutory NHS body to which local authorities can delegate health-related functions with the aim of providing integrated health and social care to the local community. Care trusts are established on a voluntary partnership basis where there is a joint agreement at local level that this model will offer the best way to deliver better health and social care services. The idea is that by combining NHS and local authority health responsibilities under a single management, care trusts can improve continuity of care and simplify administration.

Care trusts can be formed from an existing NHS trust or a PCT. In the latter case the new care trust is both a provider and a commissioner of services. It is important to note that local authority services are delegated to care trusts, not transferred.

Pooled Budgets

The Department of Health's website defines pooled funds as 'the ability for partners each to contribute agreed funds to a single pot, to be spent on agreed projects for designated services'. It also states that 'the advantage of pooled budgets is that they remove the barriers between health and social care and allow for innovation in the use of funds for new services without the need to revisit traditional debates over what is a health or what is a social care responsibility'.

In practice, this means that pooled budgets exist where a local authority and an NHS body combine resources and jointly commission or manage an integrated service. Legislation that allows for this was first introduced under section 31 of the *Health Act 1999* (now section 75 of the *NHS Act 2006*) and the concept was given further backing in the *NHS Plan*. The idea is that, once a pooled budget is introduced the public will experience a seamless service with a single point of access for their health and social care needs. There are some services that are particularly well suited to pooled budgets – for example, services for people with a learning disability and for equipment stores (for instance wheelchairs or callipers). At a practical level each pooled budget needs to designate a 'host' partner.

Where a pooled budget exists, regulations for England and Wales require that the partners have written agreements setting out:

- The functions covered
- The aims agreed
- The funds that each partner will contribute
- Which partner will act as the 'host' (i.e. which organisation will manage the budget and take responsibility for the accounts and auditing).

Lead Commissioning

Under a lead commissioning arrangement, partners agree to delegate commissioning of a service to one lead organisation. Like pooled budgets, lead commissioning was made possible by section 31 of the *1999 Act* (now section 75 of the *NHS Act 2006*).

Integrated Provision

Integrated provision involves the partners joining together their staff, resources, and management structures so that the service is fully combined (or integrated) from managerial level to the front line. Again this way of working was made possible by section 31 of the *1999 Act* (now section 75 of the *NHS Act 2006*).

Government Grants

Government grants are available to the NHS for community-based projects run in conjunction with local authorities. Typically these grants are linked to regeneration and renewal programmes in deprived communities where a partnership board with representation from many elements of the local community, including NHS bodies, has successfully bid for and then managed the distribution of the grant. Examples of these types of grant include:

- Sure Start projects aimed at developing services for children
- New Deal for Community projects aimed at developing services in an urban setting at a neighbourhood level.

In terms of the financial framework for these projects, the structure is fairly straightforward – the grant is paid directly to the participating NHS body to cover the costs incurred.

Grants from the NHS to Local Authorities (section 28a grants)

NHS bodies have for many years been able to make grants to local authorities for the provision of health services. For example, a local authority operating a unit for people with learning difficulties may receive a grant from the NHS body to cover the provision of healthcare to the clients in the unit. Such grants are made under section 28a of the *National Health Service Act 1977* and must pay only for medical care. They must not involve the transfer of health functions to a local authority.

Although they have been around for many years and are quite common, section 28a grants are fairly limited in their scope – for example, it would be ultra vires for any such grant to contribute towards the provision of social care.

Grants from Local Authorities to the NHS (section 28bb grants)

Under section 28bb of the *NHS Act 1977* local authorities can make capital grants to the NHS for the provision of health services in instances where the local authority is satisfied that the payment is likely to secure a more effective use of public funds than the deployment of an equivalent amount on the provision of local authority services.

Practical Considerations

When organisations from different sectors and with different statutory and regulatory regimes work together there are a number of practical issues that need to be thought through to ensure that the partnership is a success. From a financial and stewardship viewpoint it is important that organisations think about:

- Corporate governance
- Risk sharing and control
- Financial framework
- Legal framework
- Human resources/workforce framework.

Corporate governance

Local authorities and the NHS are subject to different governance regimes: although each receives significant levels of public funding, local authorities have a democratic mandate and are accountable to the local electorate whereas NHS bodies are ultimately accountable through their boards and the Secretary of State for Health (or Monitor in the case of NHS foundation trusts) to Parliament. See the HFMA's guide – *Effective Governance in Healthcare: an Introductory Guide* – for more about governance arrangements.

Risk sharing and control

Partnerships need to decide how they will share financial and other risks. So for example if the partnership overspends there will need to be agreement around how the overspend is financed and reported. Risk sharing agreements are often difficult to negotiate and require a degree of compromise from both partners. Partnerships also imply a loss of control over the service, as partners can no longer make unilateral changes to the service itself or to the level of funding.

Financial framework

The NHS and local government operate under different financial regimes. There are two key areas where this has an impact:

- VAT: local authorities are able to recover VAT on most items of expenditure whereas the NHS may not. HM Revenue and Customs will not allow the creation of partnerships to be used as a mechanism for avoiding VAT and, therefore, it may be necessary for the partnership to account for tax as if it were still two bodies
- Charges: local authorities have the power to charge clients for the services provided, whereas the NHS does not. The partnership agreement has to be devised so that there is no loss of revenue.

Legal framework

Greater integration and joint working between the NHS and local government was first made possible by the introduction of the *Health Act 1999* – before then there were legal limitations on the powers of NHS bodies to enter into partnership agreements with local authorities. Section 31 of the 1999 Act provided the necessary legal framework for greater partnership working and these powers were extended by the *Health and Social Care Act 2001*. Section 31 has now been repealed and replaced (in England) by section 75 of the *NHS Act 2006* which has consolidated NHS legislation. This new provision is in exactly the same terms as section 31 and existing arrangements continue as if made under the new powers.

Human resources/workforce framework

Where staff from different organisations are brought together in integrated arrangements it is essential that employment arrangements, human resources policies and procedures are formalised.

Secondments from one partner organisation into another need to be treated with particular care as difficulties can arise. For example, if the secondment extends beyond two years the employee has rights of tenure within the partnership. Secondment also implies separate employing authorities and separate terms and conditions for staff working alongside each other. The introduction of *Agenda for Change* within the NHS has made this a more prominent issue.

Where staff transfer to a partnership the *Transfer of Undertakings (Protection of Employment)* or TUPE regulations may come into effect – again this could lead to difficulties in relation to staff working side by side.

Partnership Models

Partnerships can take a variety of forms – two common models are discussed below.

The quasi partnership

Some organisations have decided not to go down the pooled budget route and have instead set up shared management arrangements with NHS and local authority funding and expenditure kept as two separate streams. A variation is that the budgets for the management of the shared services covered by the agreement are pooled but the budgets for the provision of services are not.

In this way decisions relating to the service can be taken in partnership and the services themselves can appear seamless to their users. However, accountability for income and expenditure is still divided.

The diagram opposite shows a situation where there is joint management and decision making for the shared service but there is no budget pooling: accountability for the funding side remains with each partner.

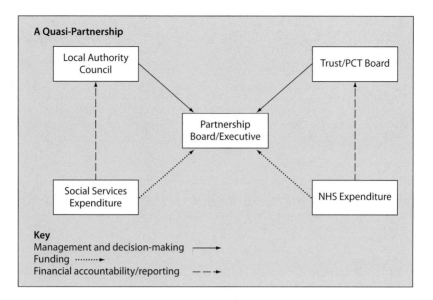

The host partner

In a partnership where pooling of budgets takes place one partner will become the host. All financial transactions will go through the host's accounts and be subject to the host's financial regime. The other partner will make payments to the host at the agreed level of funding.

The partnership agreement may call for a degree of ring fencing of the cost of the pooled service within the host's books so that the partnership board and executive can see and protect the income and expenditure that relates to the pool.

The diagram over the page shows the situation where a trust or PCT board acts as the host partner and is accountable for the ring-fenced budget. The local authority provides an agreed budget and participates in the partnership board.

Other Issues

There are a number of other areas where NHS bodies and local authorities come into close contact. These include:

- Local authority overview and scrutiny
- Delayed discharges
- Local improvement finance trusts (LIFTs).

Overview and scrutiny

Since January 2003, local authorities with social services responsibilities have been able to establish committees of councillors to provide overview and scrutiny of local NHS bodies by virtue of powers set out in section 38 of the *Local Government Act 2000*. The ultimate aim is to

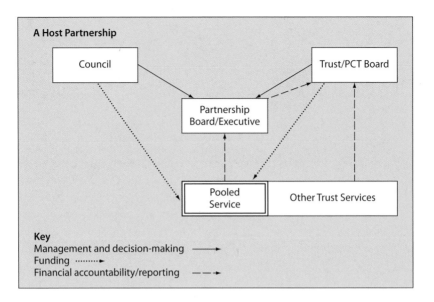

A Host Partnership

Council → Partnership Board/Executive ← Trust/PCT Board

Pooled Service | Other Trust Services

Key
Management and decision-making ———▶
Funding ·········▶
Financial accountability/reporting — — ▶

secure health improvement for local communities by encouraging authorities to look beyond their own service responsibilities to issues of wider concern to local people. This is achieved by giving democratically elected representatives the right to scrutinise how local health services are provided and developed for their constituents. Health organisations are often invited to attend formal meetings of local authorities to answer questions on key issues including financial health, present operational plans or undertake formal consultation with elected members.

Delayed discharges

Delayed discharges from hospitals (often referred to as patients who are 'bed blocking') remains a problem for the NHS and the government is keen to see the NHS, local authorities and other local organisations (including housing organisations, primary care and the independent and voluntary sectors) working together to minimise the impact of this. To encourage local authorities to do all they can to make swift discharges possible, the government introduced a system whereby if a patient is delayed in being discharged from acute services solely because supporting community care arrangements are lacking the relevant local authority must financially reimburse the trust concerned. As part of this arrangement, trusts have to notify social services departments of patients who may require community care. For more see the *Community Care (Delayed Discharges) Act, 2003* and related guidance on the reimbursement pages of the Department of Health's website.

Local improvement finance trusts

The local improvement finance trust (LIFT) initiative was launched in 2001 and is a form of public-private partnership designed to help develop and improve primary care premises. This may include the co-location of related services, including local authority social services. See chapter 10 on public private partnerships for more details.

References and Further Reading

Health Act 2006: www.opsi.gov.uk/acts/acts2006/60041-af.htm

Local Strategic Partnerships: Guidance, Department for Communities and Local Government: www.communities.gov.uk/publications/localgovernment/localstrategicpartnerships2

Strong and Prosperous Communities – The Local Government White Paper, 2006, Department for Communities and Local Government: www.communities.gov.uk/publications/localgovernment/strongprosperous

The Operating Framework for the NHS in England 2008/09: www.dh.gov.uk/en/ Publicationsandstatistics/Publications/PublicationsPolicyAndGuidance/DH_081094

Our health, Our care, Our say: a new Direction for Community Services, Department of Health, 2006: www.dh.gov.uk/en/Healthcare/Ourhealthourcareoursay/index.htm

Joint Strategic Needs Assessment, Departments of Health and Communities and Local Government guidance, 2007: www.dh.gov.uk/en/Publicationsandstatistics/Publications/ PublicationsPolicyAndGuidance/DH_081097

Local Government and Public Involvement in Health Act 2007: www.opsi.gov.uk/ACTS/acts2007/ukpga_20070028_en_1

The NHS Plan: a plan for investment, a plan for reform, Department of Health, 2000: www.dh.gov.uk/en/Publicationsandstatistics/Publications/PublicationsPolicyAndGuidance/ DH_4002960

Department of Health Care Trust web pages: www.dh.gov.uk/PolicyAndGuidance/OrganisationPolicy/IntegratedCare/CareTrusts/fs/en

Care trusts – to access links to existing trusts visit: www.nhs.uk/ServiceDirectories/Pages/CareTrustListing.aspx

Integrated Care Network: www.integratedcarenetwork.gov.uk/

Health and Social Care Act 2001 section 45: www.opsi.gov.uk/ACTS/acts2001/20010015.htm

For more on Health Act Partnership Arrangements: www.dh.gov.uk/en/Policyandguidance/ Organisationpolicy/IntegratedCare/Healthact1999partnershiparrangements/index.htm

NHS Act 1977: www.opsi.gov.uk/acts/acts1977/pdf/ukpga_19770049_en.pdf

Effective Governance in Healthcare: an Introductory Guide, HFMA, 2006: www.hfma.org.uk

HM Revenue and Customs: www.hmrc.gov.uk

Agenda for Change: www.dh.gov.uk/en/Policyandguidance/Humanresourcesandtraining/ Modernisingpay/Agendaforchange/index.htm

For more on TUPE see: www.dti.gov.uk/employment/trade-union-rights/tupe/page16289.html

Local Government Act 2000: www.opsi.gov.uk/acts/acts2000/ukpga_20000022_en_1

Overview and Scrutiny of Health – Guidance, Department of Health, 2003:
www.dh.gov.uk/en/Publicationsandstatistics/Publications/PublicationsLegislation/DH_4009607

Delayed Discharges: www.dh.gov.uk/en/Policyandguidance/Organisationpolicy/IntegratedCare/
Delayeddischarges/index.htm

LIFT: www.dh.gov.uk/en/Procurementandproposals/Publicprivatepartnership/NHSLIFT/
NHSLIFTguidance/index.htm

For more on local authority functions see the Local Government Association's website:
www.lga.gov.uk

10. Public Private Partnerships

Introduction

Partnership working with other organisations is increasingly common in the NHS and takes a variety of forms. The overall objective is the same for all approaches – to develop a comprehensive healthcare infrastructure and modern, responsive patient care environment. This chapter focuses on the main public private partnerships (PPPs) that are used in the NHS – the private finance initiative (PFI) and local improvement finance trusts (NHS LIFT).

Private Finance Initiative

Background

The PFI is a mechanism for funding major capital investments without immediate recourse to public money. Instead private companies are contracted to design and build the assets needed. These are then leased back to the NHS, usually over a period of around 30 years.

The PFI was launched over fifteen years ago in the November 1992 autumn statement of the Chancellor of the Exchequer. While there had already been a number of high profile transport related private sector infrastructure projects (for example, the Channel Tunnel and the Queen Elizabeth II Bridge for the Dartford Crossing), the 1992 announcement indicated the government's intention to apply PFI principles more widely.

The original aim of the PFI was to involve the private sector more directly in the provision of public sector services and make use of its commercial, entrepreneurial and managerial expertise. As a result, the public sector focus changed from procuring and managing infrastructure projects to enabling service delivery and guarding the interests of the users and customers of public services.

Although the PFI has evolved since 1992, it continues to play an important role in public sector infrastructure investment and has been used to deliver a range of new facilities in the NHS – for example, hospitals, staff accommodation, information management and technology (IM&T) systems, energy schemes and laboratory services. PFI projects have involved the provision of services in the form of assets and 'hard' (for example, estates) and 'soft' (for example, cleaning, domestic and catering) services.

Under the PFI responsibility for the design, construction, maintenance, operation and financing of capital assets rests with the private sector. The public sector focus is on defining the standards of service required – the private sector partner then decides how it can best deliver a service to meet those standards. The public sector client only pays for the service when it becomes operational and the payment, which is of a revenue nature, is based on the satisfactory provision of the service. Payment takes the form of an ongoing 'unitary charge' paid to the PFI provider once the services have commenced in a satisfactory manner. The financing of the construction of the asset is the responsibility of the PFI provider through a range of funding mechanisms, which may involve a loan, equity or bonds.

Another key feature of PFI is that under current accounting rules an asset provided under a PFI service contract is not deemed to be owned by the public sector organisation and does not therefore appear on its balance sheet. Instead the asset is owned by the PFI provider who is responsible for ensuring that the asset remains fit for purpose throughout the life of the contract. This means that using the PFI reduces the need for public sector capital and the public sector borrowing requirement.

The accounting treatment of PFI funded assets is expected to change when international financial reporting standards (IFRS) are followed for the preparation of accounts from 2009/10 with the end result that many more projects could appear on NHS balance sheets and in public sector borrowing figures (see 'accounting for PFI transactions' later on in this section and chapter 14).

Benefits of PFI

Supporters of the PFI argue that it helps achieve service improvements and increased value for money through:

- Better allocation of risk – risk is allocated to those best placed to manage it
- Incentives to perform – the provision of a service over a long-term contract with in-built performance clauses concentrates management attention on service quality
- Close integration of service needs with design and construction – traditionally this has not been the case with one party building a facility and another operating it
- A clearer focus on roles and responsibilities – the public sector can concentrate on what services are required and the private sector can determine how best to meet those pre-set requirements
- A continuing commercial incentive for efficiency – the private sector provider will want to achieve efficiency in the delivery of services over the entire period of the contract
- Potential for third party revenues – the PFI may improve efficiency and lead to the public sector sharing in income generating activities.

Disadvantages of PFI

PFI critics identify the following disadvantages:

- It involves an overly bureaucratic and lengthy process to gain approvals
- There can be significant revenue costs for advisory assistance – for example on the legal and financial side
- There are issues and concerns relating to the off balance sheet accounting treatment
- There is a potential for private sector partners to earn excessive profits
- Staff side trade associations can be resistant at both an ideological and practical level
- There are concerns about the affordability of new PFI schemes.

PFI in the NHS

PFI schemes involve creating partnerships between the public and private sectors that allow the NHS to focus on the provision of high quality clinical care to patients while the private sector provides investment to help deliver the modernisation agenda.

Major PFI schemes are typically design, build, finance and operate (DBFO) schemes, which mean that the private sector partner is responsible for:

- Designing the facilities (based on the requirements specified by the NHS and in line with technical guidance, regulations and standards)
- Building the facilities to time and at a fixed cost
- Financing the capital costs
- Operating the facilities (providing facilities management and other support services).

In essence a PFI project involves the agreement of a contract between an NHS body and a private sector organisation for the provision of services over an agreed contract period. The private sector organisation will normally be in the form of a special purpose vehicle (SPV) or special purpose company (SPC) established specifically for the project. The SPV may consist of a construction company, a facilities management company and a financing organisation. The exact composition will depend on the project and the prevailing circumstances. Similarly the length of the contract depends on the nature of the service to be provided – a new hospital may have a contract period of 30–35 years.

The contract will set out in detail the obligations of each party. The development of a PFI project must follow a prescribed process in the NHS and comply with EU procurement guidance. This is discussed in more detail below.

Key principles – value for money and risk

There are two fundamental requirements for a PFI project:

- Value for money (VFM) must be demonstrated for public sector expenditure
- The private sector must genuinely assume risk.

Value for money

VFM is assessed by looking at 'whole life' costs and benefits (i.e. over the period of the project). This involves a financial review of the benefits, risks and associated cash flows of public sector and PFI options. Discounted cash flow investment appraisal techniques are used to determine the relative net present values – i.e. the total value in today's terms of all benefits and costs associated with a project or option. The costs are subtracted from the benefits to give a net value.

The Treasury's 2006 document *Value for Money Assessment Guidance* sets out a framework that organisations should use to consider whether the PFI procurement route will deliver VFM and how best to achieve it. This guide emphasises that 'procuring authorities should begin detailed assessments of the VFM of PFI projects at the earliest stage possible'.

The Guide is available on the Treasury's website.

Risk

A risk matrix is used to determine those risks to be taken by the public sector, those assumed by the private sector and those that are shared. The key principle is to allocate risk to the party that is best able to manage it. In particular, there needs to be an assessment in VFM terms of whether a risk should be transferred, retained, managed or insured against. It is also important to remember that every risk transferred has a price. The key risks that need to be considered when assessing a project include:

- Design and construction risk – failure to meet requirements, time and cost overruns
- Commissioning and operating risks – operating costs, availability and performance
- Demand, volume or usage risks
- Risk associated with the asset's residual value at the end of the PFI arrangement
- Technology or obsolescence risk
- Regulatory risk – for example, taxation and planning permission
- Project financing risk.

How a PFI scheme works

The development of a PFI project can be a lengthy and time-consuming process and there is a wealth of detailed practical guidance available to NHS organisations contemplating going down this route. The best place to start is the Department of Health's website which also provides links to other key sources, including the Treasury whose *Green Book* sets out the approach that the public sector should take to investment appraisal generally, including PFI transactions. Organisations also need to think about appointing technical, financial and legal advisers to help support and guide them through the process.

A PFI scheme in the NHS follows the same principles and procedures that have been established to ensure that all investment in the NHS is soundly based whether it is publicly or privately funded. This means the development of robust business cases using the Office of Government Commerce's (OGC) *Five Case Model* which is designed to ensure that schemes:

- Are supported by a robust case for change that provides strategic synergy – the strategic case
- Optimise value for money – the economic case
- Are commercially viable – the commercial case
- Are financially affordable – the financial case
- Are achievable – the management case.

The HFMA has published a toolkit designed to help organisations implement the *Five Case Model*.

For a PFI scheme the process is as follows:

- Establish the strategic context, assess the options and, for major schemes, make the case for change in a strategic outline case (SOC) and get approval
- Identify and develop a preferred option through an investment appraisal, make the case in an outline business case (OBC), and get approval
- Prepare for procurement by turning the approved option into a detailed specification of outputs, outcomes and desired allocation of risks
- Advertise the project in the Official Journal of the European Union (OJEU), identify potential providers and the best privately financed solution

- Select a preferred bidder with whom negotiations can be completed involving stakeholders in the assessment of the proposals
- Complete the definitive investment appraisal and full business case (FBC) to obtain approval
- Finalise, award and implement the contract
- Evaluate and monitor the project.

The steps described above are affected to a certain degree by the 'competitive dialogue' process introduced by EU Directive 2004/18/EC. This came into effect for OJEU notices placed after January 2006 and is designed to identify far more detail of what is required to deliver the project (for example, design, shape, size, functionality) at the point of submitting tenders. For detailed guidance trusts should consult the Private Finance Unit (PFU) at the Department of Health.

In the early stages of potential PFI schemes (for example at SOC or OBC stage), it may be difficult to achieve a consensus view within an organisation about what exactly is required, what the timescales should be and what resources are needed to ensure success. It is important that agreement is reached through a robust process that tests and challenges current and projected levels of service provision and service configuration – otherwise there is a danger that the organisation's requirements will be over- or under-estimated. The business case process should drive a consideration of changing circumstances, future requirements and opportunities and lead to an agreed corporate view on the best way forward backed up by sound and reasoned assumptions and projections.

Potential PFI providers need to have a sound grasp of an organisation's requirements as articulated in invitations to negotiate (ITN). The documentation of assumptions from an early stage of a project support the development of output specifications and the ITN. For example, in the case of health sector schemes the use of activity data and performance indicators will assist in the sizing of projects. Changes in inpatient to day case ratios, shorter lengths of stay for inpatients and improved occupancy levels need to be modelled to determine the optimum size of new or upgraded facilities. These factors will clearly have an impact on the demand for services. Similarly, there is often an opportunity to provide services in a more efficient and effective way in a new setting. Improved design of facilities coupled with investment in technology may allow new models of service to be developed. Organisations should use the early stages of PFI projects to consider these opportunities and develop robust assumptions.

The capital value of a project determines what approvals are required – current requirements as set out in the Department of Health's 2007 guidance *Delegated Limits for Capital Investment* are:

- Business cases for projects with a capital value over £100m require approval from HM Treasury
- Department of Health approval is required for cases valued between £35m and £100m
- SHAs can approve cases up to £35m.

Individual trust approval limits depend on turnover and the Healthcare Commission's performance ratings (see chapter 15). For example, a trust with a turnover of £130m and performance ratings of 'good' for use of resources and 'fair' for quality can approve cases up to £8m. The most a trust can approve without recourse to the SHA is £12m. Smaller value schemes are unlikely to be approved on their own for PFI but in certain circumstances they can be batched and a single partner identified for all schemes. This has the advantage that fees can be shared over more than one scheme.

Accounting for PFI transactions

The accounting treatment of agreed PFI deals must be in line with latest Treasury guidance. Factors to be taken into account in assessing whether a transaction is on or off balance sheet include:

- Is the contract separable into different elements?
- What are the qualitative indicators – arrangements for operator default, nature of the operator's financing and who determines the nature of the property?
- What are the quantitative indicators in terms of real commercial risk to the operator – demand risk, third party revenues, design and construction risks, performance regime, cost changes, obsolescence risk, end of contract/residual value risk?
- What is the overall assessment in terms of VFM?

As mentioned earlier, it is expected that the accounting treatment of PFI funded assets will change when IFRS is introduced for the preparation of accounts from 2009/10.

For the latest position on IFRS see the Treasury's website.

Management of PFI projects

The operational phase of a PFI scheme is often taken for granted even though it tends to involve organisational change and new ways of doing things. Although standard guidance is available from the Department of Health for many aspects of the PFI process, each scheme is unique in terms of its detailed content. For example, the services covered, availability and performance regimes, payment method and timing, how changes will be dealt with, indexation agreements (i.e. the rate at which payments rise) and monitoring regimes will differ from contract to contract.

The onus for the delivery of services, in accordance with output specifications, lies with the SPC. However, it is incumbent on the purchaser of the services to determine how it is going to manage the contract. For example, the performance and availability regimes will operate on an on-going basis throughout the contract period and purchasers need to have processes in place to highlight performance failure and the 'unavailability' of facilities from day-to-day or even hour-to-hour. Indexation is likely to occur on an annual basis, while benchmarking and market testing to ensure that the service remains competitive may be on a seven-year cycle. Dealing with changes will be driven by strategic and operational need. The purchaser of services needs to manage this wide range of adjustments to the unitary charge.

The complexity of the agreed elements of the unitary charge payments mechanism will also have an impact on the level of effort needed to manage the contract successfully. An extremely detailed performance and availability regime coupled with, say, a quarterly in-advance payment of the unitary charge will require a lot more effort than a monthly-in-arrears payment on account process with a reconciled balancing payment within an agreed period.

Key issues that need to be considered in the management of PFI schemes include:

- Contract awareness – performance and availability regimes, services, change control
- Organisational arrangements – purchaser representative, SPC interface, roles and responsibilities
- Monitoring
- Payments mechanism and process
- Systems and procedures.

Contract awareness

In many organisations the development of the PFI scheme and the negotiation of the PFI project agreement will be undertaken by a relatively small number of key staff supported by external financial, legal and technical advisers. Many of the organisation's staff, who will be involved in day-to-day contact with the SPC's service providers, will be unaware of the detailed content of the PFI project agreement. In particular, the output specifications for services and the availability and performance regimes will be critical to ensuring that services are delivered to the required quality standards. If staff are unaware of the agreed standards, they will be unable to judge the quality of the services delivered and the extent to which the output specification standards are being achieved.

Similarly, the advent of a PFI project may have a significant impact on the way in which services are delivered within an organisation. Innovative solutions or the transfer of duties will require change within the organisation and a full understanding of the implications. Processes for ordering specific outputs, with a potential impact on the unitary charge, may not be readily understood by those who have not been involved in the contract development and negotiations.

There is therefore a need to raise contract awareness throughout the organisation via a good communication process that informs staff of the implications of the PFI contract and the impact it will have on how the organisation operates.

Organisational arrangements

Organisational arrangements will differ depending upon the type and scale of scheme. However, for all PFI projects it is essential that:

- There is clarity over the detail of the payment mechanism. What services does it cover, what are the financial penalties and what are the time limits on corrective action?
- Roles, responsibilities and accountabilities for contract management (including how the organisation works with the provider of services at a strategic and operational level) are clear. For example, who is the senior purchaser representative for the contract? What are the key interfaces with the provider at an operational level?
- The roles and functions of staff in checking and authorising payments to the provider of services are set out and understood

- There is clarity over the detail of what is covered in any 'soft' arrangements – for example, maintenance or light bulb replacement.

Monitoring

Responsibility for delivering services to the prescribed standards and the monitoring of services lies with the SPC which is expected to produce monthly reports setting out information on compliance and identifying failures. This forms a key element in the calculation of the monthly unitary charge. The purchaser of services needs to consider how to monitor the SPC's processes and the extent of any random test checking of service delivery to ensure robustness and compliance with output specifications.

Payments mechanism and process

The unitary payment changes regularly in response to a range of general, annual and monthly adjustments. The payments process also needs to be in line with the timings set out in the PFI contract. Depending on the nature of the payment mechanism, the timescales may be relatively tight so both purchaser and provider need to have systems in place that can cope. In developing these systems, it is essential that organisations think about payments that may exceed normal standing order and standing financial instruction levels and require special authorisation procedures.

Systems and procedures

In keeping with good practice, organisations should document the systems and procedures associated with the management of PFI contracts in order to ensure clarity, continuity, accountability and 'auditability' of processes. This may seem self-evident but can be overlooked, particularly in the short term. A failure to document processes can lead to a lack of effective control of the contract.

The implications of payment by results

Payment by results (PbR) has been rolled out across the NHS with 2007/08 being the last year of the transitional arrangements. Under this regime, payments are made by commissioners to provider trusts for individual spells of patient care charged at a nationally set tariff for each healthcare resource group (HRG – a grouping of similar clinical procedures that require approximately similar levels of resource input).

Provider trusts have to meet contractual payments in relation to PFI schemes from the income derived from the activity undertaken at national tariff values. Clearly this income also has to cover the costs associated with providing the patient related activity.

Organisations embarking on PFI schemes need to ensure that projects remain affordable under PbR. In practice, this may be difficult to guarantee and PFI schemes may be less attractive and prevalent as a result. However, there is some support available in the form of 'tariff relief' via the NHS Bank. This relief will be given to those trusts that are going through the PFI process and who may struggle to cover their costs in the early years of operation whilst only receiving average tariff prices. The relief will equate to 7.5% of capital expenditure spread over 5 to 7 years on a tapering basis.

NHS LIFT

Background

NHS LIFT aims to improve and develop front line primary and community care facilities. It was developed to try and tackle the problem of sub-standard premises whose condition and functionality mean that quality and access are often below an acceptable standard, with a knock on effect on the potential for service development and improvement.

To develop this new market for investment, the Department of Health entered into a national joint venture with Partnerships UK (itself a joint venture between the Treasury, the Scottish Executive and the private sector) and established Partnerships for Health (PfH). PfH completed waves 1–3 of the programme, delivering 42 local NHS LIFT companies, plus another 8 approvals from wave 4. In 2006, the Department of Health purchased Partnerships UK's 20% stake in PfH, making PfH 100% owned by the Department.

PfH delivers NHS LIFT, on behalf of the Department in partnership with the local health economy through the establishment of a LIFT company. This is a limited company with the local NHS, PfH and the private sector partner as shareholders. This limited company – the LIFTco – owns and maintains the building and leases the premises to PCTs, GPs, local authority social services, dentists and pharmacists, often creating a 'super health centre'. The local PCTs are shareholders in the LIFTco to protect the public interest.

At local level, a management board comprising private sector partners, local NHS nominees and PfH works together to agree and develop investment programmes.

Objectives

The aim of LIFT is to increase investment to help improve both the quality of care provided and the environment in which it is delivered. In particular, NHS LIFT is designed to help deliver new one stop primary care centres and new, refurbished or upgraded GP premises.

NHS LIFT's stated objectives are to:

* Contribute to *NHS Plan* targets
* Efficiently deliver local investment and improved services
* Concentrate on the areas of greatest need
* Improve the primary care estate
* Own and lease premises to GPs
* Assist in the regeneration of local communities.

How NHS LIFT works

In terms of assessing the case for investment all new LIFT schemes must follow a process set down by the Department for Health in its guidance document *NHS LIFT Business Case Approval Process*. This emphasises that 'the process should be 'light touch' and always proportionate to the scale of the proposed investment'. As with PFI schemes, NHS LIFT proposals must demonstrate that they will achieve VFM and provide improved services, in line with the *NHS Plan* targets and objectives.

The current state of play

Some 50 projects, in four waves, had been approved as at February 2007. The Department of Health website includes a progress report on specific schemes containing such information as the financial-close date and capital values.

Local Partnerships

It is possible to construct local partnership arrangements with private sector developers for schemes such as residential accommodation. Business cases are developed as in PFI schemes and approved by the SHA, which also gives the authority to proceed. There are no unitary payments as the partner receives income from tenants. However, the trust may have to give some guarantees on occupancy levels.

References and Further Reading

Department of Health Guidance on PFI:
www.dh.gov.uk/procurementandproposals/publicprivatepartnership/privatefinanceinitiative/fs/en

Value for Money Assessment Guidance, HM Treasury, 2006:
www.hm-treasury.gov.uk./media/4/4/vfm_assessmentguidance061006opt.pdf

The Green Book, HM Treasury:
www.hm-treasury.gov.uk./economic_data_and_tools/greenbook/data_greenbook_index.cfm

Office of Government Commerce: www.ogc.gov.uk

Public Sector Business Cases using the Five Case Model: a toolkit, HFMA, 2007: www.hfma.org.uk

Delegated Limits for Capital Investment, Department of Health, 2007: www.dh.gov.uk/en/Publicationsandstatistics/Publications/PublicationsPolicyAndGuidance/DH_080864

EU Public Procurement Directive on Competitive Dialogue: www.dh.gov.uk/en/Procurementandproposals/Publicprivatepartnership/Privatefinanceinitiative/DH_4132174

Public Private Partnerships guidance, HM Treasury:
www.hm-treasury.gov.uk./documents/public_private_partnerships/ppp_index.cfm

Private Finance Unit, Department of Health – contact details available via:
www.dh.gov.uk/en/Procurementandproposals/Publicprivatepartnership/Privatefinanceinitiative/Standardcontract/DH_4016186

Department of Health Guidance on LIFT (including NHS LIFT Business Case Approval Process and NHS Bank support): www.dh.gov.uk/procurementandproposals/publicprivatepartnership/nhslift/fs/en

11. Commissioning

Introduction

The Department of Health's website states that 'commissioning is the process of deciding what services or products are needed, acquiring them and ensuring that they meet requirements. In the NHS, commissioners act on behalf of the public, ensuring they have access to the services they need, not only today but also in the future'.

In practical terms this means that commissioners negotiate agreements with service providers (NHS, private and voluntary sectors) to meet the health needs of a particular population. Although commissioning has existed since the start of the NHS, recent reforms to the financial regime and in particular the introduction of payment by results (PbR) and practice based commissioning (PBC) have made it more prominent. The Department of Health's 2007 document *World Class Commissioning: vision* has placed even greater emphasis on getting commissioning right and sees it as being at the heart of delivering an NHS that is 'fair, personalised, effective and safe, and which is focused relentlessly on improving the quality of care'.

As the main healthcare commissioners, primary care trusts (PCTs) are at the forefront of work to turn the world class commissioning vision into a reality, and to apply it in a way that ensures that the needs and priorities of their local populations are met.

This chapter focuses on what commissioning involves and the role of commissioners in today's NHS – but first it looks briefly at the policy background to give an insight into how commissioning has developed over recent years.

Policy Background

The internal market

Between 1991 and 1999, the NHS operated an internal market that separated the function of service provision from commissioning. Health authorities received funding allocations for their populations and commissioned services from service providers to meet the needs of their population. Service providers received payment for services usually in the form of block monthly payments for a range of services provided under a service agreement or contract.

Although, the internal market focussed attention on issues such as price, performance and deliverables, it also fragmented the NHS and hardened the demarcations between purchasers and service providers. Since 1999 the government has developed the role of primary care. PCTs now have the lead commissioning role within the NHS, managing about 80% of the service's budget, the bulk of which they use to commission services from other NHS bodies, the private sector, voluntary and 'third sector' providers. PCTs are also responsible for commissioning primary care services including ophthalmic, pharmacy, dental and a range of community health services (see chapter 6 for more details).

Commissioning at practice level has also been introduced in recent years (see later in this chapter).

The reform agenda

The government's reform agenda – first articulated in the NHS Plan – has a number of strands all designed to deliver an improved NHS that is 'locally driven, looking outwards not upwards[10]'. Effective commissioning is central to this agenda but is also affected by other key elements. In particular, the introduction of PbR for an increasing range of activities has shifted the focus of commissioning away from price negotiations to specifying quantity, quality and delivery of service targets. PbR has been developed to increase efficiency and cost-effectiveness within the NHS and to encourage investment in new capacity to help meet access targets. Under PbR, additional activity is paid for at full rather than marginal cost – as a result, effective demand management is essential. Chapter 13 looks in detail at PbR.

Patient choice and plurality of provision have also had a significant impact on commissioning. For example, since December 2005, PCTs have had to ensure that patients have a choice of four or five providers at the point of referral, in order to meet government targets – to make this possible, effective planning and demand management is essential. From April 2008, choice has been extended still further with patients effectively having a 'free choice' in relation to hospital-based services.

Commissioning decisions are affected by a range of other influences such as the requirement to reduce waiting times to a maximum of 18 weeks by no later than December 2008 and the need to adhere to condition specific 'national service frameworks', covering a wide range of areas from diabetes to long term conditions.

What is Commissioning?

In its 2006 publication Health Reform in England: Update and Commissioning Framework the Department of Health set out a framework detailing key changes designed to strengthen commissioning and ensure that it could drive health reform, improved health and healthcare and improved financial health for the NHS. This Commissioning Framework set out an over-arching vision for the commissioning role of PCTs which are responsible for commissioning the full range of health services for their populations, working in partnership with general practices to promote PBC.

The Commissioning Framework defines commissioning as the means by which the NHS secures the best value for patients and taxpayers and emphasises that if it is to be effective, commissioning must involve making 'the best use of allocated resources to achieve the following goals:

- improve health and well-being and reduce health inequalities and social exclusion
- secure access to a comprehensive range of services
- improve the quality, effectiveness and efficiency of services
- increase choice for patients and ensure a better experience of care through greater responsiveness to people's needs'.

---

[10] World Class Commissioning, Department of Health, 2007.

The focus for commissioning is therefore on achieving the best possible health outcomes (including reduced health inequalities) and the best possible healthcare within the resources made available by the taxpayer.

As it is inevitable that demand for healthcare will exceed the level of funds available, there will always be an element of 'prioritising' within commissioning. This involves a focus on local needs, targets and desired outcomes together with reviewing services in the search for greater effectiveness, economy and efficiency.

The *NHS Plan* placed particular emphasis on key government targets, as well as on the planning and commissioning process to deliver these targets. More recently, national priorities have been set out in the Department of Health's guidance documents *National Standards, Local Action: Health and Social Care Standards and Planning Framework 2005/06–2007/08* and the *Operating Frameworks* for 2007/08 and 2008/09.

The commissioning cycle

The *Commissioning Framework* makes it clear that commissioning is not a one off activity but rather a continuous cycle that involves:

- Assessing health needs
- Reviewing service provision and identifying gaps or areas where change is needed
- Deciding priorities
- Designing services
- Shaping the structure of supply
- Managing demand whilst ensuring appropriate access to care
- Ensuring effective clinical decision making
- Managing performance
- Undertaking patient and public feedback.

To be effective commissioners (both PCTs and practices under PBC) need to:

- Have access to information and skills that will support their decisions (for example population risk assessments)
- Engage with clinicians
- Improve community engagement
- Use incentives and contracts for commissioners
- Increase choice for patients.

For more detailed information on the commissioning cycle see the *Commissioning Framework*.

Commissioning approaches

PCTs are the main driving force in commissioning services for their local population. Their activities are performance managed by strategic health authorities (SHAs) in the context of the need to achieve national targets, determine local health economy priorities and agree trajectories that link to key 'vital signs' (indicators designed to show how the NHS is performing locally and nationally) set by the Department of Health in its *Operating Framework 2008/09* and *Operational Plans 2008/09–2010/11*.

There are a number of different approaches to commissioning including:

- Individual PCTs commissioning on their own
- Co-ordinating commissioners ('lead' consortia arrangements) where groups of PCTs work together formally. In this approach, a single contract is negotiated by the lead commissioner with the local service provider and it is 'performance managed' across all member PCTs
- Specialist commissioning groups (SCGs) – for specialist high cost, low volume treatments (for example, transplant surgery). Following the 2006 *Carter Review* SCGs are now co-located within SHA boundaries (i.e. there are currently 10 SCG 'hubs')
- Network arrangements (for example for cancer services) have undertaken some commissioning functions on behalf of their constituent PCTs
- Practice based commissioning (i.e. by primary care clinicians– see below)
- Partnership working with local authorities (see below).

Practice Based Commissioning

Practice based commissioning (PBC) was first introduced in 2005/06 through the document *Practice Based Commissioning: achieving universal coverage* and, as the Department of Health's website states, is about 'engaging practices and other primary care professionals in the commissioning of services'. The aim is that, by enabling primary care clinicians to take commissioning decisions themselves, patients will receive higher quality services that better suit their needs and circumstances. The underlying presumption is that primary care professionals are in the best position to decide what services their patients need and to redesign them accordingly.

As well as involving clinicians more closely in commissioning decisions, PBC is designed to incentivise improvements in services including the development and provision of services outside of hospitals. A proportion of any resources freed up through changes in commissioning practice can be used for the benefit of the practice's patients. There are also incentive payments for practices that sign up to PBC and for achieving their PBC plans.

Under PBC, responsibility for commissioning along with an associated notional budget from the PCT is allocated to primary care clinicians. This is designed to align clinical and financial responsibilities. However, because the PCT remains legally responsible for managing the money and negotiating and managing all contracts with providers, the budget allocated to primary care practitioners is notional or 'indicative'. In practice this means that although primary care clinicians determine the range of services to be provided for their population, the PCT acts as their agent to undertake any required procurements and to carry out the administrative tasks that underpin these processes.

The PCT is also responsible for the overall commissioning strategy and for ensuring that PBC is implemented. This is emphasised in the Department of Health's November 2006 guidance *Practice Based Commissioning: practical implementation*, which states that PCTs 'are charged with ensuring that PBC continues to flourish'. It also sets out a number of 'key expectations' placed on PCTs which included the need for there to be:

- A locally agreed incentive scheme offered to all practices
- Timely activity and financial information relating to practices that meet practice preferences
- Tools and support provided to practices so that they can discharge their commissioning responsibilities, either directly or through agreed alternative arrangements.

This guidance has since been enhanced with another key policy document issued in December 2007 as part of the *2008/09 Operating Framework* called *Practice Based Commissioning – budget setting refinements and clarification of health funding flexibilities, incentive schemes and governance*. This takes forward the encouragement given in the *NHS Next Stage Review Interim Report* for practice based commissioners to use NHS funds more flexibly to secure alternatives to traditional NHS provision. In particular, the guidance states that 'PCTs should agree with practice based commissioners a menu of local flexibilities, to support their achievement of local and national priorities.' A possible menu of flexibilities is included in the document along with guidance on setting practice budgets.

The Audit Commission's 2007 report – *Putting Commissioning into Practice: implementing practice based commissioning through good financial management* – identified two areas where PBC is making progress:

- Providing GPs with an understanding of the financial consequences of their decision making
- Engaging GPs in the management of secondary care usage.

The Commission also found a number of areas where further development is needed:

- PCT, practice and other stakeholders' ownership of PBC
- PCT support to practices
- Incentives and arrangements for sharing savings
- Budget setting
- Provision and quality of data and information.

The government's original aim was to have universal coverage of PBC by December 2006 but as involvement in PBC remains voluntary for primary care clinicians the expectation now is that by 2008 'most if not all' practices will be involved.

Partnership Working with Local Authorities

As many PCTs are coterminous with district or unitary council boundaries, joint commissioning between the NHS and local authorities for particular services and client groups is increasingly common. This follows changes originally introduced by the *Health Act 1999* facilitating the movement of funds between the NHS and local authorities, including the option of pooling budgets where this is considered advantageous. The focus on integrated care pathways has also given impetus to greater partnership working with local authorities. This allows services to be pulled together on a 'whole systems' basis from the perspective of the service user rather than the organisation delivering the service. In this context, lead responsibility for commissioning may now sit with the local authority and not the health organisation (see chapter 9 for more about partnership working with local authorities).

Planning and Contracting

Service planning

PCTs are required to produce three-year operational plans (known as local delivery plans – LDPs – before the 2008/09 planning round) outlining how they intend to meet *NHS Plan* targets and local priorities within the three-year financial allocations. The 2008/2009 *Operating Framework* makes clear that PCTs will be performance managed against an agreed set of indicators referred to as 'vital signs'. These comprise a variety of national and locally agreed indicators and targets. Every year PCTs prepare new three-year rolling plans which involves firming up service developments and resources at the beginning of each year.

PCTs are also expected to set out a clear medium term commissioning strategy which reflects public health needs and expectations, and a current year commissioning prospectus. These documents are supported by underpinning delivery strategies including a medium term financial strategy, procurement strategy and manpower strategy.

Contracts

Service agreements

The traditional approach to commissioning in the NHS used service agreements between commissioners and providers. These agreements set down the expectations of each party and were analogous to contracts. They included as much detail as was felt necessary – in particular, service agreements specified the activity volume, financial value and tolerances.

Service agreements are still used for some non-acute activities where PbR does not yet apply and tend to take the form of 'block contracts' specifying activity levels and payment amounts – in other words, a fixed sum is paid for access to a defined range and volume of service. Cost and volume contracts are also used – here a fixed sum is paid for access to a defined range and volume of services but if there is a variation from the intended level of activity, there is a variation in payment levels according to a variation, or threshold agreement clause. This determines the marginal rate of payment for higher or lower than target performance. The threshold agreement represents a mechanism for sharing the risk of unforeseen events between commissioner and service provider. In most contracts of this kind, the variation agreement is not enforced within a narrow range of target activity. This band of activity is called the threshold or tolerance.

Cost per case contracts identify for each episode or unit of care a payment to the service provider. Cost per case contracts are commonplace where waiting list activity is placed with private sector providers, and for individual, expensive, and bespoke care package agreements (for example, the placement of patients in medium secure mental health facilities). Cost per case contracts suit procedures that are infrequent, unpredictable, or can have significant cost variations. They are also used for treatments under the patient choice regime, where patients may choose a provider that the commissioner does not have an established contract with.

The standard/'new NHS contract'

For acute hospital services, service agreements have been superseded by a standard approach to contracting. This was first proposed in the Department of Health's 2006 document *Health Reform in England: update and commissioning framework*. Since then a standard contract has been developed to 'support the achievement of key standards and targets and ensure that commissioners and providers do not become financially exposed'. The aim is that the contract 'will create legally binding agreements between PCTs and foundation trusts (FTs), and between PCTs and independent and third sector providers. Agreements between PCTs and NHS trusts will be in exactly the same form and be treated with the same degree of rigour and seriousness as if they were legally binding'.

An interim version of the contract was trialled in 2007/08 and from April 2008 a revised version applies to agreements made by PCTs with:

- NHS trusts
- FTs – although FTs with existing contracts that extend beyond March 2008 can choose whether to adopt the standard contract or retain their existing contracts until they run out.

The Department has issued detailed guidance on how to use the standard contract which is available on its website. It is important to note that the contract has a three-part structure:

- Mandatory elements
- Elements which must be in the contract, but the details are for agreement or completion by the contracting parties
- Additional elements which can be added by local agreement.

The guidance states that 'all contracts should be agreed by 28 February before the start of the new contract year. There will be a clear and timely dispute resolution process to resolve the difficulties that may arise in some places. Parties who have not reached agreement by 28 February will enter mediation, and formal adjudication on any remaining disputes will begin at the end of March'.

Under this new approach contracts will essentially be for three years with prices 'refreshed' annually.

Working with Foundation Trusts

FTs follow a different financial regime to other provider trusts and have been operating at full PbR tariff for tariff based services longer than non-foundation organisations. However commissioning from FTs follows the same principles as with NHS trusts – good commissioning is the same whatever organisation is providing services. Agreements between PCTs and FTs are in the form of legally binding contracts which tend to focus more attention on information flows.

If a PCT has a contractual dispute with an NHS trust, the SHA arbitrates. If there is a dispute between a PCT and an FT, the initial approach is for the SHA and Monitor (the independent regulator of FTs) to mediate. The option exists to invite the Centre for Effective Dispute Resolution (CEDR) to mediate in place of the SHA and Monitor although the costs will be borne by the parties to the dispute.

Existing three year contracts with FTs must be superseded by the new standard contract once the term finishes although FTs can choose to migrate to the new contract before the term ends.

Performance Management

Having set clear targets and priorities in line with the *Operating Framework*, the government has strengthened the processes for monitoring and managing performance. In addition to service providers' internal management processes, the commissioning activity within PCTs entails managing performance against contracts and service agreements. PCTs are performance managed by SHAs in terms of the agreed operational plan. Performance information is aggregated at SHA level as part of monitoring government targets and delivery of each SHA's own area plan.

Information

Accurate information is essential to effective commissioning in the new environment and particularly with the roll-out of PbR and PBC. Key information includes historical referral patterns, historical spend and how these compare with other practices in the PCT. PCTs and practices increasingly need access to up-to-date and even real time information so they can monitor actual activity against plans and expenditure against budgets. A national information system developed by NHS Connecting for Health and known as the 'secondary uses service' (SUS) is designed to collect patient level activity information from providers and make it available to commissioners. This system then applies the tariff to providers' activity information, calculates the payment due and notifies each commissioner. The Department of Health's *Operating Framework for 2008/09* says that by April 2009 the NHS should be using SUS as 'the standard repository for activity for performance monitoring, reconciliation and payments'.

Information on how PCTs spend their resources across 23 different programmes of care is also collected as part of a programme budgeting initiative. This information enables PCTs to benchmark their own spend in a particular area with that of a similar organisation covering a similar population. PCTs can then challenge their historical spending patterns and ensure they are commissioning the right level and mix of services.

Commissioning in the Future

As mentioned earlier, the focus in commissioning is now on improving its application so that it becomes world class. The Department of Health's vision document describes what achieving this aim will involve and identifies 11 organisational competencies that underpin effective commissioning. The Department of Health's website states that these competencies 'describe the knowledge, skills, behaviours and characteristics that PCTs will need to develop to reach world class status. In summary world class commissioning will:

- lead the NHS at a local level
- work collaboratively with partners
- engage with the community
- work closely with clinicians
- manage knowledge and assess needs
- prioritise for improved outcomes
- influence and shape the market
- promote innovation and improvement
- procure robust contracts
- support and manage providers
- demonstrate sound financial management'.

As part of the world class commissioning agenda, the Department of Health has developed a framework enabling PCTs to procure expert commissioning support services. The *Framework for Procuring External Support for Commissioners* (FESC) will provide PCTs with easy access to a range of external suppliers who can support them in undertaking their commissioning functions.

References and Further Reading

Commissioning Arrangements in the NHS – Department of Health web pages:
www.dh.gov.uk/en/Policyandguidance/Organisationpolicy/Commissioning/index.htm

Payment by Results: www.dh.gov.uk/PolicyAndGuidance/OrganisationPolicy/
FinanceAndPlanning/NHSFinancialReforms/fs/en

World Class Commissioning: www.dh.gov.uk/en/Policyandguidance/Organisationpolicy/
Commissioning/Worldclasscommissioning/index.htm

The NHS Plan: a plan for investment, a plan for reform, Department of Health, 2000:
www.dh.gov.uk/en/Publicationsandstatistics/Publications/PublicationsPolicyAndGuidance/
DH_4002960

Patient Choice: www.dh.gov.uk/PolicyAndGuidance/PatientChoice/fs/en

Health Reform in England: Update and Commissioning Framework, Department of Health, 2006:
www.dh.gov.uk/en/Publicationsandstatistics/Publications/PublicationsPolicyAndGuidance/
DH_4137229

National Standards, Local Action: Health and Social Care Standards and Planning Framework 2005/06–2007/08. Available via the publications, policy and guidance pages of the Department of Health's website:
www.dh.gov.uk/PublicationsAndStatistics/Publications/PublicationsPolicyAndGuidance/fs/en

The NHS in England: the Operating Framework for 2008/09, Department of health, 2007:
www.dh.gov.uk/en/Publicationsandstatistics/Publications/PublicationsPolicyAndGuidance/
DH_081094

Operational Plans 2008/09–2010/11, Department of Health, 2008:
www.dh.gov.uk:80/en/Publicationsandstatistics/Publications/PublicationsPolicyAndGuidance/
DH_082542

Specialised Services Commissioning (including the Carter Review): www.dh.gov.uk/en/
Managingyourorganisation/Commissioning/Commissioningspecialisedservices/DH_080938

Practice Based Commissioning: www.dh.gov.uk/en/Policyandguidance/Organisationpolicy/
Commissioning/Practice-basedcommissioning/index.htm

Practice Based Commissioning – Department of Health Guidance (including Achieving Universal
Coverage and Practical Implementation): www.dh.gov.uk/en/Managingyourorganisation/
Commissioning/Practice-basedcommissioning/DH_4127126

Practice Based Commissioning – budget setting refinements and clarification of health funding
flexibilities, incentive schemes and governance, Department of Health, 2007: www.dh.gov.uk/
en/Publicationsandstatistics/Publications/PublicationsPolicyAndGuidance/DH_081101

Our NHS, Our Future: NHS Next Stage Review Interim Report, Department of Health, 2007:
www.dh.gov.uk/en/Publicationsandstatistics/Publications/PublicationsPolicyAndGuidance/
DH_079077

Putting Commissioning into Practice: implementing practice based commissioning through
good financial management, Audit Commission, 2007: www.audit-commission.gov.uk

The Standard NHS Contract for Acute Hospital Services and Supporting Guidance:
www.dh.gov.uk/en/Publicationsandstatistics/Publications/PublicationsPolicyAndGuidance/
DH_081100

Foundation Trusts:
www.dh.gov.uk/PolicyAndGuidance/OrganisationPolicy/SecondaryCare/NHSFoundationTrust/fs/en

Monitor: www.monitor-nhsft.gov.uk

Centre for Effective Dispute Resolution: www.cedr.co.uk/

Secondary Uses Service: www.connectingforhealth.nhs.uk/systemsandservices/sus

Programme Budgeting: www.dh.gov.uk/PolicyAndGuidance/OrganisationPolicy/
FinanceAndPlanning/ProgrammeBudgeting/fs/en

The Framework for Procuring External Support for Commissioners, Department of Health, 2007:
www.dh.gov.uk/en/Publicationsandstatistics/Publications/PublicationsPolicyAndGuidance/
DH_065818

12. Costing

Introduction

This chapter looks at an activity that is becoming increasingly prominent in today's NHS. Although costing has always been important, the introduction of payment by results (PbR) means that the production of accurate cost information is now of critical importance, not only because the Department of Health uses costing information supplied by NHS organisations to develop the national tariff but also because NHS organisations need to have a detailed understanding of their own cost base so that they can manage their activities effectively.

What is Costing?

Costing is all to do with quantifying, in financial terms, the value of resources consumed in carrying out a particular activity or producing a certain unit of output. Costing therefore involves:

- Being clear about the activity whose costs you are seeking to identify – it must be defined clearly and unambiguously
- Making sure that the 'right' costs of everything and everyone involved in carrying out that activity are included in the costing calculation.

It is also important to analyse the costs themselves – not all costs are the same and before you can cost an activity or product you need to be clear about the types of cost involved. The classification most often used involves a distinction between:

- Direct costs – those costs that can be readily and easily identified with an activity
- Indirect costs and overheads – those costs that still contribute to the cost of an activity but in a less clear cut way.

Costs also behave differently – some are fixed (i.e. they do not change with activity levels); others are variable (i.e. they increase/decrease in line with changes in activity) and some are 'semi fixed' (i.e. they stay the same until activity increases above a certain amount – often referred to as 'step' changes).

We will look in more detail at the cost classifications used in the NHS later on in this chapter.

What is Costing Information used for?

In the NHS, costing involves looking closely at healthcare services and identifying how much they cost. This can be at a variety of levels – for example, the total annual cost of the orthopaedic department in a hospital; the cost of a particular activity or group of procedures within that department (for instance, hip replacements) or the cost of an individual patient undergoing that hip replacement.

The key message is that costing is not an end in itself – it is only worth doing if the information generated is used in a meaningful way to deliver improvements in healthcare services. In the NHS, costing information is used both within organisations and at a national level.

NHS organisations need costing information for a variety of reasons – for example to:

- Help run their businesses effectively
- Help decision makers, managers and budget holders decide how services should develop in the future
- Manage 'services lines' (see later in this chapter)
- Understand how the costs of providing a particular activity compare with the income received for undertaking that activity
- Identify the costs of different activities at different levels (for example, for a particular specialty/department or for an individual patient)
- Develop commissioning strategies
- Compare potential investment opportunities
- Build up realistic budgets and plans
- Monitor performance and benchmark services
- Support negotiations for funding.

At a national level, the Department of Health uses costing information provided by NHS bodies to develop:

- Reference costs
- The tariff for activities covered by PbR
- National service frameworks
- Programme budgeting data
- Comparative data
- Efficiency targets
- Healthcare resource groups (HRGs).

What does Costing involve?

An important element of any approach to costing is identifying the activities that are to be costed. Rather than record every cost incurred separately (which would clearly be unmanageable) costs are categorised into a number of distinct headings referred to as 'cost centres'. The cost centres used by organisations will vary according to their size, structure and range of activities but – as a general rule – tend to be in line with budget headings in the general ledger.

Costing in the NHS in England must be carried out in accordance with the Department of Health's *Costing Manual*. This is revised and updated on a regular basis and is designed to ensure consistency of approach across all organisations that provide healthcare services.

The *Costing Manual* states that costs and income have to be:

- Calculated on a full absorption basis to identify the full cost of services delivered – in other words, all income and costs must be attributed to an activity or 'cost centre'. This means that the full cost of each activity is identified and all costs are allocated somewhere

- Charged directly to the relevant activity wherever this is possible – for example a general surgeon's costs will be charged to a cost centre for general surgery. Where direct charging is not possible the manual sets out standard methods of apportionment/ allocation that must be used. Generally apportionments tend to be used when dealing with indirect costs that relate to a range of activities – for example, ward costs that need to be spread across a range of specialties in proportion to the bed days used by each. Allocations are used most commonly for overheads (for example, finance or human resources) that relate to the overall running of the organisation. These costs must still be absorbed by activities but are charged out on a more general basis
- Matched with the services that generate them to avoid cross subsidisation (i.e. the costs of a particular service or activity are not artificially lowered by loading costs that relate to it to another service or activity).

The *Manual* also states that the costing process should 'be transparent with a clear audit trail' and includes a detailed appendix which lists those costs that must be charged directly and those that may be indirect or an overhead.

Although the *Costing Manual* is prescriptive in terms of the financial costing approach that must be followed, it does not prescribe cost centres or activities – these will vary according to the structure and nature of an organisation. For example, a large acute trust may well have a general surgery cost centre or budget head whereas a small cottage hospital may have a single ward that deals with a range of patients including some who have had general surgery. The *Manual* does emphasise that whatever cost centres an organisation chooses it is important that they can map them to the definitions required in the reference cost collection guidance (see later in this chapter).

Cost classifications

All NHS costs are classified as direct, indirect or overhead costs within each specialty and care programme. Although this may vary between NHS providers depending on the quality of local information systems, a minimum standard classification for each cost has been identified to achieve a consistent approach to the costing of services for all providers. The *Costing Manual* sets out these minimum standards of classification. The only acceptable deviation is for an overhead cost to move to being categorised as an indirect or direct cost. Under no circumstances should costs identified as 'direct' be allocated indirectly or apportioned as overheads.

Where the full cost of an activity is calculated, some costs can be allocated directly to that activity's cost centre, but others (indirect and overhead costs) need to be apportioned on a systematic basis.

Direct costs

Direct costs are those costs that can be directly attributed to the particular activity or output being measured. For example, within a hospital ward the cost of drugs supplied and consumed can be directly attributed to that ward by the pharmacy system. Hence, the drugs would be a direct cost of the ward cost centre.

Indirect costs

Indirect costs cannot be directly attributed to a particular cost centre but can be associated with a number of centres. Such costs need to be allocated to individual cost centres, and this is generally achieved through apportioning the costs using a unit of activity or work measure appropriate to the area concerned. For example, where linen costs cannot be directly attributed to wards these may be allocated using occupied bed days.

Overheads

Overhead costs are those costs that contribute to the general running of the organisation but cannot be directly related to an activity or service. For example, the total heating costs of a hospital may be apportioned to individual departments using floor area or cubic capacity; the costs of finance or human resources may be spread across all cost centres in proportion to those cost centres' total direct and indirect costs.

Cost pools

For indirect and overhead costs that relate to identifiable activities, 'cost pools' tend to be used to collect the costs (examples are theatres and diagnostics). The costs are then shared out to the cost centres/activities that they have provided a service or resources to. In other words, as the *Manual* explains: 'cost pools aggregate costs from more than one cost centre separately identified in the general ledger. For instance the employee services costing pool may aggregate the costs of personnel, crèche, staff restaurant, welfare services and these may then be apportioned to a clinical cost centre'. Again the *Costing Manual* sets out guidance on the pooling of costs, but each organisation decides which cost pools it needs depending on its structure and range of activities.

Cost analysis

All NHS costs must be analysed into their fixed, semi-fixed and variable components. This relates to the manner in which costs respond within a given period to the changes in level of activity. The descriptions from the *Costing Manual* are:

- 'fixed. Where they are not affected by in-year changes in activity. For example, costs such as rent and rates
- semi-fixed. Where costs are fixed for a given level of activity but change in steps, when activity levels exceed or fall below these given levels. For example, costs such as nursing staff
- variable. Where costs vary directly with changes in activity. For example, costs such as drugs'.

Approach required

The *Costing Manual* states that NHS providers must identify three key elements as part of the compilation of overall cost:

- 'a high level control total' based on actual costs by services identifying direct, indirect and overhead costs in line with the national minimum standards. The national high level

control totals should be able to be mapped to the national classification found in the current reference costs guidance
- a continuous reconciliation process at all stages of the costing process is required to ensure all costs are recovered, and that costs can be matched to relevant services and final accounts
- a 'resource profile' analysis of the key conditions which represent a minimum of 80% of the high level control total in both activity and cost terms. Specific reference should be made to clinicians' and nurses' knowledge of the:
  - conditions they treat
  - frequency with which they are performed
  - resources used to perform them.

See the *Costing Manual* for more details.

Healthcare Resource Groups

Within the NHS there is a vast range of specific interventions and diagnoses (around 23,000 codes exist) that have a cost and have to be paid for. Rather than have a separate tariff for each (which would be unworkable) a 'currency' is used to collate them into common groupings to which tariffs can be applied. In England the chosen currency is healthcare resource groups or HRGs. HRGs place patient procedures and/or diagnoses into bands, which are 'resource homogenous', that is, clinically similar and consuming similar levels of resources.

HRGs come between top-level specialities and individual patient procedures and treatments, thus reducing the number of individual care profiles that need to be costed. One of the key aims of HRGs is to provide a practical currency to enable sensible discussions between clinicians and managers about the costs of delivering healthcare – it is therefore essential that HRGs are clinically meaningful.

Since 2006/07 a new version of HRGs (version 4) has been used for costing purposes in the reference cost collection. HRG4 has been designed and endorsed by clinicians and developed with the involvement of 33 expert working groups and four expert reference panels. It was developed 'to accurately capture clinical activity in the NHS, irrespective of setting (the place of treatment)' and the expectation is that it will be used as the basis of the national tariff from 2009/10.

HRG4 comprises more than 1400 groupings arranged into 22 chapters each covering a specialty area such as the nervous system or cardiac surgery. The groupings take account of recent developments in healthcare and new interventions, as well as adding a number of previously uncovered areas such as chemotherapy, rehabilitation and critical care.

The HFMA has produced a detailed briefing on HRG4 (in conjunction with the NHS Information Centre for Health and Social Care) which looks at each HRG chapter in turn and is available via the HFMA's website: www.hfma.org.uk

Procedure Costing

The costing of an activity is not specifically required at procedure level, but may still be calculated. The procedure costs within the HRG are added together and averaged for the particular HRG. This enables more detailed costings to be used for service planning and is of particular relevance for paying patient services and specialised services to facilitate negotiations with commissioners.

The Two Part Costing Process

The costing process is broken down into two distinct parts – specialty costing and HRG/procedure costing.

Specialty costing

The specialty costing process breaks down the overall cost of providing healthcare into the costs for delivering care within the different healthcare specialties provided. Some costs can be assigned directly. For instance the cost of an orthopaedic surgeon can be assigned directly to the orthopaedic cost centre. Other costs have to be pooled and then apportioned using an appropriate method. For instance theatre costs could be apportioned on the basis of the time spent in theatre or the sessions used. Ward costs could be apportioned on the basis of bed days consumed. Overheads and support costs are also apportioned.

At this point a trust has established its specialty cost totals and also knows the various cost pools within that specialty, for instance the theatre costs. The next stage of the process attempts to break down these specialty costs among all the HRGs within that specialty. For instance within orthopaedics, a trust might typically undertake more than 40 different orthopaedic HRGs.

HRG/procedure costing

The HRG/procedure costing process looks at the costing process from the HRG perspective. HRG/procedure costing generally uses a mixture of top-down and bottom-up costing to derive the HRG/procedure cost.

Top down costing – where cost pool costs are allocated to HRGs using the total cost of that cost pool weighted for each HRG/procedure based upon the best available data/clinical estimates

Bottom up costing – the process which looks to build up the costs of that HRG from the bottom up where the actual costs are known, for instance prosthesis costs in hip replacement HRGs.

Reference Costs

References costs record activity levels, unit cost data and average length of stay for a range of specified activities and are collected each year from all providers of health services (acute, community and paramedic) to NHS patients using NHS resources. This includes any activity that has been commissioned from or sub-contracted to non-NHS providers (including independent sector providers). From 2006/07, HRG4 has been used as the currency for the reference cost collection and admitted patient care has been recorded at both finished consultant episode (FCE) and 'spell' level (a spell is the time from entry to discharge – it is used as the basic denominator for PbR as a patient can pass from one consultant to another during a hospital stay).

Increasingly, NHS organisations are using more detailed 'patient information and costing systems' (PLICS) that go beyond FCE and spell costing. The Department of Health guidance for the 2007/08 reference cost collection acknowledges that PLICS are becoming increasingly common and emphasises that they must be fully compatible with HRG4 resource groupings (for reference costs purposes).

Reference costs were originally intended for management information purposes, but now also form the basis of the PbR tariff.

National schedule of reference costs

The submission of reference costs is a mandatory part of the financial regime for NHS trusts, NHS foundation trusts, PCTs and care trusts. The information submitted is collated by the Department of Health and published annually as the national schedule of reference costs (NSRC). The NSRC shows the national average cost for a range of treatments and procedures and can be used by organisations for comparative purposes.

National reference cost index

In addition to the NSRC, a national reference cost index (RCI or NRCI) is published. The RCI gives a single figure (effectively a ranking) for each NHS provider organisation enabling comparison of their activity with similar providers (for example, district general hospitals) and with providers in their local health economy. In most cases activity is measured in HRGs.

In the index there are a range of scores. For example an organisation with costs equal to the national average for its casemix will score 100; if it scores 125 it shows that costs are 25% above the national average and a score of 75 shows that its costs are 25% below the national average.

A market forces factor (MFF) is also published to recognise the differences in costs in different geographical areas that are outside NHS control. Index scores are published pre and post application of the MFF. The post MFF index is the one generally used.

On the whole, with all other factors being equal, an organisation with a reference cost score (MFF adjusted) of less than 100 can expect to gain financially under PbR as their costs are lower than the tariff (see chapter 13 for more on PbR).

The range of services included in future index calculations will continue to expand until all services are covered.

Costing for reference costs

As mentioned above, reference costs is a mandatory annual exercise which captures the total cost to an organisation of the patient contacts that it has had in the previous financial year. Financial costs are allocated and apportioned to the HRGs that the organisation has performed in line with the prescribed classification as set out in guidance issued by the Department of Health each year.

Clinical staff feed into the process by identifying the key drivers of costs and the weights which need to be applied to HRGs to reflect the cost of these drivers.

To ensure that all NHS providers' costs are compared on a consistent basis, details of the definitions to be used and refinements to the standard costing approach are set out in the *Costing Manual*.

Reference costs are based on full costs and all relevant costs are included. The main emphasis is on the cost of delivering a service and not the funding streams that are used to recover the costs.

Cost variations

The most recent reference costs for 2006/07 show that the organisation wide RCI (adjusted for MFF and including excess bed days) ranged from 163 to 69 for trusts and from 174 to 64 for PCTs. The huge variation can be attributed to a number of factors. Some of the variation will be a result of differences in efficiency and effectiveness leading to real cost differences between providers. However, some of the variation (particularly in relation to outliers) will be the result of poor data quality, inconsistency in the costing and recording of activity between different organisations and because HRGs do not adequately reflect many specialist services.

There was also substantial variation in the different procedure costs included in the NSRC – for example, the national average unit cost of cochlea implants (without complications or co-morbidities) was £13,391, but the inter-quartile range (i.e. the costs of the middle 50% of trusts) stretched from £3,226 to £19,577.

Data quality is a particular cause for concern – in its latest reference costs guidance for 2007/08, the Department of Health states that 'there are still a number of organisations where data quality issues are unresolved (for example, levels of unclassified data, erroneous clinical coding, etc). The onus on the production of sound, accurate and timely data rests with each NHS organisation… The implications of poor quality activity and cost data are now far-reaching and will influence the financial position of each NHS organisation under the PbR programme. The need for high quality data cannot be underestimated'.

Service Line Management (SLM)

Another level of costing that is becoming more common in the NHS involves focussing on 'service lines' – in other words looking in detail at the income and costs of an organisation's services in much the same way as a private sector company analyses its business units. In practice, this means that the focus is on profitability information by specialty. SLM is considered best practice in the FT sector and is also used in other non foundation trusts. Monitor's guidance in this area lists the characteristics of a typical service line as being:

- Distinct patient groups
- Distinct product/services/procedures
- Designated staff
- Clearly identified profit and loss responsibilities.

The information gleaned from costing at this level is then used to 'manage' each service line (hence 'service line management' or SLM) and develop business plans.

For more about SLM see chapter 9 and Monitor's website.

Patient Level Information and Costing Systems (PLICS)

At an even more detailed level, systems have been developed that can identify and record the cost of individual patients. This can provide organisations with an extremely rich source of data on which to base their activity and business plans.

The Department of Health's website states that 'PLICS represent a change in the costing methodology in the NHS from a predominantly top down allocation approach, based on averages and apportionments, to a more direct and sophisticated approach based on the actual interactions and events related to individual patients and the associated costs'. Once costs have been identified at individual patient level, they can still be aggregated to HRG-level for wider comparison and to inform the national tariff.

PLICS systems are becoming increasingly common and are encouraged by the Department which identifies the key benefits as being:

- 'service-level economics reporting
- an understanding of the variations
- a major improvement in clinical ownership of resource decisions
- provision of information to enable improved HRG classification
- improved funding policy and evidence-based analysis in discussions with commissioners'.

Information about PLICS is available on the Department's website.

Cost Return and Programme Budgeting

NHS organisations are required to submit a costing return to the Department of Health each year that analyses costs by cost type – for example medical staff and drugs. Since 2004/05 there have also been 'programme budgeting' requirements.

The aim of programme budgeting is to provide a source of information that can be used by all NHS bodies to give a greater understanding of 'where the money is going' and 'what we are getting for the money we invest in the NHS'. Programme budgeting covers all expenditure channelled through a PCT. This includes hospital expenditure, community expenditure, GP prescribing and other components all broken down into 23 broad healthcare headings (for example infectious diseases and cancer and tumours). Programme budgeting enables commissioners to benchmark their use of resources across providers and with other commissioners. It also enables a higher level of benchmarking by more strategic organisations such as the Department of Health.

References and Further Reading

Payment by Results: www.dh.gov.uk/PolicyAndGuidance/OrganisationPolicy/ FinanceAndPlanning/NHSFinancialReforms/fs/en

National Service Frameworks: www.dh.gov.uk/en/Healthcare/NationalServiceFrameworks/index.htm

NHS Costing Manual: www.dh.gov.uk/PolicyAndGuidance/OrganisationPolicy/ FinanceAndPlanning/NHSCostingManual/fs/en

Healthcare Resource Groups Version 4: www.icservices.nhs.uk/casemix/pages/hrg.asp

HRG 4, HFMA Briefing, March 2008: www.hfma.org.uk

The Information Centre for Health and Social Care: www.ic.nhs.uk

Reference Costs: www.dh.gov.uk/PolicyAndGuidance/OrganisationPolicy/FinanceAndPlanning/ NHSCostingManual/fs/en

NHS Reference Costs 2006/07 (includes the RCI): www.dh.gov.uk/en/Publicationsandstatistics/ Publications/PublicationsPolicyAndGuidance/DH_082571

Monitor (for guidance on service line reporting and management): www.monitor-nhsft.gov.uk

Patient Level Information and Costing Systems (PLICS): www.dh.gov.uk/en/ Managingyourorganisation/Financeandplanning/NHScostingmanual/DH_080056

Programme budgeting: www.dh.gov.uk/PolicyAndGuidance/OrganisationPolicy/ FinanceAndPlanning/ProgrammeBudgeting/fs/en

13. Payment by Results

Introduction

In 2002, the Department of Health announced that it was to introduce a system of payment by results (PbR) in England. This decision was based on the belief that the 'old' system of financial flows was not sufficiently responsive or flexible to meet the needs of the government's reform agenda.

PbR is limited to the English NHS – other countries in the UK have not adopted, nor given any indication that they will adopt this system. However some limited use of tariff payments is used in Scotland (for activity flows between health boards – see chapter 18) and Wales is currently undertaking a review of financial flows (see chapter 19).

The stated aims of PbR are to provide a system that supports patient choice and is fair, transparent and 'rules based'. By implication, these were regarded as deficiencies in the 'old' system, where financial issues and difficulties were dealt with in an ad-hoc and less transparent way. In effect, good performance was not recognised and bad performance did not lead to change.

Under PbR, payments made to providers of care for NHS patients are linked to the activity and services actually provided. Payment is based on a national tariff that recognises the type, mix and severity of the treatment. It is intended to be a fair and consistent basis for financing providers, rather than one based on historical budgets and negotiating skills.

PbR does not in itself affect the way funding is allocated to commissioners (PCTs) – they still receive allocations from the Department of Health based on a weighted capitation formula (see chapter 3). However, PbR does require PCTs to develop a stronger focus on service quality and demand management reflecting the move away from their previous responsibility for price negotiation.

Why was PbR introduced?

The 2002 budget settlement announced a large and sustained increase in NHS funding, and guaranteed this for a five-year period. The government needed to be assured that these resources would be utilised to develop and deliver more and better services. To achieve this aim there needed to be a financial system that contained the right balance of reward, incentive and equity to underpin the *NHS Plan* – hence the introduction of PbR.

Under the 'traditional' approach, many PCTs had simple 'block contracts' with the hospitals that their patients used. Many of these were not based on activity, work done and/or achievement of plans – the hospital effectively received a block of funding irrespective of the number of patients treated. Providers were not rewarded for achieving budgets or increasing activity. Management of demand was variable and costs and benefits of different patterns of activity were not always clear.

Block contracts were generally based on historical patterns of care and reflected local costs irrespective of relative cost efficiency when compared to the rest of the NHS. Because service level agreements (SLAs) were set at local prices, PCTs' real purchasing power was affected as much by the relative costs of their principal providers as by the resource allocation formula. Block contracts were also very limited in their ability to respond to changes in patterns of service provision or patient casemix.

The flow of funds under the 'old' system is shown below. In this example, trust A has high costs and trust B low costs – as a result, PCT1 is commissioning at high local prices and PCT2 at low local prices:

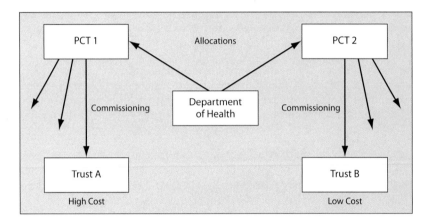

PbR is designed to overcome these limitations by:

- Reimbursing providers fairly and transparently for the services they deliver
- Encouraging PCTs to plan and manage demand for services more effectively
- Rewarding efficiency and quality in service provision
- Enabling patients to be treated at the provider of their choice as payment will be at a fixed price and will follow the patient
- Applying to all providers of healthcare to NHS patients irrespective of their organisational/legal status, be they public or private providers.

PbR is therefore a critical tool in the delivery of the NHS reform agenda as set out in the *NHS Plan*. It provides a clear and efficient financial framework that underpins choice, plurality of provision, access and equity. The flow of funds under PbR is shown in the diagram opposite – as in the previous diagram, trust A is high cost and trust B low cost:

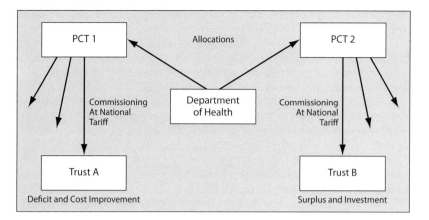

International Context

Over the past 20 years, a growing number of countries (including Germany, the USA, Australia, Sweden and Eire) have used tariff systems to pay for acute healthcare. The tariffs are based on casemix measures, with a separate rate set for groups of procedures and treatments that are both clinically similar and consume similar levels of resources. Internationally, casemix measures based on initial diagnosis have been used (often called diagnosis-related groups) although in England bespoke healthcare resource groups (HRGs) have been developed, giving greater weight to the procedures carried out on patients (see below).

This international experience has been drawn on in developing the PbR system for England, although its scope far exceeds systems used elsewhere.

What is Payment by Results?

PbR is based around the use of a prospective, tariff-based system that links a preset price to a defined measure of output or activity. The two key issues are therefore:

* How is the activity measure defined?
* How is the tariff determined?

Activity measurement is not uncommon or new in the NHS. It is more advanced in acute services, where models of defining and measuring casemix have been developed over the past 30 years. These have generally used, as a starting point, the methods and methodologies developed by Fetter and colleagues in the USA in the 1970s, which led to the development of diagnosis-related groups (DRGs). English variants, known as HRGs were developed by the NHS Information Authority (now the NHS Information Centre for Health and Social Care). PbR uses the HRG classification of casemix as the basis for making payments as they are the most developed and comprehensive tools in England for classifying the outputs of the health system. HRGs mainly cover the acute sector, with significant gaps for instance for mental health services. However the latest version of groups (HRG4) has been designed to be setting independent and to support the provision of components of healthcare outside of hospitals through the use of unbundled tariffs.

HRGs group services that are clinically similar and require similar resources for treatment and care. They are often referred to as the 'currency' that is used for commissioning. They have been developed by clinicians in order to provide clinically meaningful groups of patients who require similar levels of resources. There are some 1400 HRGs in HRG4. If you want to know more, the HFMA has produced a detailed briefing on HRG4 (in conjunction with the NHS Information Centre for Health and Social Care) which looks at each HRG chapter in turn.

The national tariff is based on the average reference cost for these HRGs as reported by the NHS. Reference costs are discussed in chapter 12 and the NHS has collected these for a number of years. The tariff prices therefore reflect the reported cost of services and are reviewed annually. They include uplifts for generic cost pressures, changes in technology and practice (for example, the cost of recommendations made by the National Institute for Health and Clinical Excellence – NICE) and an assumption on efficiency improvements.

A tariff for reimbursement – effectively a national set of prices – is published annually by the Department of Health. The table below shows some examples of the elective tariff for 2007/08 and 2008/09. In both these years the tariff was still based on HRG version 3.5 with HRG4 due to be introduced as the basis for the tariff from 2009/10. The differences in prices between the two years are a result of two influencing factors. First there is the uplift for cost increases, already discussed. However, each year the tariff uses a more recent set of reference costs as its basis. In theory, as costing practices improve, reference costs should become more accurate leading to more accurate tariffs. This practice of refreshing the reference costs can lead to more major changes in tariff rates, both up and down.

HRG	Service	Tariff (£) 2007/08	Tariff (£) 2008/09
C04	Minor mouth or throat procedures	543	558
H01	Bilateral hip replacement	6496	7599
H04	Primary knee replacement	5613	5663
Q11	Varicose vein procedures	1018	1074
J29	Major reconstructive surgery	4515	4892

How the Tariff is set

The tariff is based on information provided by NHS organisations. There is effectively a four stage process:

- Stage 1 – activity coded. Clinical coders assign a diagnosis or procedure code to activity based on the patient notes or discharge summary

- Stage 2 – HRG assigned. Activity is automatically assigned to an HRG (via software called the HRG grouper) based on the diagnosis or procedure codes – as logged by the clinical coder
- Stage 3: local costs submitted to Department of Health. At the end of June each year, all providers have to submit details of their activity, costed locally, to the Department of Health for all their provided services (this includes commissioners who provide services). Costs and activity are based on the previous financial year – for example, for the June 2008 submission, costs and activity will be based on the 2007/08 financial year
- Stage 4: the Department of Health calculates the prospective national tariff. The Department of Health calculates the national average local cost for each HRG/service within the scope of PbR, converts finished consultant episode costs to spells costs for admitted patients (a spell is the time from entry to discharge – it is used as the basic denominator for PbR as a patient can pass from one consultant to another during a hospital stay and providers are moving towards submitting costs on a spell basis) and uplifts them to create a prospective tariff for the coming financial year. For example, reference costs submitted to the Department of Health in June 2007 are the basis for the 2008/09 national tariff. The tariff is calculated annually based on the reference cost submission. As mentioned earlier in this chapter, the tariff is uplifted/adjusted to reflect:
  - generic cost pressures
  - inflation
  - changes in technology and practice (for example, NICE guidance)
  - assumptions on efficiency improvements.

  The Department may also make a number of 'normative' changes to specific tariffs to correct known problems or to provide an incentive to drive a specific behaviour.

Cost Differences

As the tariff is the average cost of each HRG, providers will receive either more or less than they need to cover their costs. There can be a number of reasons why costs vary including casemix (for instance a hospital that undertakes more of the higher cost procedures within a particular HRG may not cover its higher costs from a tariff set on average costs), clinical practice, local initiatives and market forces.

The area that generates most debate is the impact of market forces on an organisation's costs – it is simply a matter of fact that organisations in some parts of the country have higher costs purely because of their location and because labour, land, buildings and even equipment cost more. These differences are unavoidable and to ensure equity, a compensating adjustment is made. This adjustment is called the market forces factor or MFF. The most obvious area affected is London and the South East.

In the past the MFF has been used to adjust commissioners' allocations, reflecting the higher costs they had to pay for services in their locality. The actual unavoidable costs differences faced by providers were reflected in local prices and contracts. However under PbR, all providers receive the same national tariff, and so a mechanism is needed to ensure providers are not disadvantaged because of their location. Under PbR, the PbR element of the market forces adjustment (i.e. the MFF relating to activity covered by PbR) is paid directly to providers as a separate sum rather than making an adjustment to the tariff. If the tariff were adjusted it would effectively mean commissioners would still be paying different prices depending on the MFF of the provider they were commissioning with. This could lead to price-based competition with an incentive for PCTs to direct patients to services provided by trusts in a lower MFF zone.

How PbR was introduced

PbR is a fundamental change to the way money moves around the NHS. To allow time for organisations to prepare and manage any transitional issues, a five-year programme was set for its introduction with the original aim that by 2008 all commissioning would be within the framework of PbR.

Preparation 2003 to 2005

During the preparation period, the national tariff was applied only to activity in a limited number of HRGs (15 in 2003/04 and 48 in 2004/05). PCTs were required to commission for any changes in activity around the agreed baseline at the tariff rate. The baseline activity was paid for at an agreed locally negotiated rate.

The transition – 2005 to 2008

The original intention for 2005/06 was to include elective and non-elective activity, accident and emergency attendances and outpatient appointments. This would have meant that for large district general hospitals some 70% of income would have been covered by the national tariff. However with concerns over financial volatility, the Department of Health decided to delay the expansion of the tariff coverage for non-NHS foundation trusts (FTs) and concentrate purely on elective activity. This meant that about 30% of a typical hospital's income was actually covered by the tariff. FTs continued with the originally planned full system. NHS trusts joined FTs in using the wider ranging tariff for 2006/07.

During the transitional period the key issue for trusts was that any under activity (other than for emergency care which was treated differently) was not paid for. In other words, failure to meet SLA volumes resulted in withdrawal of funds. Trusts therefore faced potential financial risks and rewards depending on their cost levels:

- If costs were greater than average (i.e. above national tariff) a trust faced a potential deficit
- If costs were below average the trust had a potential gain.

A trust's reference cost index provides a rough indication of how it fares under the tariff. A reference cost of 105 suggests that a trust is 5% more expensive than average and needs to cut 5% from its running costs if the national tariff is to cover its expenditure. Similarly a reference cost of 95 suggests that a trust is 5% cheaper than tariff rates and makes a surplus for reinvestment. Few trusts operate exactly at national average costs, so essentially every trust gains or loses under PbR. Trusts therefore need to contain their total expenditure within their income, but in the knowledge that the income is a function of activity multiplied by the nationally set tariffs.

PbR is meant to incentivise high cost trusts to reduce costs. However, in recognition of the fact that most NHS organisations needed time to adjust to the new system, a number of principles were applied during the transitional period:

- The overall revenue impact of the transition was minimised (i.e. gainers supported the losers)
- Transition arrangements resolved only issues associated with the impact of PbR (i.e. they did not deal with any underlying financial problems)
- PCTs' purchasing powers were maintained in the first instance (i.e. for 2005/06), regardless of distance from target (i.e. allocations were adjusted initially to neutralise the impact of PbR). In 2006/07 PCTs received only 50% of this protection, known as the purchaser parity adjustment, with the aim that it would be phased out by 2008/09
- Trusts moved in four equal steps towards the full tariff (i.e. in the first year a gaining trust kept one quarter of the gains it made from being paid at tariff prices. A losing trust lost just a quarter of the full losses implied by being paid at tariff rates).

PbR in the Future

Although the original intention was to have all commissioning within the framework of PbR by 2008, there are still a number of activities that are excluded – for example, community, mental health and ambulance services. There are also a number of other issues under discussion relating to how PbR moves forward as set out in the 2007 consultation paper *Options for the Future of Payment by Results: 2008/09 to 20010/11*. The objectives of the consultation were to:

- Incentivise better health and healthcare
- Drive innovation, productivity and responsiveness
- Help maintain a clinically sound, transparent and sustainable transactional framework for commissioning NHS services.

To meet these objectives, three basic principles were set out:

- PbR must make clinical sense and to this end HRG4 has been developed
- NHS organisations require stability and predictability as PbR continues to grow
- Local innovation should be encouraged in pursuit of national objectives.

One key proposal in the consultation was for PbR to mean more than simply a national tariff. It was proposed that depending on the services covered, three models were possible:

- National currency and price
- National currency, local price
- Local currency and price.

The consultation also raised the possibility of using costs from a sample of providers to set the tariff, rather than using national averages, and of expanding the use of normative pricing (i.e.

setting a tariff price based on a judgement about what efficiencies can be achieved or to encourage the take-up or dropping of particular treatments/activities).

In January 2008, the Department of Health issued its response to the consultation by outlining key themes for future work in PbR. These are to:

- Get the building blocks right – ensuring that the PbR infrastructure (i.e. classifications, coding, casemix, costing and currencies) is as robust as possible
- Ensure that future work fits with the findings of Lord Darzi's review (*Our NHS, Our Future*). This means developing a tariff that 'supports the localising of care where possible and the centralising of treatment where necessary'. This will also involve examining 'the effect on casemix of shifting care out of hospitals' and looking at 'how PbR can better support the functioning of clinical networks and co-operation between providers'
- Expand the scope – the five priority areas identified are mental health, community services, critical care, urgent and emergency care and long term conditions
- Encourage local involvement in the development of PbR (i.e. so that it is locally driven)
- Involve clinicians at all levels so that PbR is 'clinically led'.

References and Further Reading

The Department of Health publications referred to in this chapter are available on the Payment by Results pages of its website: www.dh.gov.uk/en/Managingyourorganisation/Financeandplanning/NHSFinancialReforms/DH_077249

Budget 2002, HM Treasury, 2002:
www.hm-treasury.gov.uk/budget/bud_bud02/bud_bud02_index.cfm

The NHS Plan: a plan for investment, a plan for reform, Department of health, 2000:
www.dh.gov.uk/en/Publicationsandstatistics/Publications/PublicationsPolicyAndGuidance/DH_4002960

Fetter R.B: DRGs, their design and development, Health, Administration Press, Ann Arbor, Michigan 1991

DRGs and Healthcare, Bardsley, Coles, Jenkins (eds) Kings Fund, London 1987

For information about the latest version of HRGs, go to the Health and Social Care Information Centre: www.ic.nhs.uk/casemix

HFMA Briefing: HRG4 www.hfma.org.uk/TrainingAndDevelopment/InformationServices/

Reference Costs, Department of Health: www.dh.gov.uk/en/Publicationsandstatistics/Publications/PublicationsPolicyAndGuidance/DH_082571

PbR Guidance for 2008/09 (including the MFF), Department of Health: www.dh.gov.uk/en/Managingyourorganisation/Financeandplanning/NHSFinancialReforms/DH_081238

Our NHS, Our Future (the Darzi Review), Department of Health, 2007: www.dh.gov.uk/en/Publicationsandstatistics/Publications/PublicationsPolicyAndGuidance/DH_079077

Options for the Future of PbR – 2008/09 to 2010/11 (consultation paper and response): www.dh.gov.uk/en/Consultations/Responsestoconsultations/DH_082424

14. Financial Reporting and Performance

Introduction

Every NHS organisation needs to provide timely, accurate and balanced information about its stewardship and use of resources and its non-financial performance to the organisation's different stakeholders. Also, to run organisations effectively, top management needs up-to-date financial and non-financial performance information on a timely basis. It should be presented in a form that is tailored to user needs, is easy to understand and highlights the key financial issues that they need to be aware of.

This chapter considers the nature of financial reporting and performance in the NHS and looks at the following issues:

- External reporting
- Internal reporting
- Financial performance targets
- Non-financial performance standards and targets
- Performance assessment
- Financial performance management.

External Reporting

Statutory requirements

All NHS bodies have a statutory duty to produce annual accounts. For NHS trusts, primary care trusts (PCTs) and strategic health authorities (SHAs) the relevant legislation is section 232 and paragraph 3(1) of schedule 15 of the *NHS Act 2006* and for NHS foundation trusts (FTs) section 30 and paragraph 25(1) of schedule 7 of the *NHS Act 2006*. The form and content of the accounts is prescribed by the Secretary of State for Health – or the independent regulator Monitor for FTs – and is largely consistent with UK generally accepted accounting practice (UK GAAP). The production of the statutory annual accounts is the principal means by which NHS bodies discharge their accountability to taxpayers and users of services for their stewardship of public money.

NHS accounting framework

NHS bodies are expected to adhere to the accounting standards issued or adopted by the Accounting Standards Board (ASB). However, the government has the final say on how these standards are applied to the public sector, including NHS bodies. The Treasury has developed a *Financial Reporting Manual* setting out how the accounting standards should be implemented in the public sector. The Department of Health produces a *Manual for Accounts* for SHAs, PCTs and NHS trusts that is consistent with the requirements of the *Financial Reporting Manual* and which NHS bodies are required to follow. Monitor produces a similar manual for FTs, called the *NHS Foundation Trust Financial Reporting Manual*. These manuals are updated each year. The manuals provide a summary of the relevant accounting standards, but NHS bodies will refer to the standards themselves if a more detailed understanding is required. Accounting standards are intended to provide a framework for good practice and the common disclosure of information. They provide the benchmark against which an organisation's audited accounts are judged. A list of current standards, issued as statements of standard accounting practice (SSAPs), financial reporting standards (FRSs) or reporting statements (RSs), and their applicability to the NHS is shown below.

SSAP	Title	Applicable?
4	Accounting for Government Grants	Yes
5	Accounting for VAT	Yes
9	Stocks and Long Term Contracts	Yes
13	Accounting for Research and Development	Yes
17	Accounting for Post Balance Sheet Events	Yes – but superseded by FRS21 in 2006/07
19	Accounting for Investment Properties	Yes – but only where bodies are authorised to hold such assets by the Secretary of State
20	Foreign Currency Translation	Yes
21	Accounting for Leases and Hire Purchase Contracts	Yes
25	Segmental Reporting	Yes

FRS	Title	Applicable?
1	Cash Flow Statements (revised)	Yes
2	Accounting for Subsidiary Undertakings	Yes – in principle
3	Reporting Financial Performance	Yes
4	Capital Instruments	Yes
5	Reporting of Substance of Transactions (revised)	Yes
6	Acquisitions and Mergers	Yes – in principle
7	Fair Values in Acquisition Accounting	Yes – in principle
8	Related Party Disclosures	Yes
9	Associates and Joint Ventures	Yes – in part
10	Goodwill and Intangible Assets	Yes – in part
11	Impairment of Fixed Assets and Goodwill	Yes – in part
12	Provisions, Contingent Liabilities and Contingent Assets	Yes
13	Derivatives and other Financial Instruments	Yes
14	Earnings per Share	Withdrawn
15	Tangible Fixed Assets	Yes
16	Current Tax	No
17	Retirement Benefits	Yes
18	Accounting Policies	Yes
19	Deferred Tax	No
20	Share Based Payments	No
21	Events after the Balance Sheet Date	Yes
22	(IAS 33) Earnings per Share	No
27	Life Assurance	No
28	Corresponding Amounts	Yes

RS	Title	Applicable?
1	Operating and Financial Review	Yes

These standards apply for the 2007/08 and 2008/09 financial years.

In its *Budget 2008*, the Treasury announced that international financial reporting standards (IFRS) will be followed for the preparation of accounts from 2009/10. It is expected that implementation of IFRS will mean that the treatment of PFI funded assets will change as will the treatment of leases, holiday accruals and non-current assets. There will also be a number of other changes in disclosure rules.

Annual accounts

The *Manual for Accounts* and the *NHS Foundation Trust Financial Reporting Manual* specify the format and timing of the annual accounts. The format of the accounts differs slightly depending upon the type of NHS body concerned, but will consist of:

- The foreword to the accounts
- The four primary statements:
  - the balance sheet
  - the revenue account (called the income and expenditure statement for NHS trusts and FTs and the operating cost statement for PCTs and SHAs)
  - the statement of recognised gains and losses
  - the cash flow statement
- Notes to the accounts
- Statements and certificates: directors' statement of responsibilities (for FTs – the accounting officer's statement of responsibilities); the statement on internal control (SIC); the auditors' report.

To help non-executive directors and others to understand the accounts of PCTs, NHS trusts and FTs, the HFMA and the Audit Commission have produced a series of practical guides – see their websites for details.

Once the NHS body has prepared the annual accounts they must be audited. After the accounts have been audited and the necessary amendments made, the board is required to formally adopt the accounts. The certificates will be signed at the same time. The auditor will then sign the audit report. More information on the work of auditors is contained in chapter 15.

NHS bodies must publish an annual report and audited accounts as one document and present it at a public meeting. NHS bodies still have the option to prepare and distribute an annual report and summary financial statements, however this is additional to the annual report and accounts, which must be available if requested by a member of the public. The auditors must be given a copy of the annual report along with the accounts and working papers at the start of the audit so that they have sufficient time to carry out the required work before the completion of the auditor's opinion. Other quantitative aspects of the annual report are reviewed by auditors to ensure consistency with the annual accounts.

As well as preparing the statutory annual accounts, NHS trusts, PCTs and SHAs are also required to submit summarisation schedules to the Department of Health. The summarisation schedules are consistent with the annual accounts, but contain slightly different information and are used by the Department to prepare the summarised accounts for each type of NHS body and the Department's own resource account. Similarly FTs have to complete consolidation schedules which are used by Monitor to produce a summary of FT accounts. The use of summarisation and consolidation schedules also facilitates the preparation of whole of government accounts (WGA).

The *Manuals for Accounts* set out the timetable for completion of the accounts and audit. The 2006/07 accounts were prepared and submitted for audit by early May and the audit was completed by late June. FTs currently work to a slightly quicker timetable. As a result of the Treasury's faster closing initiative, NHS bodies and auditors are under increasing pressure to produce audited accounts sooner after the year-end. The accounts timetable has already moved forward over recent years and is likely to continue to do so.

Annual report

All NHS bodies are required to produce an annual report which must be published with the full set of audited accounts. The annual report is primarily a narrative document similar to the directors' report described in the *Companies Act*, but with additional information reflecting the NHS body's position in the community. The report gives an account of the body's activities and performance over the last financial year.

Although the layout of the annual report is not prescribed, the *Manuals for Accounts* specify the areas that should be covered – these are *Companies Act* requirements which apply to NHS bodies.

From 2005 a requirement had been incorporated into the *Companies Act 1985* for the annual report to contain an operating and financial review (OFR). Then in November 2005, the Chancellor abolished this requirement in an attempt to reduce the administrative burden facing companies. However for the public sector it remains best practice to produce an OFR. A reporting statement by the ASB makes it clear that the detailed content of the OFR must be decided by the board. It is therefore the responsibility of the directors of each NHS body to ensure that the OFR includes reference to current performance and policy targets. The OFR should include details of performance that are not reported in the annual accounts including useful non-financial and financial information. The HFMA has produced guidance on preparing OFRs which is available on its website.

The annual report must be approved by the NHS body's board of directors before presentation at a public meeting. This meeting must be held before 30 September following the end of the relevant financial year. There is no requirement for SHAs to hold a public meeting. For FTs, the annual report and accounts must be presented to a meeting of the board of governors. This meeting should be convened within a reasonable timescale after the end of the financial year, but must not be before the FT has laid its annual report and accounts before Parliament.

Internal Reporting

Reporting to budget holders

The reporting of performance against the budget and any corrective action taken as a result is an essential element of financial management in the NHS. Budget reporting to budget holders should be sufficiently detailed to ensure that all significant variances are identified and to properly identify any issues requiring corrective action.

While the nature and format of budget monitoring information will vary between different levels in the organisation, the over-riding factors must be that the information is timely and accurate. To ensure accuracy, financial commitments should be recognised as soon as possible and be reflected in the monthly financial reports. Without accurate budget reporting at budget holder level, costs cannot be properly controlled.

The information is produced at a range of levels, allowing managers to see not only summary performance, but also the performance of individual departments and teams. The exact nature of this reporting depends on the organisation's management structure. These reports on income and expenditure are often referred to as the 'management accounts'.

A recent development in management accounting has introduced the concepts of service line reporting (SLR) and patient level costing. A service line is a distinct clinical operating unit of a trust, with clearly definable income and costs. SLR is made possible through the payment by results (PbR) system and allows a trust to see the profitability of each of its service lines, not just the overall position. This approach allows clinicians and managers to better understand cost drivers and the financial effect of clinical decisions. It also provides the evidence to support strategic decisions such as investment and expansion of particular service lines.

Patient level costing is the natural extension of service line reporting. Where service line reporting analyses costs and revenues at departmental level, patient level costing attempts to assign costs and revenues to individual patient spells. This is more complex and requires detailed recording of all activity relating to a patient spell, for instance, operating theatre time; the time spent by individual clinicians and the amount of drugs and other medical supplies used. However, the benefit is increased accuracy of reporting and more accurate reference cost returns, on which the PbR tariff is based (see chapter 13 for more on PbR).

NHS bodies should ensure that budget holders receive continuous training so that they have sufficient skills to undertake the task of budget management.

Reporting to NHS boards

NHS boards need financial information to properly direct the organisation. This information has to be accurate and timely so that the board can take early and corrective action where necessary. The form and content of board financial reports will vary and it is for the board to identify the format, content and frequency of the financial information that it is to receive. The types of information NHS bodies may report to their boards include:

- Performance against the achievement of statutory and departmental duties and targets (including performance against resource limits, compliance with the *Better Payment Practice Code* and performance against external financing limits)

- In-year income and expenditure position and year-end forecasts, including an analysis of financial risks, the likelihood of them arising and how they will be managed
- Activity levels linked to financial data
- Progress on the achievement of any cost improvement programmes and financial recovery plans
- Balance sheet
- Cash forecast
- Losses
- Performance of outsourced services
- Progress against internal and external audit recommendations
- Progress on major capital schemes
- Staffing and establishment reports.

As well as considering the above on a monthly basis, there will also be financial information that the board will need to consider every year, including:

- Annual accounts
- Financial plans
- Annual audit letters.

The board should also be regularly updated and advised on the nature and development of new systems within the NHS (recent examples include the introduction of PbR and practice based commissioning) so that they are better able to understand their potential impact and well prepared to manage the real impact when implementation has taken place.

Information produced for both internal and external purposes should be derived from the same financial system, ensuring that there is only one version of the truth and that decisions throughout the organisation are being made consistently on the basis of the same information.

Financial Performance Targets

NHS bodies face a range of statutory and departmental financial targets. The targets and their nature vary according to the type of NHS body – as shown below:

NHS trusts

Statutory (i.e. duties that are a formal requirement of trusts as laid down in statute through Parliament)	• Income and expenditure balance (the 'break-even duty'). Every trust has to ensure that its revenue is not less than sufficient, taking one financial year with another, to meet outgoings properly charged to the income and expenditure account. 'Taking one financial year with another' has been interpreted to mean that over a three (or exceptionally a five) year period, trusts are required to achieve break-even position in their income and expenditure account. Further details on trusts' financial duties and about trust surpluses and deficits can be found in chapter 7.

Departmental (i.e. an additional rule and regulation set down by the Department of Health that clarifies or specifies how a trust will operate)	• Every trust must break-even each and every year • The external financing limit. The external financing limit (EFL) can be defined as the difference between what a trust plans to spend on capital in a year and what it can generate internally from its operations. The EFL can be either positive or negative. A positive EFL arises when a trust is required to draw down additional government funding above what it can generate internally to support its capital expenditure plans. A negative EFL arises where the trust is required to repay public dividend capital (PDC) or save cash. The target EFL will be set at the start of the financial year by the Department of Health and the trust will be expected to manage its resources to ensure it achieves the target (see chapters 7 and 16) • Capital cost absorption. Trusts are required to achieve a cost of capital absorption equivalent to 3.5% of average relevant net assets. Net relevant assets are calculated as follows:

Total capital and reserves	X
minus donated asset reserve	(−)
minus assets in the course of construction	(−)
minus cash held in paymaster accounts	(−)
Total relevant net assets	Y

• Contain expenditure, measured on an accruals basis, within capital resource limits (CRLs). The CRL is set by the Department of Health for accrued capital expenditure in year. The trust is required to stay within this limit when measuring gross capital expenditure less the book value of assets disposed of during the year
• Apply the *Better Payment Practice Code*. Trusts have to achieve a public sector payment standard of valid invoices paid within 30 days of the receipt of the invoice. A target (currently 95%) is set at the start of the year by the Department of Health for the value and volume of invoices that must be paid within 30 days.

PCTs and SHAs

Statutory	• Contain expenditure, measured on an accruals basis, within revenue resource limits. The revenue resource limit (RRL) is set by the Department of Health for accrued revenue expenditure. PCTs and SHAs are required to stay within this limit when measuring gross revenue expenditure less miscellaneous income • Contain expenditure, measured on an accruals basis, within capital resource limits. The CRL is set by the Department of Health for accrued capital expenditure in year. PCTs and SHAs

	are required to stay within this limit when measuring gross capital expenditure less the book value of assets disposed of during the year • Remain within cash limits. There is a combined cash limit for both revenue and capital.
Departmental	• Apply the *Better Payment Practice Code*. PCTs and SHAs have to achieve a public sector payment standard of valid invoices paid within 30 days of the receipt of the invoice. A target (currently 95%) is set at the start of the year by the Department of Health for the value and volume of invoices that must be paid within 30 days • For PCTs only – to recover the full cost of their provider activities.

NHS foundation trusts

FTs' financial targets differ significantly from NHS trusts. There is no requirement for FTs to break-even, remain within the external financing limit, achieve a predetermined capital cost absorption rate or remain within a capital resource limit. This reflects the different financial regime that FTs operate within. FTs are allowed to incur deficits and operate on a similar basis to commercial organisations. FTs are required under their authorisation, amongst other things, to 'operate effectively, efficiently and economically and as a going concern' and to 'comply with a range of operational and financial requirements'. The main financial target is therefore to remain solvent.

FTs have a statutory limit on the increase in income from private patient activity. The proportion of income from private activity as a proportion of total income must be no greater than it was for the predecessor NHS trust.

FTs must also comply with Monitor's *Prudential Borrowing Code*. Each FT is set a prudential borrowing limit (PBL) by Monitor which is reviewed at least annually. FTs must keep the total of all their borrowing from all sources within the set PBL.

More details on FTs and their financial regime are set out in chapter 8.

Non-financial Performance Standards and Targets

As well as the financial targets there are a number of other targets that NHS bodies are required to meet. The *Health and Social Care (Community Health and Standards) Act 2003* established the power for the Secretary of State for Health to set standards. The Department of Health publishes standards and targets for healthcare organisations – for example, in *National Standards, Local Action: Health and Social Care Standards and Planning Framework 2005/06 – 2007/08* in July 2004 which focused on standards aimed at driving continuous improvements in quality, national targets and local priorities. Since 2007/08, the Department of Health has also published annual *Operating Frameworks* that set priorities for the year ahead and reiterate existing commitments (see below).

Healthcare standards

Standards for Better Health, published as part of the 2004 *Standards and Planning Framework*, identified two types of standard:

- Core standards which bring together and rationalise existing requirements for the NHS, setting out the minimum level of service patients and service users have a right to expect
- Developmental standards that signal the direction of travel and provide a framework for NHS bodies to plan the delivery of services that continue to improve in line with increasing patient expectations.

Guidance issued by the National Institute for Health and Clinical Excellence (NICE) and in national service frameworks (NSFs) is an important element of the standards system and consequently form an integral element of the standards.

National targets and indicators

The 2004 *Standards and Planning Framework* set out 20 national targets covering four national priority areas:

- Health and well-being of the population
- Long-term conditions
- Access to services
- Patient/user experience.

These targets varied according to the type of organisation and in most cases ran until 2008. There are a few (mostly relating to public health) with timescales stretching until 2010.

From 2008/09 the approach has changed with the Department of Health setting out in its *Operating Framework* 'health and service priorities for the year ahead'. The 2008/09 *Operating Framework* identifies five key priority areas:

- 'improving cleanliness and reducing healthcare associated infections (HCAIs)
- improving access through achievement of the 18-week referral to treatment pledge, and improving access (including at evenings and weekends) to GP services
- keeping adults and children well, improving their health and reducing health inequalities
- improving patient experience, staff satisfaction, and engagement
- preparing to respond in a state of emergency, such as an outbreak of pandemic flu'.

Linked to these priorities, there is a range of indicators spread across three tiers:

- National requirements – or 'must dos' – which are set nationally and cascaded to either SHA or PCT level. There are 13 indicators in this tier including the 18 week referral to delivery pledge and improving access to primary care

- National priorities where targets are agreed locally with SHAs. Here there are 17 indicators covering issues like childhood obesity and immunisation levels
- Local action – a range of 34 indicators from which PCTs 'can choose where they want to focus their effort' – for example, timeliness of social care assessments and numbers of delayed transfers.

For full details see the Department's guidance as set out in *Operational Plans 2008/09–2010/11*.

Performance Assessment

The Healthcare Commission

As well as establishing the power for the Secretary of State for Health to set standards, the *Health and Social Care (Community Health and Standards) Act 2003* established the Healthcare Commission and set out its functions. The Healthcare Commission, whose legal name is the Commission for Healthcare Audit and Inspection, is an independent body that operates at arm's length from the government and is responsible for (amongst other activities) undertaking an annual review of the provision of healthcare by each NHS body in England, including FTs (see below).

In 2006 the Department of Health announced a review of healthcare regulation and a consultation paper was published outlining the proposed merger of the Healthcare Commission, the Commission for Social Care Inspection and the Mental Health Act Commission. It is expected that these organisations will be replaced by a new body (the Care Quality Commission) in October 2008 and that the new Commission will take over the regulation of health and social care from April 2009.

The annual health check

In 2004, *Standards for Better Health* was introduced to form a key part of the new performance assessment framework undertaken for the Department of Health by the Healthcare Commission. This assessment is known as the annual health check and involves reviewing and rating the performance of each NHS trust in England.

The health check looks at four elements:

- Performance against core standards which set out the minimum level of service patients and service users have a right to expect
- Performance against existing national targets
- Performance against new national targets
- The use of resources.

As mentioned earlier, **core standards** were set out by the Department of Health in 2004 and describe the level of quality that healthcare bodies (including FTs, private and voluntary providers of care) are expected to meet in seven 'domains':

- Safety
- Clinical effectiveness

- Governance
- Patient focus
- Accessible and responsive care
- Care environment and amenities
- Public health.

Existing national targets cover both existing commitments as set out in *National Standards, Local Action: Health and Social Care Standards and Planning Framework 2005/06–2007/08* and the national requirements and priorities identified in the *Operating Framework* and associated implementation guidance.

New national targets are set out on the Healthcare Commission's website and for 2007/08 were framed in terms of 'ultimate public health outcomes'.

The use of resources element of the assessment uses the results of the auditor's local evaluation (ALE) provided by the Audit Commission (see below) or the assessment for FTs provided by Monitor.

The annual health check requires NHS bodies to complete a declaration of compliance with core standards, which ideally should be signed by all members of the board including the non-executive directors.

PCTs, NHS trusts and FTs are required to invite comments on their achievement against core standards from their local patient and public involvement forums (local involvement networks from April 2008) and overview and scrutiny committees (and the SHA for non FTs).

A comprehensive list of current standards and targets and more information on the annual health check is available on the Healthcare Commission's website.

Auditors' local evaluation

The use of resources element of the annual health check is the result of the Audit Commission's auditors' local evaluation (ALE) for NHS trusts and PCTs and Monitor's financial risk rating for FTs.

Using ALE, auditors assess how well PCTs and NHS trusts manage and use their financial resources. ALE has been developed to enable auditors to make scored judgements on five key themes:

- Financial reporting
- Financial management
- Financial standing
- Internal control
- Value for money.

In each of the five themes there are a number of key lines of enquiry (KLOEs). The KLOEs are set out below.

Theme	Key Line of Enquiry
Financial Reporting	The organisation produces annual accounts in accordance with relevant standards and timetables, supported by comprehensive working papers
	The organisation promotes external accountability
Financial Management	The organisation's medium-term financial strategy/plan, budgets and capital programme are soundly based and designed to deliver its strategic priorities
	The organisation manages performance against budgets
	The organisation manages its asset base
Financial Standing	The organisation manages its spending within the available resources
Internal Control	The organisation manages its significant business risks
	The organisation has arrangements in place to maintain a sound system of internal control
	The organisation has arrangements in place that are designed to promote and ensure probity and propriety in the conduct of its business
Value for Money	The organisation has put in place proper arrangements for securing strategic and operational objectives
	The organisation has put in place proper arrangements to ensure that services meet the needs of patients and taxpayers, and for engaging with the wider community
	The organisation has put in place proper arrangements for monitoring and reviewing performance, including arrangements to ensure data quality
	The organisation has established arrangements for managing its financial and other resources which demonstrate value for money is being managed and achieved

The Audit Commission has also published the descriptions of the levels of performance against each key line of enquiry. The levels are:

1 – Below minimum requirements – inadequate performance
2 – Only at minimum requirements – adequate performance
3 – Consistently above minimum requirements – performing well
4 – Well above minimum requirements – performing strongly

Auditors make assessments based on these descriptions for each of the thirteen KLOEs and make an overall assessment in each of the five themes set out above. The five assessments are converted into an overall score by the Audit Commission. There are a number of rules in place to determine the overall score. For example if the score for any of financial management, financial standing or value for money is one, then the overall score will be one.

For 2006/07 the scores were published in October 2007.

From 2008/09, the Audit Commission will be using a new approach to the assessment of PCTs as part of the development of 'comprehensive area assessments'.

More details on the work of auditors can be found in chapter 15. For more information about ALE and comprehensive area assessments visit the Audit Commission's website.

Financial Performance Management

NHS bodies should have their own arrangements in place to manage their financial performance. NHS boards are responsible for ensuring that there are high standards of financial stewardship through effective financial planning, financial control and ensuring value for money.

To carry this out NHS boards require an effective system of financial and performance reporting. It is for the board to decide the form and content of the financial and performance reports it requires; it should agree the information it wants to receive and this should be regularly reviewed. The board should also make use of assessments made by external bodies, including the ALE scores.

The Department of Health requires the financial performance of NHS bodies to be monitored on a regular basis. The first element of the financial performance management process is the financial plan. All NHS organisations must set an annual financial plan. In doing so, the organisation must plan to achieve its financial duties. This plan must cover all expected sources of income and expenditure and the full range of responsibilities under the management of the organisation. The plans for PCTs and NHS trusts are submitted to the organisation's host SHA. These plans form the basis of the in-year external reporting that PCTs and NHS trusts are required to undertake.

One of the key roles of SHAs is to 'performance monitor' and 'performance manage' PCTs and NHS trusts. This is carried out to ensure that there is effective financial management of NHS resources. If an individual PCT or NHS trust has significant variances from plan, they will need to agree a recovery plan with their SHA.

The SHA is viewed as being an outpost of the Department of Health and the chief executive and finance director have specific responsibilities to the national NHS chief executive and finance director. The Department of Health expects the director of finance at the SHA to alert it immediately if there are any significant variances against plans and to ensure that appropriate recovery plans are put into place.

The Department of Health established a 'turnaround programme' for those organisations experiencing financial difficulties – in 2006/07, 104 PCTs and NHS trusts were included. The

Department of Health did not run a formal national turnaround programme for the 2007/08 financial year. Instead each SHA has put in place its own monitoring and reporting procedures to identify and challenge organisations that are experiencing financial difficulties. The Department of Health identified 17 turnaround trusts with severe financial difficulties – SHAs are working with these trusts to identify a long-term solution, which is expected to be tailored to the trusts' individual circumstances.

On a regular basis, SHAs require PCTs and NHS trusts to report their financial performance against the plan submitted at the start of the financial year. This information is collated by the SHA and reported to the Department of Health. The timing of the reporting to the Department is designed to reflect the information requirements of Parliament. The Parliamentary requirements are:

- Reporting the national revenue and capital financial position
- To inform Parliamentary estimates
- To ensure effective management of the Department of Health vote.

Monitor does not performance manage FTs. However, Monitor does receive information on a regular basis from FTs with the frequency depending on each FT's risk rating. Monitor will compare the information received against the annual plan submitted at the beginning of the year and will take action if there are significant deviations from the plan (see chapter 8 for more about FTs and the role of Monitor).

References and Further Reading

NHS Act 2006: www.opsi.gov.uk/Acts/acts2006/pdf/ukpga_20060041_en.pdf

Financial Reporting Council and Accounting Standards Board: www.frc.org.uk

Financial Reporting Manual, HM Treasury: www.financial-reporting.gov.uk

NHS Manual for Accounts 2007/08 for SHAs, PCTs and NHS trusts and Guide to Resource Accounting and Budgeting: www.info.doh.gov.uk/doh/finman.nsf

Details about the NHS foundation trust financial regime (including the NHS Foundation Trust Financial Reporting Manual, Prudential Borrowing Code and Risk Ratings) are available on Monitor's website: www.monitor-nhsft.gov.uk

Budget 2008: Stability and Opportunity: building a strong, sustainable future, HM Treasury, 2008: www.hm-treasury.gov.uk./budget/budget_08/report/bud_bud08_repindex.cfm

PCT, NHS Trust and FT Accounts: Guides for Non-executives, HFMA and the Audit Commission: www.hfma.org.uk www.audit-commission.gov.uk

A Guide to Good Practice on the Annual Report/Review incorporating requirements under Reporting Standard 1 (RS 1) for NHS Organisations including the Operating and Financial Review (OFR) – available from the HFMA: www.hfma.org.uk

Better Payment Practice Code: www.payontime.co.uk

HSC 1999/146 Guidance to Health Authorities and NHS Trusts on Break-Even Duty; Provisions and Accumulated Deficits. Available via the HSC pages of the Department of Health's website: www.dh.gov.uk/PublicationsAndStatistics/LettersAndCirculars/HealthServiceCirculars/fs/en

Health and Social Care (Community Health and Standards) Act 2003: www.opsi.gov.uk/acts/acts2003/ukpga_20030043_en_1

National Standards, Local Action: Health and Social Care Standards and Planning Framework 2005/06–2007/08, Department of Health, 2004. Available via the publications, policy and guidance pages of the Department of Health's website: www.dh.gov.uk/PublicationsAndStatistics/Publications/PublicationsPolicyAndGuidance/fs/en

Operational Plans 2008/09–2010/11, Department of Health, 2008: www.dh.gov.uk:80/en/Publicationsandstatistics/Publications/PublicationsPolicyAndGuidance/DH_082542

National Institute for Health and Clinical Excellence (NICE): www.nice.org.uk

National Service Frameworks, Department of Health: www.dh.gov.uk/en/Healthcare/NationalServiceFrameworks/index.htm

Care Quality Commission (includes consultation paper), Department of Health: www.dh.gov.uk/en/Publicationsandstatistics/Legislation/Actsandbills/HealthandSocialCareBill/DH_080438

Assessment for Improvement: the Annual Health Check – available from the Healthcare Commission's website: www.healthcarecommission.org.uk/Homepage/fs/en

Auditors' Local Evaluations (ALE) – Guidance for NHS organisations, Audit Commission, 2007. Details available from the health pages of the Audit Commission's website: www.audit-commission.gov.uk

Financial Management in the NHS 2004–05, NAO and Audit Commission, 2006: www.audit-commission.gov.uk

Review of the NHS Financial Year 2006/07, Audit Commission, 2007: www.audit-commission.gov.uk

World Class Financial Management, Audit Commission, 2005: www.audit-commission.gov.uk

Achieving First-class Financial Management in the NHS, Audit Commission, 2004: www.audit-commission.gov.uk

15. Governance

Introduction

This chapter explains the concept of governance and looks at the need for and aims of the different elements that are found in the NHS, with a particular focus on aspects relating to finance and financial management.

Governance is concerned with all that an organisation does, not just its administrative and support functions – in the NHS this means that effective governance is as much of a concern to a nurse or consultant as it is to an accountant or manager. The most important message here is that achieving the highest standards of governance depends on everyone, both as individuals and as members of any corporate entity within or connected with the NHS.

What is Governance?

A clear understanding of what governance is all about and what makes an effective approach to governance in practice is critical to all organisations across the public, private and voluntary sectors – without this, stakeholders cannot be sure that their interests are being safeguarded, that their organisations are being well managed and that their objectives will be met.

The terms governance and corporate governance are now used interchangeably but it was the use of corporate governance as a phrase in the 1992 *Cadbury Committee Report* that initiated debate in this area. Corporate governance was defined in that report as 'the system by which companies are directed and controlled'. In essence it is all about how an organisation is run – how it structures itself, how it is led and how it is held to account. Organisational culture is also a key factor – the principles of good governance must permeate to all levels.

What this means in practice is that, on the structural side, governance is concerned with the systems, processes and controls that are in place to provide a sound framework for clear and accountable decision making by senior managers across an organisation. In terms of leadership, governance is to do with the responsibilities, behaviour and approach of senior managers and with the organisation's underlying culture and values. And in terms of accountability, governance is both to do with how those running the organisation account for their actions to their stakeholders and how stakeholders can hold them to account.

The Cadbury definition is still widely used and has been adapted to suit specific circumstances. Of particular interest to the NHS is the Organisation for Economic Co-operation and Development's (OECD) interpretation, which emphasises the linkage to achieving objectives and monitoring performance: '...the corporate governance structure specifies the distribution of rights and responsibilities among different participants in the corporation, such as, the board, managers, shareholders and other stakeholders, and spells out the rules and procedures for making decisions on corporate affairs. By doing this, it also provides the structure through which the company objectives are set and the means for attaining those objectives and monitoring performance'.

The key point to bear in mind is that governance is not a tick box bureaucratic process that can be carried out periodically and then forgotten about. Instead its aims and principles must underlie all that an organisation does – good governance should be a natural way of life embedded at all levels.

Governance over the Years

The NHS has been well aware of the importance of governance for many years with a wide range of separate regulatory frameworks and ethical codes in operation for the different professions working in NHS bodies. The NHS has also been swift to learn from and respond to private sector developments – partly because, as the governance structures of NHS bodies are similar to those of listed companies, the principles adopted have a more direct application.

However, the focus on governance has strengthened in recent years, largely as a result of a series of high profile scandals across all sectors of the economy that have revealed governance failings of various kinds – for example, in the business world, Enron and Worldcom came to light and in the NHS, the Bristol and Alder Hey inquiries, and the Shipman crimes have dented the public's confidence.

Although good governance is critical to the success and reputation of NHS bodies, a fragmented approach to the different aspects of governance has been common until fairly recently. The publication of the *Integrated Governance Handbook* in 2006 was designed to encourage organisations to focus on establishing a comprehensive corporate governance framework covering all elements – clinical, financial and organisational. The *Handbook* defines integrated governance as 'systems, processes and behaviours by which trusts lead, direct and control their functions in order to achieve organisational objectives, safety and quality of service and in which they relate to patients and carers, the wider community and partner organisations'. The *Handbook* is not prescriptive but seeks to set out a best practice approach that supports boards as they review their governance and assurance arrangements. It emphasises that whilst the presence of well defined structures is important, treating governance issues through functional or compartmentalised processes is unlikely to be effective. Integrated governance seeks to pull together the potentially disparate systems process and behaviours to:

- Allow the board to clearly define its own purpose and strategic direction, within the context of the overall goals established for the NHS
- Ensure fitness for purpose, by considering the assurance requirements and the information needs of the board and its supporting structures, including committees.

The *Handbook* includes a self assessment matrix that boards can use to review their position and progress and is supported by a 'board development programme'. In 2007 a further contribution to the governance debate was published by the HFMA: *Integrated Governance: Delivering Reform on two and a half days a month*. This guide focuses on the practical application of integrated governance with an emphasis on board behaviours, structures and systems.

Governance from a Financial Perspective

Governance underpins all activities and consists of a number of different elements. The HFMA's guide – *Effective Governance in Healthcare* – identifies these as:

- Culture and values (the people issues – for example, leadership style and codes of practice)
- Policies, structures and processes (for example, statutory and regulatory requirements, committee structures)
- Control frameworks (for example, risk management and assurance, audit, clinical governance, counter fraud and corruption).

As this guide's focus is finance, the remainder of this chapter looks at governance from this narrower perspective. In particular it looks at:

- Risk management and assurance
- *Standards for Better Health*
- Statement on internal control
- The board's role
- The accountable officer
- The finance director
- Codes of conduct
- Committees
- Audit – external and internal
- Organisational processes and controls
- Counter fraud and corruption.

Risk management and assurance

In 2003 the Department of Health issued guidance on board assurance frameworks to provide a structure for focusing the board's attention on the main risks to meeting its organisation's objectives. This guidance – *Building an Assurance framework: a Practical Guide* – sets out practical steps for boards to follow when setting up their own assurance framework.

A key element of an effective assurance framework is a sound approach to risk management. Although a lot of jargon has grown up around risk management it is actually something that happens all the time – it is about being aware of potential problems, thinking through what effect they could have and planning ahead to prevent the worst-case scenario. In this context it is important to recognise that no approach to managing risks can give an absolute guarantee that nothing will ever go wrong. It is also worth remembering that risk is about opportunities as well as threats. Good risk management encourages organisations to take well-managed risks that allow safe development, growth and change.

As well as underpinning an organisation's system of internal control, risk management also plays a key role in the assurance framework and in the regimes of external regulators such as auditors, the Healthcare Commission and Monitor.

Risk management is now a high profile industry in its own right but the basics are simple – every organisation needs to:

- Identify the strategic objectives and aims of the organisation
- Identify existing and future risks that may affect those aims
- Evaluate the potential impact

- Identify ways of mitigating or reducing risks (for example, in its *Orange Book: Management of Risk – Principles and Concepts*, the Treasury suggests the five Ts – treat, transfer, tolerate, terminate or take)
- Manage risks by putting in place controls and warning mechanisms
- Continuously review the effectiveness of the approach and update as necessary.

Good risk management requires leadership and commitment from the top and ownership throughout the organisation. It is not about putting risks in a register and forgetting about them, it is about identifying and managing those risks, particularly those that present the biggest challenge in management terms.

The application of an appropriate risk management model, the establishment of a process to identify risks, the setting of control standards (such as standing financial instructions) and the use of benchmarking are all risk management techniques that together provide reassurance to board members.

The benefits of an effective approach to risk management and assurance include:

- Reduction in risk exposure through more effective targeting of resources to address key risk areas
- Improvements in economy, efficiency and effectiveness resulting from a reduction in the frequency and/or severity of incidents, complaints, claims, staff absence and other loss
- Demonstrable compliance with applicable laws and regulations
- Enhanced reputation and increased public confidence in the quality of NHS services.

Standards for Better Health

A key consideration in the overall risk management and assurance framework for the NHS is the need to achieve pre-set standards designed to underpin the delivery of high quality services. In 2004, *Standards for Better Health* were introduced to form a key part of the new performance assessment framework undertaken for the Department of Health by the Healthcare Commission.

This assessment is known as 'the annual health check' and involves reviewing and rating the performance of each NHS trust in England. The health check looks at four elements:

- Performance against core standards which set out the minimum level of service patients and service users have a right to expect
- Performance against existing national targets
- Performance against new national targets
- The use of resources.

Core standards were set out by the Department of Health in 2004 and describe the level of quality that healthcare bodies (including NHS foundation trusts, private and voluntary providers of care) are expected to meet in seven 'domains':

- Safety
- Clinical effectiveness

- Governance
- Patient focus
- Accessible and responsive care
- Care environment and amenities
- Public health.

Existing national targets are those set out in *National Standards, Local Action: Health and Social Care Standards and Planning Framework 2005/06–2007/08* and the national requirements and priorities identified in the *Operating Framework* and associated implementation guidance.

New national targets are set out on the Healthcare Commission's website and for 2007/08 were framed in terms of 'ultimate public health outcomes'.

The use of resources element of the assessment uses the results of the auditor's local evaluation (ALE) provided by the Audit Commission or the assessment for FTs provided by Monitor.

The annual performance ratings are derived from these assessments – for each trust there is a two part rating:

- Quality of services based on performance against core standards, existing and new national targets (and the results of any improvement reviews)
- The use of resources.

The ratings use a four point scale – excellent; good; fair or weak.

All trusts are required to make an annual declaration of compliance with the core standards.

The Healthcare Commission reviews its approach to the health check each year – for more details see chapter 14 and the Healthcare Commission's website.

In October 2008, the Healthcare Commission, the Commission for Social Care Inspection and the Mental Health Act Commission are expected to merge and form a new body (the Care Quality Commission) that will take over the regulation of health and social care from April 2009.

Statement on internal control

The focus on risk management and assurance finds formal expression in the statement on internal control (SIC). Since 2001/02, NHS bodies have had to submit a SIC as part of their annual financial statements. The SIC requires the following disclosures:

- The scope of the accountable officer's responsibility
- The purpose of the system of internal control
- The organisation's capacity to handle risk
- A description of the risk and control framework
- Confirmation that a review of effectiveness has been undertaken
- Any significant internal control issues.

The SIC must be signed off by the chief executive, as the accountable officer, on behalf of the board. The head of internal audit provides an annual opinion to the accountable officer and the audit committee on the adequacy and effectiveness of the risk management, control and governance processes to support the SIC. The SIC is an extremely important statement that covers the whole of an organisation. Chief executives and boards will be held to account if they sign a statement that subsequent events show they did not understand or take seriously.

The board's role

Every NHS organisation (including FTs) must have a board comprising a non-executive chair, non-executive directors and executive directors. Boards take corporate responsibility for the strategies and actions of their organisations and are accountable to the public, Secretary of State (or Monitor in FTs) and Parliament.

A board's prime duty is to 'add value to the organisation, enabling it to deliver healthcare and health improvement within the law and without causing harm. It does this by providing a framework within which the organisation can thrive and grow'. As the board is the pre-eminent governing body there is a range of responsibilities and decisions that it cannot delegate. These are sometimes referred to as being 'reserved' to the board and include:

- Financial stewardship responsibilities, including adopting the annual report and accounts
- Determining the organisation's strategy and policies and setting its strategic direction
- Appointing senior executives
- Overseeing the delivery of services
- Standards of governance and behaviour.

The board is free to agree other issues that only it will deal with and must also decide which responsibilities it will delegate.

The accountable officer

The Department of Health has formally given chief executives the status of accountable officers for their organisations and they are sent a memorandum setting out their responsibilities. The accountable officer must sign a statement confirming that he or she has properly discharged the responsibilities set out in this memorandum. These are that chief executives must ensure that their organisations:

- Operate effectively, economically and with probity
- Make good use of their resources
- Keep proper accounts.

The chief executive is accountable to Parliament via the Department of Health accounting officer and the Secretary of State for Health.

In FTs the line of accountability is different as the chief executive is the accounting officer responsible to Parliament via Monitor. Monitor has issued its own accounting officer memorandum which emphasises that 'accounting officers are responsible to Parliament for the resources under their control.'

The finance director

Finance directors of health bodies are automatically executive directors with a seat on the board. Their three key responsibilities as identified in the Finance Staff Development Board's guide to *The Role of the Finance Director in a Patient-led NHS – a Guide for NHS Boards* are:

- To provide financial governance and assurance
- To provide business and commercial advice to the board
- Corporate responsibilities as an executive director of the board.

In practice this means that finance directors have a role to play in:

- Corporate management – finance directors take part in: setting the strategic direction of the organisation; drawing up its plans; presenting information to the board to show how their plans are being actioned; helping to shape new initiatives by finding cost-effective solutions; and managing the finances in support of the corporate objectives
- Financial management – finance directors are responsible to the chief executive and board for formulating, monitoring and reviewing the financial strategy, as an integral part of the business plan
- Public accountability and stewardship – finance directors have a special responsibility for preparing the annual financial statements and returns; for ensuring that the highest standards of conduct are maintained within their organisations and that there is probity in the use of public money
- Finance directorate management – finance directors need to lead the way in adopting the best possible standards of management in order to provide a finance function that is highly motivated, well trained, and dedicated to quality and excellent service.

Codes of conduct

Code of Conduct: Code of Accountability in the NHS

These codes were originally issued in 1994 and revised in 2004. They define the public service values that must underpin the work of NHS boards, set out accountability regimes and describe the basis on which NHS organisations should fulfil their statutory duties.

Code of Practice on Openness in the NHS

This 2003 code sets out the basic principles underlying public access to information about the NHS. It defines openness in NHS management as a natural part of its accountability to the local population and sets out the minimum documents and matters that are expected to be disclosed publicly and those that must not, such as confidential patient information.

Code of Conduct for NHS Managers

The *Code of Conduct for NHS Managers* was issued in October 2002 following a recommendation in the Kennedy Report (the *Inquiry into the Management of Care of Children*

Receiving Complex Heart Surgery at the Bristol Royal Infirmary). It sets out core standards of conduct expected of NHS managers to guide them and employing health bodies in the work they do and the decisions and choices they have to make. It also reassures the public that these important decisions are being taken against a background of professional standards and accountability.

Code of Business Conduct (Standards of Business Conduct for NHS Staff)

This code was developed and issued in 1993 and defines the relationships between NHS officers and third parties, including:

- Declaration of interests – employees must declare if they have an interest/relationship in contracts or other organisations that could affect business
- Awarding contracts – strict rules are laid down about how contracts should be awarded to prevent bias
- Rules on the acceptability of commercial sponsorship.

Committees

To help the board discharge its duties effectively, a number of committees exist in NHS bodies. It is up to each organisation to decide what committee structure best suits its needs. However, within the finance area, there are two mandatory committees:

Remuneration and terms of service committee

A key function of management is to appoint, appraise and reward its employees fairly and equitably. NHS boards carry out this function by establishing a terms of service and remuneration committee. This is a mandatory committee that reports to the board. The committee must comprise the organisation's chair and at least two other non-executive directors.

Audit committee

Audit committees provide an independent and objective review of the organisation's overall internal control system including financial systems, its financial information and compliance with legislation. The audit committee is a sub-group of the board, comprising non-executives and excluding the chair of the NHS body. A revised *NHS Audit Committee Handbook* was published in 2005 which includes specimen terms of reference and a self assessment checklist.

PCT professional executive committee

PCTs must also have a professional executive committee (PEC) – a committee of the board which is designed to bring together clinical and managerial perspectives.

Charitable funds committee

NHS organisations with charitable funds will usually have a dedicated charitable funds committee that reviews the use of charitable funds and investment performance. Such charitable funds are legally separate from NHS monies, but the trustees of the charity are usually the directors – the charitable funds committee is therefore a committee of board directors, but not formally a sub-committee of the organisation (see chapter 17 for more on charitable funds).

External audit

The public is entitled to expect that money raised by local or national taxation is properly accounted for. To provide an assurance that this is the case, there is a need, among other things, for a wide-ranging and independent external audit covering both the audit of the financial statements and work in relation to the organisation's arrangements for securing value for money from its use of resources.

The Audit Commission is responsible for ensuring that public money is spent economically, efficiently and effectively to achieve high quality local and national services for the public except in relation to FTs which select and appoint their own external auditors who are regulated by Monitor in line with its own Audit Code. In relation to the NHS it is the Audit Commission that is responsible for the audit of SHAs, PCTs and NHS trusts.

The Audit Commission's role includes the appointment of external auditors (its own staff or accountancy firms) to SHAs, PCTs and NHS trusts. These appointed auditors audit each body's annual financial statements and must follow the Audit Commission's Code of Audit Practice which requires them to review and report on:

- The annual accounts, annual report and SIC
- Arrangements for securing economy, efficiency and effectiveness in the use of resources.

They must also undertake an annual auditors' local evaluation (ALE) at PCTs and NHS trusts, the judgements from which form the use of resources assessment within the Healthcare Commission's annual health check. ALE assessments focus on financial reporting, financial management, financial standing, internal control and value for money. A new approach to the assessment of PCTs will be taken by the Audit Commission from 2008/09 as part of the development of 'comprehensive area assessments'.

The external auditor is also required to issue an annual audit letter to board members at the conclusion of each year's audit. The letter acts as a brief for the board and brings together the major issues arising from the audit which the auditor wishes to raise.

The Audit Commission Act 1998 provides auditors with the power to report where they have specific concerns arising from their audits:

- Section 8 requires auditors to consider whether, in the public interest, they should report on any matter coming to their notice
- Section 19 requires the auditor to refer matters to the Secretary of State for Health if he or she has reason to believe that an NHS organisation has made a decision that involves, or may involve, unlawful expenditure.

Internal audit

All NHS bodies must have an internal audit service to provide an independent and objective opinion to the accountable officer, board and audit committee on the extent to which risk management, control and governance arrangements support the aims of the organisation. Internal audit also provides an independent and objective consultancy service specifically to help line management improve the organisation's risk management, control and governance.

In practice this means that the role of internal audit includes:

- Reviewing the adequacy and effectiveness of internal control
- Assisting management in identifying problem or risky areas
- Helping safeguard assets and resources
- Highlighting areas of concern to the audit committee/board
- Carrying out reviews/investigations
- Liaising with external auditors/other regulators
- Providing assurance to management/audit committee/board that controls are operating effectively.

Organisational processes and controls

Board reports

Boards must ensure that they receive regular financial and other information in a succinct and efficient form so they can make informed decisions on spending. It is for the board to decide the form and content of the reports – however, they must ensure that they have what they need to fulfil their responsibilities.

In particular, they need 'intelligent information' as reflected in *The Intelligent Board*, produced by the independent research and analysis body, Dr Foster, in conjunction with the Appointments Commission. This guidance proposes a number of principles for board reporting, as well as providing a framework for strategic issues and operational performance – it states that 'the key tests of the success of any information resource for the board will be the extent to which it:

- prompts relevant and constructive challenge
- supports informed decision-making
- is effective in providing early warning of potential financial or other problems
- develops all directors' understanding of the organisation and its performance.'

Annual accounts

All NHS bodies have a statutory duty to produce annual accounts. For NHS trusts, PCTs and SHAs the relevant legislation is section 232 and paragraph 3(1) of schedule 15 of the *NHS Act 2006* and for FTs section 30 and paragraph 25(1) of schedule 7 of the *NHS Act 2006*. The form and content of the accounts is prescribed by the Secretary of State for Health – or Monitor for FTs – and is largely consistent with UK generally accepted accounting practice (UK GAAP). The production of the statutory annual accounts is the principal means by which NHS bodies discharge their accountability to taxpayers and users of services for their stewardship of public money.

Standing orders (SOs)

Standing orders (SOs) provide a comprehensive framework for carrying out activities within NHS bodies and are therefore a critical element in the governance framework. For SHAs, PCTs and NHS trusts, SOs are the link to an organisation's statutory powers and translate these powers into a series of practical rules designed to protect the interests of both the organisation and its staff. In many ways SOs are similar to the memorandum and articles of association of a company. In FTs SOs form part of their constitution.

The majority of provisions set out within SOs relate to the business of the board and structure of its committees. This includes procedural issues such as:

- The composition of the board and committees
- How meetings are run
- Form, content and frequency of reports submitted to the board
- What constitutes a quorum
- Record of attendance
- Voting procedures.

Other areas covered in SOs include:

- Appointment of committees and sub–committees
- Scheme of delegation
- Decisions reserved to the board
- Standards of business conduct
- Declarations of interest
- Register of interests and hospitality
- Duties and obligations of board members.

One area covered by SOs that often receives particular attention relates to standards of business conduct, declarations of interest and hospitality. The fact that this is deliberately included in SOs rather than delegated to standing financial instructions (SFIs) indicates to managers and staff how important it is to follow the procedures set down and the importance attributed to probity.

Reserved decisions and schemes of delegation

An NHS body's SOs must include a schedule of decisions reserved to the board and a scheme of delegation to other committees or officers. This is literally a detailed listing of what the board alone can decide on and who the board empowers to take actions or make decisions on its behalf. Examples of decisions reserved to the board include:

- Approving of SOs
- Establishing terms of reference and reporting arrangements for all committees
- Agreeing the schedule of reserved decisions and scheme of delegation

- Approving standing financial instructions
- Appointing the board's vice chair
- Defining the organisation's strategic aims
- Approving business cases for capital investment
- Approving budgets
- Receiving and approving the annual report and annual accounts.

Standing financial instructions (SFIs)

The *Code of Accountability* requires the boards of SHAs, PCTs and NHS trusts to draw up standing financial instructions (SFIs), which have the same statutory backing as SOs. SFIs cover financial aspects in more detail and set out detailed procedures and responsibilities. SFIs are designed to ensure that NHS organisations account fully and openly for all that they do.

Model SFIs for SHAs, PCTs and NHS trusts are available on the Department of Health's website. Many organisations inform their staff of the agreed SOs and SFIs using their intranet sites, supplemented by summarised handbooks and presentations on key points. It is good practice to ensure that new employees are made aware of these documents as part of the induction process.

FTs do not have to have SFIs – however, they do have written financial procedures that fulfil the same function.

Counter fraud and corruption

The emphasis on dealing with fraud and corruption in the NHS has increased significantly over the last few years. As a result, NHS bodies are now required to have a local counter fraud specialist (LCFS) and to adhere to national guidelines set by the NHS Counter Fraud and Security Management Service (CFSMS). Although FTs are not bound by these directions they have LCFSs through the terms of their healthcare contracts.

The role of the LCFS is to take forward work to counter fraud and corruption in the health body for which they are the nominated officer. Activity should take place in seven generic areas:

- Developing an anti fraud culture
- Deterrence
- Prevention
- Detection
- Investigation
- Sanction
- Redress.

Counter fraud work should take place within a clear ethical framework. This describes principles of professionalism, propriety, fairness, objectivity, vision, and expertise. All LCFSs have to undergo training on this ethical framework if they are to receive their professional accreditation as 'accredited counter fraud specialists'.

Other policies/procedures

For NHS bodies to run smoothly, many more policies and procedures (both financial and non-financial) are required; and these are usually pulled together in organisational policy and procedure manuals. These cover a wide variety of areas from banking procedures, use of credit cards to health and safety and equal opportunities policies.

References and Further Reading

The Financial Aspects of Corporate Governance (the Cadbury Committee Report), 1992: www.ecgi.org/codes/code.php?code_id=132

OECD: www.oecd.org

Integrated Governance Handbook, Department of Health, 2006: www.dh.gov.uk/en/Policyandguidance/Organisationpolicy/Governance/index.htm

Integrated Governance: delivering reform on two and a half days a month, HFMA, 2007: www.hfma.org.uk

Effective Governance in Healthcare: an Introductory Guide, HFMA, 2006: www.hfma.org.uk

Assurance: The Board Agenda, 2002. Available from the governance pages of the Department of Health's website: www.dh.gov.uk/en/Policyandguidance/Organisationpolicy/Governance/index.htm

Building an Assurance Framework: A Practical Guide, 2003. Available from the governance pages of the Department of Health's website: www.dh.gov.uk/en/Policyandguidance/Organisationpolicy/Governance/index.htm

The Orange Book: Management of Risk – Principles and Concepts, HM Treasury, 2004: www.hm-treasury.gov.uk/media/3/5/FE66035B-BCDC-D4B3-11057A7707D2521F.pdf

Better Standards for Health: guidance is available via the Healthcare Commission's website: www.healthcarecommission.org.uk

National Standards, Local Action: Health and Social Care Standards and Planning Framework 2005/06–2007/08, Department of Health, 2004. Available via the publications, policy and guidance pages of the Department of Health's website: www.dh.gov.uk/PublicationsAndStatistics/Publications/PublicationsPolicyAndGuidance/fs/en

The NHS in England: the Operating Framework for 2008/09, Department of health, 2007: www.dh.gov.uk/en/Publicationsandstatistics/Publications/PublicationsPolicyAndGuidance/DH_081094

Auditors' Local Evaluations (ALE) – Guidance for NHS organisations, Audit Commission, 2007. Details available from the health pages of the Audit Commission's website: www.audit-commission.gov.uk

Statement on Internal Control, Department of Health, 2007:
www.dh.gov.uk/en/Publicationsandstatistics/Lettersandcirculars/Dearcolleagueletters/DH_073559

The Role of the Finance Director in a Patient Led NHS, Finance Staff Development Network:
www.fsdnetwork.com/documents/roleofdf.pdf

The Code of Conduct: Code of Accountability in the NHS, Department of Health:
www.dh.gov.uk/en/Publicationsandstatistics/Publications/PublicationsPolicyAndGuidance/
DH_4093864

Code of Practice on Openness in the NHS, 2003: www.dh.gov.uk/en/Publicationsandstatistics/
Publications/PublicationsPolicyAndGuidance/DH_4050490

Code of Conduct for NHS Managers: www.dh.gov.uk/en/Publicationsandstatistics/Publications/
PublicationsPolicyAndGuidance/DH_4005410

Bristol Royal Infirmary Inquiry (The Kennedy Report): www.bristol-inquiry.org.uk/

Standards of Business Conduct for NHS Staff, Department of Health, 1993: www.dh.gov.uk/en/
Publicationsandstatistics/Lettersandcirculars/Healthserviceguidelines/DH_4017845

The NHS Audit Committee Handbook, Department of Health and HFMA, (2005), available to
order from the HFMA and to download from the governance pages of the Department of
Health's website:
www.dh.gov.uk/en/Policyandguidance/Organisationpolicy/Governance/index.htm

Audit Commission (including details of ALE, the Code of Audit Practice and Comprehensive
Area Assessments): www.audit-commission.gov.uk

Monitor (including the Governance and Audit Codes for NHS Foundation Trusts):
www.monitor-nhsft.gov.uk

Internal Audit Standards for the National Health Service, 2002: Available from the governance
pages of the Department of Health's website:
www.dh.gov.uk/en/Policyandguidance/Organisationpolicy/Governance/index.htm

The Intelligent Board, Doctor Foster, 2006: www.drfoster.co.uk/

NHS Act 2006: www.opsi.gov.uk/acts/acts2006/ukpga_20060041_en_1

Model Standing Orders, Reservation and Delegation of Powers for SHAs, PCTs and NHS Trusts,
Department of Health, 2006. Available from the governance pages of the Department of
Health's website:
www.dh.gov.uk/en/Policyandguidance/Organisationpolicy/Governance/index.htm

Counter Fraud and Security Management Service: www.cfsms.nhs.uk

16. Capital Investment

Introduction

This chapter looks at capital investment – what it is and how it is managed across the NHS. It concentrates on capital investment in (non foundation) NHS trusts and public capital – those assets that have been purchased with public funds. An alternative to using public funds is the use of public private partnerships – this is covered in chapter 10. Reference is also made to capital investment in PCTs and other sources of funding. Accounting treatment is covered and the chapter concludes with a brief look at the alternatives to asset ownership.

The capital regime followed by foundation trusts (FTs) is covered in chapter 8.

Capital Investment – Definition

Expenditure may be classified as either revenue or capital. Where expenditure is significant and is incurred to acquire an asset intended for use on a continued basis then it is classified as capital and is described as capital investment. Materiality and consistency of classification across the NHS is important – this is achieved through the use of the *NHS Capital Accounting Manual* published by the Department of Health which defines capital assets as:

- An individual asset with a cost of £5,000 or more
- Generally having a life greater than one year
- A system or group of functionally interdependent assets of £5,000 or more (for example, IT hardware attached to a network).

The £5,000 includes VAT where this is not recoverable, installation costs and external fees.

The main categories of capital assets are:

- Land
- Buildings
- Assets in the course of construction
- Equipment (including vehicles)
- Computing and IT equipment.

Capital expenditure is charged to the balance sheet since the assets purchased are used over a number of years. Operational (day-to-day or revenue) expenditure is charged to the revenue account – i.e. to the income and expenditure account in NHS trusts and the operating cost statement in PCTs and SHAs.

Capital Funding Process

Capital Investment is funded from one of three sources:

- Public capital
- Public/private partnerships (including the private finance initiative (PFI), joint ventures and LIFT – see chapter 10)
- Charitable funds where an asset is gifted to an NHS organisation.

The Treasury caps public capital by setting an annual spending limit. Prior to 2007/08 the majority of public capital was allocated on a formulaic basis to trusts and PCTs as 'operational capital' (for buildings and equipment replacement and renewal) and to SHAs as 'strategic capital' (for bigger, more strategic schemes). These allocations took the form of public dividend capital (or PDC) which attracted dividend payments. An element of capital funding is managed centrally to target particular investment objectives.

Since 2007/08 the approach to allocating capital to NHS trusts has changed so as to increase the financial rigour of investment decisions and assist trusts in making the transition to FT status. Through the introduction of an approach similar to that followed by FTs, access to capital and working capital[11] is more closely tied to financial performance and affordability with a 'prudential borrowing limit' or PBL set for each trust each year – the PBL is the maximum amount that a trust can borrow to fund additional capital investment.

For allocation purposes, public capital is divided into a number of different elements which are shown in the table that follows, along with an indication of the changes introduced from 2007/08.

Source of Capital Funding		Description	Trusts	PCTs
Department of Health allocation	Investment by the Department	Where it is commercially and operationally appropriate the Department of Health invests capital for the overall benefit of NHS organisations This is accounted for by the Department – for example, the IT structure used across the NHS. Costs are borne centrally.		
	Operational capital	Allocated on an unconditional formulaic basis and used mainly for buildings and equipment replacement and renewal. There is no upfront charge for the funds. However, trusts are required to make a return of 3.5% on the assets as well as including a charge for depreciation in their revenue accounts.	Approach no longer used.	Approach continues to be used.

---

[11] Working capital is the money and assets that an organisation can call upon to finance its day-to-day operations (it is the difference between current assets and liabilities and is reported in the balance sheet as net current assets (liabilities)). If working capital dips too low, organisations risk running out of cash and may need a working capital loan to smooth out the troughs.

	Strategic capital	Allocated on an unconditional formulaic basis to SHAs so that they can target larger investments within their geographic area. Trusts are required to make a 3.5% return on any assets funded in this way as well as charging for depreciation.	Approach no longer used.	Funding of PCT business cases approved by SHAs.
	Targeted investment objectives	Achievement of some key targets is aided through targeted capital investment. Trusts are required to make a 3.5% return on any assets funded in this way plus depreciation.	Used to complete announced programmes of investment. Increasingly replaced by PBL.	Approach continues to be used.
Internally generated	Based on forecast depreciation	Trusts have to break-even having included a charge for asset depreciation in their revenue expenditure. Depreciation is a notional charge (i.e. it involves no cash payment) and the cash 'generated' can be used for capital investment.	Unconditionally available to invest in building maintenance, replacement equipment and other developments (but subject to capital controls – see later in this chapter and chapter 7).	PCTs account for depreciation and retain the cash 'generated' for capital investment.
	Surplus	Trusts can make surpluses.	Any surplus generated by trusts can be used for capital investment.	
Borrowing (from Department of Health)	Based on prudential borrowing limit – the maximum level of borrowings from all sources that a trust may have.	Enables trusts to invest in locally determined priorities.	Subject to affordability and approval of business case – the size of the scheme dictates the approval mechanism with SHAs able to approve up to £35m (see chapter 10).	Approach not used.

For PCTs the expectation is that from 2008/09 they will bid each year for the capital they require through their SHAs to the Department of Health based on robust and affordable (i.e. sustainable from a revenue consequences perspective) capital investment plans.

For NHS trusts the new approach gives more freedom to plan on the basis of affordability as the PBL is set on the assumption that the trust could afford the costs of borrowing to this level both in terms of the interest payments and the principal repayment. Access to these interest bearing loans is controlled firstly through PBL and then by the SHA business case approval process. The loan interest is in accordance with the National Loans Fund rate – currently (March 2008) about 4.7%. The period of loans will generally be the same as the life of the assets to which they relate. The loan is repaid in equal instalments in September and March each year and interest (calculated on the outstanding balance) is paid twice a year. Trusts must generate surpluses to create the cash to repay the principal while the interest on the loans is a revenue charge.

The PBL for each trust is published annually by the Department but is not an annual limit – instead it indicates the maximum cumulative borrowing that a trust may have to fund additional capital investment. Using a system that mirrors arrangements for FTs, this maximum borrowing is calculated using information from the previous year's financial accounts and financial plan and applying a series of financial ratios to calculate an overall financial risk rating for each trust. This risk rating corresponds to a maximum borrowing limit expressed as a percentage of the trust's net assets (also known as the trust's 'gearing'). PBLs are reviewed at least annually when the latest accounts data becomes available.

At the time of writing (March 2008), PBLs for 2008/09 had not been announced. However, it is understood that the Department of Health is looking at adopting the new risk rating weightings used for foundation trusts from April 2007 to recalculate PBLs for 2008/09.

The four criteria (comprising five ratios – there are two ratios for criterion C) used to establish the risk rating for 2007/08 are set out below:

Achievement of plan (criterion A)

Actual earnings before interest, tax, dividend and amortisation (actual EBITDA)/planned EBITDA – expressed as a %.

Score	<25%	>25%, <60%	>60%, <80%	>80%, <100%	>100%
Rating	1	2	3	4	5

Underlying performance (criterion B)

Actual EBITDA/income – expressed as a %.

Score	<0%	>0%, <4%	>4%, <8%	>8%, <9.99%	>9.99%
Rating	1	2	3	4	5

Financial efficiency (criterion C)

(EBITDA/average net relevant assets) – expressed as a %. This indicator is also known as the 'return on capital employed'.

Score	<1.5%	>1.5%, <2.5%	>2.5%, <3.0%	>3.0%, <3.5%	>3.5%
Rating	1	2	3	4	5

Income and expenditure (I&E) surplus/income – expressed as a %. This indicator is also referred to as the 'I&E surplus margin ratio'.

Score	<−3%	>−3%, <0%	>0%, <1%	>1%, <1.99%	>1.99%
Rating	1	2	3	4	5

The overall financial efficiency rating is calculated by adding together both criterion C indicators and dividing by two.

Liquidity (criterion D)

(Cash at bank plus debtors <1 year less creditors <1 year) plus (12/365 × total operating expenses/total operating expenses) × 365.

Score	<10	>10, <15	>15, <25	>25, <34.99	>34.99
Rating	1	2	3	4	5

The overall rating that results from taking the A to D ratios and dividing the total by four determines the maximum loan as a percentage of net assets – as shown below:

Risk Rating	1 (high)	2	3	4	5 (low)
Maximum gearing (%)	0	10	15	25	40

As explained earlier, the Treasury caps spending on public capital by setting an annual spending limit for health – this is referred to as the capital departmental expenditure limit (DEL). In order to contain overall expenditure within this limit both PCTs and NHS trusts are set annual capital resource limits (CRL) by the Department of Health which they must stay within.

For trusts there is also a control mechanism called the external financing limit (EFL) – this limits the amount a trust can spend on capital in a year over and above what it can generate from its own operations.

For further details on CRLs and EFLs refer to chapter 14.

The Cost of Capital and Capital Charges

What is the cost of capital?

Any capital investment, whether in the public or private sector, has an 'opportunity cost' (in other words, the money could have been used for alternative purposes or not raised as taxes). The NHS therefore has a system of capital charges to recognise and account for its cost of capital. Capital charges comprise two key elements – a **return** (similar to debt interest) and **deprecation**. Both elements are explained in greater detail below. They are levied on all capital assets owned by the NHS, except for assets acquired by donation or with a net book value of zero. Capital charges are included in trust revenue costs and budgets, and recovered through the prices charged to commissioner PCTs and other bodies.

Capital charges are designed to:

- Ensure that there is a consistent awareness of the costs of capital in the NHS
- Provide incentives to use capital efficiently and dispose of surplus assets
- Ensure the costs of capital are fully reflected in the costing of healthcare services, so that fair comparisons are possible, both within the NHS and between the NHS and the private sector
- Promote effective planning for the replacement of capital assets.

The system of capital charges ensures that the cost of capital is reflected in the costs of healthcare services and in this way aids decision-making when alternative service provision options are discussed. It also provides an incentive to improve asset utilisation – savings in capital charges arising from better utilisation are 'real' savings available for deployment as service developments or to meet other cost pressures.

Rate of return

The rate of return is calculated on 'net relevant assets' – the average of the value of assets held at the beginning and end of the year. Under the old capital system, a trust would buy assets using capital allocations from the Department of Health. The asset purchased would attract a rate of return charge (paid through the PDC dividend) of 3.5%. Under the new system of prudential borrowing, the trust faces direct capital charges through the interest payments it is required to make. It does not pay an additional 3.5% on these assets. In practice the loan liability reduces the trust's overall net assets on which the capital charges are calculated.

Depreciation

Depreciation is calculated annually to spread the cost of the assets over their expected economic life. Annual depreciation is charged to the income and expenditure account. It also forms part of the costs recovered in service agreements or contracts.

Capital Charges – Example

Capital charges have two elements:

- The rate of return on average relevant net assets
- The depreciation (or wearing out) of those assets.

Consider a simplified example of a trust with average relevant net assets (the average of the assets held at the beginning of the year and at the end of the year) of £158m.

The rate of return or cost of capital = 3.5% of £158m = £5.5m.

Depreciation will be calculated on the mix of fixed assets the trust holds, all of which are depreciated at different rates. Consider that the depreciation in this trust was estimated to be £6m.

Total NHS capital charges (combining rate of return and depreciation) is estimated at £11.5m.

Impact of changes to the rate of return

When capital charges were first introduced to the NHS in 1991, the rate of return was set at 6%. In 2003 this was changed to 3.5%. Under the capital funding regime for FTs (and NHS trusts from 2007/08), the cost of capital is approximately 4.7%. Changes in the cost of capital have several effects including:

- The relative attractiveness of public and private options will change when assessing NHS investments
- The attractiveness of leasing options will alter – generally, the higher the cost of public capital the more attractive leasing options are.

Estimating capital charges

Trusts and PCTs are required to estimate and submit their capital charges for the following financial year. These estimates are aggregated nationally and used to:

- Calculate the total funding required to meet capital charges – generally PCT baselines are adjusted to reflect changes arising from price movements (but not volume changes)
- Determine trust dividend payments paid in cash by trusts to the Department of Health generally in two equal amounts in September and March the next year – these payments are based on the trust's rate of return element
- Inform the Department of the capital base and cost of capital in the NHS.

Assets operated under PFI agreements are not NHS assets and are therefore 'off balance sheet' and not subject to capital charges. The costs are recovered by the private partner as part of the revenue charge for the use of facilities. The balance sheet treatment of PFI funded assets is expected to change when international financial reporting standards (IFRS) are used for accounting purposes from 2009/10.

The preparation of accurate capital charges estimates is challenging but essential. As the estimates are prepared prior to the financial year to which they relate, trusts must think through the acquisitions, disposals and depreciation that they expect to take place for the remainder of the current year and the following year. In the annual accounts, actual depreciation is recorded. Differences from the estimate can arise (for example, due to changes in the timing of the completion of projects) and result in unplanned surpluses or deficits.

Accounting for Capital Investment

NHS capital accounting follows closely the relevant accounting standards. Of particular importance in this context are the financial reporting standards – FRS 5 *Reporting of Substance of Transactions*, FRS 11 *Impairment of Fixed Assets and Goodwill* and FRS 15 *Tangible Fixed Assets*. The *NHS Capital Accounting Manual* provides detailed guidance on all aspects of NHS capital accounting. From 2009/10 NHS accounts will also comply with IFRS – of relevance here is *IAS 16 Property, Plant and Equipment*, and *IAS 17 Leases*. See chapter 14 for more about financial reporting.

Asset Registers

Every NHS body maintains an asset register of all its capital assets. This is used in the preparation of annual accounts and maintains and improves management control, information and accountability. The asset register is usually kept using the same computer software that is used to calculate depreciation.

The main information recorded in an asset register includes:

- Asset identification, description and location
- Date and method of acquisition and initial capital outlay
- Replacement costs, cumulative depreciation charges and estimated life
- Revaluation and indexation adjustments.

Valuation

On acquisition, capital assets are recorded in the asset register at their purchase cost. To comply with FRS 15, valuations are revised annually using national indices provided by the Department of Health. The indices are applied to tangible assets (i.e. land, buildings etc) and assets under construction so that they reflect their current replacement value. Every five years, land and buildings are re-valued by the District Valuer (DV) to ensure that local and regional variations in land values and building costs are reflected in the asset registers. DV valuation is also required where, for example, trusts merge or there is a major change in use. Assets transferred between NHS bodies are recorded at the same book value in the receiving trust, as they were valued in the former trust.

Most intangible assets (i.e. software licences, trademarks etc) are recorded at cost less 'amortisation' (the process of charging the cost of an intangible asset over its useful life – equivalent to depreciation). However, where a readily ascertainable market value is available then this should be used.

Asset lives and depreciation charges

Depreciation is the mechanism used to reflect the fact that assets wear out over time or are 'consumed' over their useful economic life. Depreciation is an accounting charge and involves no cash payment.

The Department of Health has produced a list of standard lives for various classes of asset and these are normally adopted by trusts unless individual asset lives can be justified or the asset does not fit into one of the standard categories. Examples of these standard asset lives are:

- Short life engineering equipment, medical equipment, office and IT equipment – five years
- Medium life medical and engineering equipment and furniture – ten years
- Long life medical and engineering equipment – fifteen years
- Vehicles and soft furnishings – seven years
- Mainframe-type IT installations – eight years.

FRS 15: Tangible Fixed Assets specifies that the expected life of equipment should be reviewed annually. If there is a 'significant' difference between the remaining standard and actual asset life, the accounting entries relating to asset value, life, accumulated depreciation and reserves must reflect the current asset life.

Depreciation in the NHS is charged on a straight-line basis over the life of the assets. The *NHS Capital Accounting Manual* specifies the following arrangements:

- Land is considered to have an infinite life and is not depreciated
- Buildings, installations and fittings are depreciated over their assessed lives, with both the value and the life expectancy determined periodically by the DV
- Assets in the course of construction are not depreciated until they are in operational use
- Equipment is depreciated over its useful economic life
- Leased assets classified as capital are depreciated over the shorter of the lease term remaining or the asset's remaining economic life.

It is important to note that while the straight line basis of depreciation usually means by equal instalments, because depreciation is calculated on asset values adjusted by indices, the depreciation charged to the income and expenditure account each year will not be the same. The difference between this and the calculation without the indices is an annual adjustment between the income and expenditure reserve and the revaluation reserve.

Indexation

The table below shows the recent indices used for asset valuation and gives an idea of the impact of inflation in building values.

	Land 2004/05 = 100	Buildings/assets under construction 1985/86 = 100	Equipment (other than IT equipment which has a zero indexation rate) 1992/93 = 100
2005/06	105	222	145
2006/07	111	240	149
2007/08	117	260	153

A simplified example showing how these indices are used is given below:

Indexation – an Example

Assume:

- A building with a book value of £2m and a life of 20 years
- Straight line depreciation is £0.1m per annum.

In 2007/08 indexation is $(260 - 240)/240\% = 8.333\%$

Revised book value is £2.167m

Depreciation for the year is 2.167m/20 = £0.108m.

Accounting entries

Dr: Building asset: £0.167m
Cr: Revaluation reserve: £0.167m

Dr: Depreciation income and expenditure account: £0.108m
Cr: Asset book value £0.108m

Dr: Revaluation reserve £0.008m (the difference between the straight line depreciation calculated on the original value and the current value)
Cr: Income and expenditure reserve £0.008m

Consider some of the complications that may occur and why the example is a simplification:

- When a building is first commissioned its value may be assessed as less than cost
- A building consists of different elements – for example, the outside walls, roof and the doors and walls inside the building. These may all have different life expectancies and therefore depreciation and indexation calculations (the DV uses 26 different elements in its valuation work)
- An asset is unlikely to become operational conveniently on the first day of a financial year. Usual practice is to index an asset the year after it becomes operational and commence depreciation the quarter after it becomes operational

- The DV may revise the valuation of the building. Usually this will be an adjustment between the asset's book value and the revaluation reserve – however, there may be circumstances where the change in value affects income and expenditure
- A decision may be taken that a building is surplus. This may lead to an 'impairment' (i.e. a loss in the asset's value) or if the decision is that the building will be surplus in a number of years time give rise to what is termed 'accelerated depreciation'. That is the annual depreciation is adjusted to reduce the value of the building to that expected when it is no longer needed
- When a building becomes surplus land may also be surplus and this is included when adjusting the accounts.

Indexation adjustments are recorded in the asset register thus providing a clear link between each asset and the revaluation reserve.

As each asset is different the appropriate accounting treatment will also vary. It is important that the *Capital Accounting Manual* and the full text of relevant accounting standards are referred to. The table below sets out some of the most common accounting transactions:

Dividend payment

The rate of return capital charges calculation becomes the trust's dividend payment:

Dr: Income and expenditure account – dividend payment
Cr: Cash

PBL loan

Dr: Cash
Cr: Creditors (Department of Health – creditors long term or payable within a year as appropriate)

As the loan is repaid these entries are reversed.

PBL loan – interest

Dr: Income and expenditure account – interest charges
Cr: Cash

Depreciation

Dr: Income and expenditure account – depreciation
Cr: Asset value.

Capital Investment – the Procurement Process

Business cases

NHS trusts and PCTs have rolling programmes of capital investment to ensure that their asset bases are fit for purpose. The table earlier in this chapter highlighted how public capital is made available for this. When additional capital investment is needed to further modernise or develop a new service, the first stage is usually to develop a business case.

In the context of capital investment, a business case is a written statement of the need for investment in capital. It sets out the process of selection of the asset (as there are likely to be several options or solutions), and the costs of ownership of the asset.

When preparing business cases it is important to include:

- The strategic 'fit' of the proposed investment within the local health economy, including a clear and concise statement of need
- Effective project management arrangements, clear lines of communication and details of key individuals who will be personally accountable
- An indication that the proposal has the support and approval of key stakeholders including commissioners, staff and patients
- Quantified analyses of the investment and its lifetime costs, benefits and cash flows (using techniques such as discounted cash flow and net present value where appropriate)
- Evidence-based information supporting the proposal in terms of priority, cost-effectiveness, clinical service management and best use of scarce resources given alternative procurement routes.

Of particular interest to the SHA in their approval process is strategic fit and affordability within the trust's borrowing limit. SHAs also use the Department's checklist of those aspects that need to be tackled before giving approval – this is particularly relevant for larger schemes.

The HFMA has also published detailed guidance to the business case process in its toolkit: *Public Sector Business Cases using the Five Case Model.*

Procurement

The Department of Health *Capital Investment Manual* outlines the procurement process for capital and emphasises the importance of affordability and value for money. The size and scope of any scheme determines the approval process but regardless of the type, size and funding of capital investment the following procurement principles and processes should be borne in mind:

- The proposed investment should be placed in a strategic context
- Different capital investment options should be evaluated in an outline business case (OBC) using economic appraisals including discounted cash flows to identify the financially preferred option
- The approved option should be prepared for procurement focusing on detailed specifications of outputs, outcomes and risk allocation

- The proposed scheme should be advertised to prospective providers (PFI projects and other large proposed procurements need to be advertised in the Official Journal of the European Union – OJEU)
- Once a preferred bidder has been chosen, agreement must be reached on contractual arrangements. Under PFI schemes the contracts will cover the facility's useful life (normally between 25 to 30 years for projects based on building an asset)
- The full business case (FBC) should bring together the arguments for the preferred planned investment including current and future service requirements, affordability, the trust's competitive service position and the ability to complete the project within the specified budget and time scale
- Once the contract is finalised and awarded the contract can be enforced
- The contract will need to be monitored throughout its life
- A post-project evaluation is required to review the procurement procedure from the initial planning and project appraisals to the contract monitoring and actual service outcomes. The purpose is to inform and improve future capital investment decisions.

Capital Investment Control

To give an idea of how the capital investment control mechanisms referred to in this chapter fit together, a simplified example is shown below:

Capital Investment Control Process – Example

Assumptions

- Average net relevant assets of £158m
- Depreciation calculated on the mix of fixed assets the trust holds (all of which are depreciated at different rates) is estimated to be £6m
- Income and expenditure budgets are in balance
- An existing rolling programme and other schemes underway total £5m
- Anticipated funding for national objectives is £0.5m
- A risk rating of 2 which gives a PBL of 10% of net relevant assets – the trust may therefore borrow up to £15.8m
- A new capital investment is identified that could be completed in year at a cost of £2m
- Depreciation at year end totals £6.2m.

Capital charges estimate	The rate of return or cost of capital = 3.5% of £158m = £5.5m	This determines the trust's dividend payment for the next year generally payable in two equal instalments of £2.75m in September and March.
	Depreciation of £6m	Depreciation is budgeted at £6m. As income and expenditure is in balance the trust has £6m that it may invest in capital assets.
	Total forecast capital charges of £11.5m	

Capital resource limit	£5m is needed for the rolling programme.	As this is less than the budgeted depreciation and the trust's income and expenditure budget is in balance, cash will be available from service agreement and contract income.
	£0.5m is expected for a specific national objective.	The CRL will be increased during the year for any further awards relating to national objectives.
	£2m is needed for the new investment.	CRL will be needed for the new investment.
	The initial capital resource limit (CRL) is set at £7.5m.	The initial CRL is used by the Department to plan the annual position across the NHS enabling early adjustment should the initial assessment exceed the overall capital departmental expenditure limit (DEL).
Prudential borrowing limit	The trust can borrow up to a maximum of £15.8m. This year it has £6m from depreciation and £0.5m from national funding so will need to borrow £1m against its capital expenditure needs of £7.5m.	Where specific sizable capital projects are involved, full business case approval is required from the SHA.
	The trust will be keen to keep loans to a minimum as interest is charged at about 4.7%. The trust will ensure the loan is only taken when the cash is needed to fund the scheme.	
Capital external financing limit	The sources of funding outside of trust operational activities are: £0.5 for central objectives £1.0 towards the new investment (within PBL) **Total EFL = £1.5m**	The next year's EFL will include the first repayment of the loan. Therefore assuming no new schemes or central objectives the EFL for next year will be a minus figure.
Depreciation	Assume the actual depreciation in the year totals £6.2m.	The trust's budget for depreciation will be £0.2m overspent. Assuming no other budget variances the trust accounts for the year will show £0.2m overspending. This has no impact on the trust's capital control limits.

It is worth thinking through some of the complications and risks within the above example:

- The final CRL is unlikely to be that set at the start of the year. There may be changes necessary early on to control the overall NHS total. During the year there may be adjustments for central initiatives or transfers between PCTs/trusts
- There may be significant slippage in capital expenditure that may result in the Department withdrawing funds from a trust. Trusts will be aware of this possibility and be prepared to bring forward other future investments
- An approved business case will take a number of months to prepare. The financial position of the trust may change during this period resulting in PBL being withdrawn
- In developing business cases the cost of capital is 3.5% but it is important that trusts plan income and expenditure budgets and cash flow on the basis of interest payments on loans at the national loans fund rate (about 4.7%). Cash flow planning must also include loan repayments
- Capital investment may be needed to help deliver financial stability to a trust yet the trust may have a risk rating that does not allow access to PBL
- Trusts may also obtain loans to fund working capital. This affects average net relevant assets and the amount needed to achieve the 3.5% rate of return
- The example takes no account of any working capital loans that exist, which would score against the trust's PBL.

Alternatives to Asset Ownership

The NHS can use assets without legal ownership. The main alternatives are by leasing and PFI schemes.

Leases

A lease may be defined as 'a contract between two parties (the 'lessor' and the 'lessee') for the hire of a specific asset'. The lessor owns the asset, but conveys the right to use the asset to the lessee for an agreed period of time in return for the payment of specified rentals. One of the main attractions of leasing is that it may enable an asset to be excluded from the balance sheet and hence from any restrictions relating to capital expenditure. Whether or not a lease has to be included on the balance sheet as a capital asset depends on the nature of the lease – NHS guidance on this follows FRS 5.

The two types of lease are:

- Where the lessor transfers to the lessee substantially all the economic benefits and risks of asset ownership, the asset should be recorded in the trust's asset register together with a corresponding lease creditor. The asset is in effect treated as if it had been bought outright. It will attract capital charges and be subject to depreciation, indexation and appropriate revaluations. Assets also count towards the CRL and impact on the EFL. Such leases are therefore on the balance sheet and are often referred to as **finance leases**
- Where the lessor retains the risks of ownership, the asset should not be capitalised and the payments are charged to revenue. Such leases are often referred to as **operating**

leases. The discounted value of the lease payments (i.e. the total cost of lease payments in today's terms) will normally be less than 90% of the fair value of the asset.

The classification of leases is under constant scrutiny and it is expected that IFRS will have an impact in this area when they are introduced for accounting purposes from 2009/10.

Private finance initiative (PFI) and local improvement finance trusts (LIFT)

PFI schemes involve creating partnerships between the public and private sectors. In the NHS, PFI is an important element in the government's plans to renew the NHS estate. Local improvement finance trusts (LIFTs) are also used to develop and improve primary care premises.

PFI capital investment in the NHS typically involves the private sector partner providing the capital asset (design, build, construction and financing), facilities and the associated support services that will be used by the NHS in its provision of clinical patient care.

At the planning stages of proposed capital investments, schemes should be tested for their suitability for PFI arrangements. For a scheme to be regarded as suitable, it must demonstrate value for money and be affordable. Although the private sector is likely to have a higher cost of capital than the NHS, it may achieve compensating savings – for example, by providing more cost-effective management, efficiency savings or managing risk more effectively. See chapter 10 for more details about the PFI.

PFI and LIFTs have encouraged the spread of more complex asset types, including:

- Deferred assets, including those financed by PFI schemes where asset ownership reverts back to the NHS in the future
- Intangible (non-physical) assets, generating economic benefit from the 'right' of ownership, for example expenditure on software or research and development
- Assets that are held on leases
- Donated and assets funded by the new opportunities fund.

Assets may be transferred to PFI and LIFT partners. This will normally be at the DV's valuation so that the NHS receives a cash receipt with the costs to the partner being recovered in charges over the agreed contract period. PFI and LIFT is covered in more detail in chapter 10.

References and Further Reading

Capital Accounting Manual, Department of Health, 2004: www.info.doh.gov.uk/doh/finman.nsf

Public Private Partnerships – PFI and LIFT, Department of Health web pages: www.dh.gov.uk/ProcurementAndProposals/PublicPrivatePartnership/fs/en

Capital Investment Manual, Department of Health, 1994: www.dh.gov.uk/en/Procurementandproposals/Publicprivatepartnership/Privatefinanceinitiative/ InvestmentGuidanceRouteMap/DH_4133176

NHS Allocations, Department of Health web pages: NHS Allocations (including the weighted capitation formula), Department of Health: www.dh.gov.uk/en/Policyandguidance/ Organisationpolicy/Financeandplanning/Allocations/index.htm

The Operating Framework for the NHS in England 2008/09: www.dh.gov.uk/en/ Publicationsandstatistics/Publications/PublicationsPolicyAndGuidance/DH_081094

Delegated limits for capital investment, Department of Health, 2007: www.dh.gov.uk/en/ Publicationsandstatistics/Publications/PublicationsPolicyAndGuidance/DH_080864

Budget 2008: Stability and Opportunity: Building a Strong, Sustainable Future, HM Treasury, 2008: www.hm-treasury.gov.uk./budget/budget_08/report/bud_bud08_repindex.cfm

Accounting Standards Board (for details of accounting standards): www.asb.org.uk

Public Sector Business Cases using the Five Case Model: a Toolkit, HFMA, 2007: www.hfma.org.uk

Monitor (including the Prudential Borrowing Code): www.monitor-nhsft.gov.uk

17. NHS Charitable Funds

Introduction

This chapter looks at the management of funds held on trust and is based on the legislative framework as it applies to England and Wales. The *Charities Act* was passed in November 2006 and the first tranche of provisions, which included raising the audit threshold, were effective for financial years beginning on or after 27 February 2007. There are different regulatory regimes in Scotland and Northern Ireland.

History and Background

There are around 300 NHS charities and the overall level of funds held is significant. The accumulation of these funds is, to a large degree, a consequence of the historical funding of early health services through charitable sources. More recently these funds have been boosted through capital growth and income from investments, legacies and donations and fund-raising appeals.

When the NHS was created, most existing charitable assets were pooled into the Hospital Endowments Fund. The main exceptions to this were teaching and university hospitals, which retained control of their endowments through boards of governors and management committees respectively.

The Nature and Purpose of Charitable Funds

A trust is created when funds are accepted by a trustee to be held and used for the benefit of a beneficiary. The arrangement is usually governed by an instrument that sets out the terms of the trust and the purpose to which funds are to be applied by the trustee. Trustees are not obliged to receive funds on trust and may refuse where conditions imposed by the donor are too onerous. In order to be deemed charitable, funds held on trust must have purposes that are for the general public good and are exclusively charitable.

The *Charities Act 2006* amended the *Charities Act 1993* in various ways. It also listed thirteen categories of charitable purpose:

- The prevention or relief of poverty
- The advancement of education
- The advancement of religion
- The advancement of health or saving lives
- The advancement of citizenship or community development
- The advancement of the arts, culture, heritage or science
- The advancement of amateur sport
- The advancement of human rights, conflict resolution or reconciliation or the promotion of religious or racial harmony or equality or diversity
- The advancement of environmental protection or improvement
- The relief of those in need by reason of youth, age, ill-health, disability, financial hardship or other disadvantage

- The advancement of animal welfare
- The promotion of the efficiency of the armed forces of the Crown, or of the efficiency of the police, fire and rescue service or ambulance services
- Other purposes beneficial to the community not falling under any of the other headings.

The Act also provides for the continuing admission of other categories that are analogous to these principal categories. The categories are subject to the overriding requirement of demonstrable public benefit. Funds that do not fall under one or more of the thirteen charitable purposes listed above are likely to be non-charitable but if there is a doubt advice should be sought from the Charity Commission.

Previous guidance from the Department of Health questioned whether non-charitable funds had a place within the NHS and suggested that they should more properly lie in the exchequer accounts as income generation schemes or taken outside the NHS boundary. It is therefore not expected that health service bodies would hold non-charitable trusts. This might, for example, include funds held on trust for the benefit of a single named patient (which has insufficient public benefit to be charitable in law).

There are three main types of charitable funds recognised in law. These are:

- Unrestricted funds – which may be spent at the discretion of the trustees in line with the charity's objectives. Designated funds (see below) count as a subset of unrestricted funds
- Restricted income funds – which can only be spent in accordance with restrictions imposed by the donor when the funds were granted to or raised for the charity
- Endowment funds – where capital funds are made available to a charity and trustees are legally required to invest or retain them. Endowment funds can be 'permanent' (trustees cannot spend the capital, only the income generated through its investment) or 'expendable' (here capital can be converted to income).

Funds may also be 'designated' which means that trustees can earmark unrestricted funds for a specific purpose. Designating funds can be useful where it is planned to build up funds through periodic transfers from unrestricted funds over time for a significant project or where funds are needed to meet ongoing costs (for example, staffing) to which formal commitments have been made. It may also be a useful way to recognise the apparent 'wishes' of donors (which do not create 'restrictions').

Where Charitable Funds come from

Trustees are not obliged to receive funds on trust and may refuse where the conditions imposed by the donor are too onerous or where they are unlikely to be able to use funds as directed. To avoid criticism and safeguard their own position, trustees are advised to seek advice from the Charity Commission before refusing a donation. Acceptance of all donations should be tested against the general principle that it does not, nor appears to, place an NHS body or the Department of Health/Welsh Assembly Government under an inappropriate obligation.

There are five main sources of new money for charitable funds. These are:

- Donations
- Fund-raising
- Legacies
- Grants
- Investment income and interest.

Donations

Donations can be solicited (for example, through posters, leaflets or other appeals) or unsolicited (for example, where, at the end of a hospital stay, a patient asks how they can donate to the ward or hospital charity).

Donations of both types can be unrestricted or restricted. An unrestricted donation would arise when, for example, a patient or relative gives money 'for the hospital charity' or 'for the ward funds' without specifying how it should be used. Even if there is a particular use suggested, it will only be a 'restriction' if the terms are strictly limited – for example, 'it must be used' or 'must only be used' – and are formalised in writing. A donation made in response to a fund-raising leaflet soliciting donations for a general fund would also be unrestricted.

It is desirable to minimise the proportion of donations received as 'restricted' funds because restricted funds limit spending flexibilities. One way to do this is to use a standard form of receipt that invites donors to record how they 'wish' their donation to be used 'without imposing any trust'. The wishes expressed can be reflected through the designation of donations, but donations on these terms will be 'unrestricted'. The Charity Commission can supply a sample format. Such a receipting system can also assist with accountability and the receipt can incorporate an invitation to donate under 'Gift Aid' arrangements.

Fund-raising

Fund-raising income results from events (anything from coffee mornings and sponsored swims through to high profile celebrity events) and targeted appeals. If the money is sought for an explicit purpose (for example, if tickets or a poster for a charity dinner state 'all proceeds from this event will be used to buy monitors for the special care baby unit') then it must be used for that and nothing else. The power of NHS trustees to raise funds is set out in section 222 of the *NHS Act 2006* and the Act does permit funds to be used more flexibly where there is an insufficient response (a failed appeal) or an excess of funds over and above the appeal target, provided certain safeguards are met.

Legacies

Legacies can be restricted or unrestricted depending on the terms on which the bequest is made. The 'wishes' or 'desires' of a donor are normally non-binding designations, however reference should be made to the terms of the gift to ensure that a binding restriction does not mean that the legacy is restricted funds.

If the legacy cannot be fulfilled (for example, if the function it was intended for no longer exists or has been transferred to another body) the NHS trustee(s) concerned should consider whether they received the legacy under section 91 of the *NHS Act 1977* (re-enacted as section 218 of the *NHS Act 2006*), which may provide a power to redirect the funds. Advice may be sought from the Charity Commission. If it appears that section 91/section 218 does not apply then an application must be made to the Charity Commission for a scheme that allows the legacy to be used in another way.

Where a service transfers to another NHS body, the Department of Health or Welsh Assembly Government should be contacted, where appropriate, to organise a transfer of the related charitable funds. This is a separate issue from seeking the Charity Commission's authority to amend the trusts affecting restricted funds. Normally the service transfer (and consequent transfer of charitable funds) authorised by the Department of Health would precede and inform the Charity Commission's decisions on how to amend the trusts of linked restricted funds.

Grants

Grants are usually restricted income given for a specific purpose. As well as the general principles which apply to the use of and accounting for restricted funds, grants often have additional requirements attached.

Investment income and interest

Investment income and interest (and any gains or investment losses) must be apportioned to the restricted fund that generates it. Where the trustee(s) administer(s) more than one charity, the income and investment gains and losses must also be apportioned to the respective charities. In the case of designated unrestricted funds of a charity the trustee(s) are permitted to apply investment gains for any of the objects of the charity concerned.

Types of Trustee

There are four types of trustee in the NHS:

- **Corporate trustees**: most charitable funds in the NHS are managed by corporate trustees – in other words it is the NHS corporate body (i.e. NHS trusts or special health authorities) that is the corporate trustee. The board of the trust or authority acts on behalf of the corporate trustee in the administration of the charitable funds – they are not themselves individual trustees. NHS trusts derive their power to hold charitable funds from clause 16, part II, schedule 2 of the *NHS and Community Care Act 1990*. Primary care trusts derive their power from schedule 5A, part iii, clause 12(1) (c) of the *NHS Act 1977* – inserted into that Act by section 2 (1) of the *Health Act 1999*. Foundation trusts derive their power from sections 213, 214 and 216 of the *NHS Act 2006*
- **Special trustees**: under section 7 of the *1946 NHS Act* the endowment and trust funds were vested in the board of governors of designated teaching hospitals who acted as trustees. Subsequently the *1973 NHS Reorganisation Act* provided for the reorganisation of charitable funds held historically. In particular, section 29 permitted the appointment of

bodies of 'special trustees' appointed by the Secretary of State for Health. The terms on which special trustees hold that property are prescribed by sections 93 and 95 of the *NHS Act 1977*, as affected by section 212 of the *NHS Act 2006*. Special trustees are no longer created

- **Section 11 trustees**: under section 11 (1–3) of the *NHS and Community Care Act 1990*, (re-enacted under paragraph 10, schedule 4 to the *NHS Act 2006*) the Secretary of State for Health can appoint trustees to hold and administer the charitable funds associated with an NHS trust. Equivalent provision was made in section 7 of the *Health Act 1999* for trustees for a primary care trust
- **Section 22/51 trustees**: under section 22 of the *Health and Social Care (Community Health and Standards) Act 2003*, (re-enacted under section 51 of the *NHS Act 2006*) the Secretary of State for Health can appoint trustees to hold and administer the charitable funds associated with an NHS foundation trust.

The various provisions of the *NHS Act 2006* mentioned have parallel provisions for Wales, set out in the *NHS (Wales) Act 2006*. In Wales equivalent powers to those of the Secretary of State are exercised by Welsh ministers.

It is important to appreciate that health service bodies are not themselves charities. Only the property they hold on trust for exclusively charitable purposes constitutes a charity. The decision as to which model of trusteeship should apply in any locality (and which NHS body, or body of NHS trustees should hold funds linked to a particular NHS trust or facility) lies with the Department of Health, exercising statutory responsibility (or Welsh ministers in Wales). The Department of Health operates a policy under which charitable funds linked to an NHS body are only allocated to its trusteeship if they total more than £500,000. Below that figure the trusteeship is usually allocated to another NHS body or body of NHS trustees which already holds more than £500,000 of charitable funds.

Trustees – Roles and Responsibilities

In broad terms, trustees have a duty to ensure compliance, a duty of prudence and a duty of care.

Compliance

Trustees must ensure that:

- The charity complies with charity law and with the requirements of the Charity Commission as regulator. As part of this, they must ensure that the charity prepares its annual report, returns and accounts as required by law
- The charity does not breach any of the requirements or rules in its governing document
- Any fund-raising activity undertaken by or on behalf of the charity is properly undertaken and that funds are properly accounted for. NHS trustees have specific powers to raise funds, set out in section 222 of the *NHS Act 2006*. Guidance on the proper conduct of fund-raising can be found in the Charity Commission's leaflet *CC20: Charities and fund-raising* (published on the Commission's website).

Trustees also have a responsibility to review the charity's objects and ensure they are still relevant and workable. If they are not, trustees should ask the Charity Commission for advice on how to change them.

Duty of prudence

Trustees must:

- Ensure the charity is and will remain solvent
- Ensure the charity's income and property is applied solely for the purposes set out in its governing document and for no other purpose
- Use charitable funds and assets wisely and only in furtherance of the charity's objects
- Avoid activities that might place the charity, its assets or reputation at risk
- Take special care when investing the charity's funds
- Ensure adequate financial management and control arrangements are in place.

Duty of care

Trustees must:

- Exercise such care and skill as is reasonable in the circumstances having particular regard to:
    - any special knowledge or experience that he or she has or professes to have
    - any special knowledge or experience that it is reasonable to expect of a person acting in the course of that kind of business or profession (where he or she acts as a trustee in the course of a business or profession)
- Act with integrity and avoid any personal or organisational conflicts of interest – where trustees are required to make a decision which affects the personal interests of one of their number, that person should not be present at any discussion or vote on the matter
- Ensure they have appropriate risk management plans in place. Trustees of charities with gross annual income over £500,000 must make a statement about this in their annual report
- Consider using external professional advice where there may be a material risk to the charity.

Regulation – Roles and Responsibilities

Department of Health

The Secretary of State for Health is responsible for:

- The appointment and removal of trustees
- The terms of their office
- The establishment of section 11, section 51 or special trustee bodies
- The transfer of property between trustee bodies – no transfers of charitable funds or trustee responsibilities can be made where NHS bodies are restructured without the Department's authority or agreement.

These responsibilities are exercised through the Department of Health.

Welsh Assembly Government

In Wales Welsh ministers have equivalent powers to those of the Secretary of State in England, and exercise those responsibilities through the Welsh Assembly Government.

Charity Commission

The Charity Commission is the statutory organisation that regulates charities in England and Wales. It is responsible for regulating the proper conduct and administration of charities. Its aim is to maintain public confidence in the integrity of charity which it does by encouraging better methods of administration, giving advice to trustees and investigating and correcting abuse. The Commission has the power to change the objectives of a charity where this is necessary and where trustees do not have the power to do so themselves. It also keeps a register of charities, which is open to public inspection.

The NHS is required to register charitable funds with the Charity Commission and to file audited accounts in a prescribed form and also to produce an annual report and annual return. The Charity Commission provides advice and guidance to help charities make effective use of their resources and to help trustees fulfill their objectives and obligations.

The Management of Charitable Funds

Day-to-day management

Trustees are only able to delegate authority that is specified in their governing instrument or section 11 of the *Trustee Act 2000*. However, they cannot delegate their statutory duties and responsibilities. This means that although in practice the day-to-day management of charitable funds may be delegated to a sub-committee and staff, trustees remain accountable for all decisions relating to and the performance of the charity. It follows, therefore, that they need to be well informed about the business of the charity if they are to meet their responsibilities effectively. They will need to establish clear reporting lines and ensure that appropriate arrangements exist to enable them to oversee actions taken on their behalf.

This means that there need to be written rules and procedures covering the formal conduct of the charity's business. These will normally be set out in the form of standing orders, standing financial instructions and procedures or guidance notes, in addition to any 'scheme of delegation'. The frequency of corporate trustee meetings or of committee meetings will depend upon the size of the charitable funds being administered and the number and complexity of its transactions. Meetings need to be frequent enough to avoid any delays to the charity's administration that might lead to a failure to meet legal and regulatory requirements or to poor management of its resources.

Reserves policy

As far as the income received by the fund is concerned, trustees are under a legal duty to apply charitable funds within a reasonable time of receiving them. To be able to do this prudently, trustees need to consider, and regularly review, what level of reserves it is appropriate for them to hold. Without a sound reserves policy, trustees cannot be content that their reserves are at a level to meet current needs. If reserves are too high, the charity is retaining funds without justification and this could constitute a breach of trust. If reserves are too low, the fund's ability to meet future commitments or needs may be at risk. Trustees are required to have a formal reserves policy, review this regularly and report on it in their annual report.

Investment powers

Under the *Trustee Act 2000*, charity trustees have a general power of investment that can be used in relation to any charity property held on trust (except property of charitable companies) subject to any 'restriction or exclusion' affecting the charity. This power allows a trustee to place funds in any kind of investment, excluding land, as though he or she was the absolute owner of those funds. The *Trustee Act 2000* also gives all charity trustees power to acquire freehold or leasehold land in the UK.

Financial management

Trustees have a duty to use the income of their funds for the purpose for which they were given, unless the charity's governing document gives them the power to accumulate income or they have a specific application in mind. In order to justify the retention of income, trustees need to adopt expenditure plans. Budgets should be set with decision ceilings for fund managers and financial planning should be undertaken.

To be able to discharge their responsibilities effectively, trustees will need relevant management information to inform their decision-making. As well as the more usual financial information relating to budget and spend to date, trustees will need:

- To be informed of significant donations
- A list of large or significant transactions
- A summary investment report
- A report on slow moving or overdrawn funds
- A report on the use of the chairman's discretionary powers.

The Charity Commission booklet (CC60), *The Hallmarks of an Effective Charity*, sets out the standards the Commission believes an effective charity and its trustees will try to uphold and the principles that its regulatory framework exists to support. As such, it provides some useful pointers to trustees when reviewing their corporate governance arrangements.

Risk management

Trustees should maintain a risk register and review it on a regular basis to ensure the effectiveness of actions taken to mitigate identified risks. Detailed guidance is available on the Charity Commission's website.

VAT

VAT applies to charities in the same way that it applies to commercial enterprises. However, the activities of charitable bodies are often carried out on a 'non-business basis' and are therefore not subject to VAT. Conversely, charities may not be able to recover related VAT on expenditure. VAT is a difficult area of tax to deal with. If charities require assistance in the way they are dealing with VAT they should contact the VAT NHS Admin Team. Guidance about what specific charity reliefs are available and how they work is also available via local VAT offices.

Accounting requirements

The detailed requirements for the preparation and submission of annual accounts of individual charities that are not charitable companies depend upon their level of income or expenditure and where they are based in the UK. The key document to refer to in England and Wales is *CC15 – Charity Reporting and Accounting: the Essentials*. This is available on the Charity Commission's website. All charities in the UK that prepare accruals accounts must also follow the *Statement of Recommended Practice (SORP) 2005*.

As a minimum, all charities must:

- Prepare and maintain accounting records which must be retained for at least 6 years
- Prepare annual accounts and make these available to the public on request.

In England and Wales:

- Charities with annual income or expenditure over £10,000 must file an annual return, annual report and their accounts with the Charity Commission within 10 months of their financial year end
- In addition, charities with an income in excess of £1m must complete and submit a 'summary information return'
- The *Regulatory Reform (NHS Charitable and Non-Charitable Trust Accounts and Audit) Order 2005*, which amended the *Charities Act 1993*, regulation 3, requires all NHS charities to have a form of external scrutiny. Where gross income is £500,000 or less (or, where gross assets exceed £2.8m, the charity's gross income is £100,000 or less) the accounts may be independently examined or audited by someone appointed by the Audit Commission (England) or Auditor General (Wales) in accordance with regulation 3. Charitable funds held by special trustees established before 1973 and NHS foundation trusts acting as corporate trustee or section 51 bodies may appoint their own auditors. An annual report, return and accounts must be sent to the Charity Commission within 10 months of their financial year end
- NHS charities with income above £500,000 (or, where gross assets exceed £2.8m and gross income exceeds £100,000) must have their accounts audited by an auditor appointed by the Audit Commission or Auditor General (Wales). Charitable funds held by special trustees established before 1973 and NHS foundation trusts and section 51 bodies may appoint their own auditors. Again, an annual report, return and accounts must be sent to the Charity Commission within 10 months of their financial year-end
- Charities with a gross annual income of at least £100,000 must prepare their accounts on an accruals basis. Below this threshold, charities may elect to prepare their accounts on a receipts/payments or accruals basis.

The accruals accounts should comprise:

- A statement of financial activities (SOFA) for the year that shows all incoming and outgoing resources and reconciles all changes in its funds
- A balance sheet, showing the recognised assets, liabilities and different categories of fund of the charity
- A cash flow statement if at least two of the following apply: the charity has an annual turnover of more than £5.6m; its balance sheet shows more than £2.8m gross assets; it employs an average of 50 or more staff (from April 2008 turnover changes to £6.5m and gross assets to £3.26m or 50 or more staff)
- Notes explaining the accounting policies adopted.

Where charities have to account for more than one fund under their control, the accounts should provide a summary of the main funds. They should differentiate, in particular, between unrestricted income funds, restricted income funds and endowment funds. The columnar format of the SOFA is designed to achieve this.

The annual report

The annual report is one of the key tools available to charities to help them communicate with key stakeholders including donors, beneficiaries and the wider public. SORP 2005 provides best practice recommendations, which in England and Wales and Scotland are underpinned by law. The annual report is normally presented along with the accounts but is legally a separate document. It should cover a range of information including, for example:

- Details about how trustees are recruited and trained. Where there is a corporate trustee, or a body of individuals appointed by the Appointments Commission, this should be noted but there is no need to set out the recruitment arrangements in any more detail. Although board members of a corporate trustee are **not** trustees it is desirable to explain what training they receive to enable them to manage the charitable funds
- Details about the charity's decision making processes including, for example, what functions are delegated to sub-committees and staff
- An explanation of the charity's aims and the changes/difference it seeks to make through its work
- Details of the charity's objectives for the year and strategy for meeting these
- Details of significant activities, projects and services that contribute to the achievement of the charity's objectives
- A statement setting out its grant making policies
- Where material investments are held, details of the investment policy and objectives including the extent – if any – to which social, environmental and ethical considerations are taken into account; details of investment performance against the investment objectives set
- Where material funds have been designated, the reserves policy statement should quantify these, explain their purpose and, where they have been set aside for future expenditure, indicate when they are likely to be spent
- Plans for the future.

Guidance on the content of the annual report is available in Charity Commission booklet (CC15), *Charity Reporting and Accounting: the Essentials*.

References and Further Reading

Charities Act 2006: www.opsi.gov.uk/acts/acts2006/ukpga_20060050_en_1

Other Acts of Parliament referred to in this chapter can be found via: www.opsi.gov.uk/acts.htm

The Charity Commission offers a range of useful free publications. These can be accessed via www.charity-commission.gov.uk or ordered from its offices. Guidance available from the Charity Commission referred to in this chapter:

   CC3 – The Essential Trustee: Introduction (2007) and what you need to know (2008)
   CC20 – Charities and Fund-raising (2004)
   CC60 – The Hallmarks of an Effective Charity (2004)
   CC15 – Charity Reporting and Accounting: the Essentials (2007)

NHS Charitable Funds: A Practical Guide, HFMA, 2005: www.hfma.org.uk

VAT – for NHS connected charities the best contact is the NHS VAT team: nhsvatteam@hmrc.gsi.gov.uk

Information is also available via local VAT offices – see: www.hmrc.gov.uk

SORP 2005: www.charitycommission.gov.uk/investigations/sorp/sorp05docs.asp

Regulatory Reform (NHS Charitable and Non-Charitable Trust Accounts and Audit) Order 2005: www.opsi.gov.uk/SI/si2005/20051074.htm

Audit Commission: www.audit-commission.gov.uk

Auditor General Wales: www.wao.gov.uk/home.asp

Appointments Commission: www.appointments.org.uk/

18. The NHS in Scotland

Introduction

In operational terms much of NHSScotland is similar to England and Wales. However, there are substantial organisational differences, which this chapter looks at. More detailed information regarding the structures and processes of NHS Scotland can be found in the *Introductory Guide to NHS finance in Scotland* published by HFMA Scotland.

Organisational and Policy Changes from the Scottish NHS Plan

Partnership for Care – Scotland's Health White Paper (2003) was the blueprint for setting in place organisational and policy change within NHSScotland and built on the earlier White Paper – *Our National Health: A Plan for Action, a Plan for Change* (2000). The main changes were to encourage a more collaborative approach to managing and providing health services at both a national and local level.

The main features of the document were:

- Dissolution of NHS trusts as separate legal entities and the transfer of their functions, staff and assets intact to new operating divisions of their area NHS boards
- Introduction of a single local health plan
- A new performance and accountability framework for NHSScotland
- Revised financial framework and financial targets
- Decentralisation of decision-making to front line staff.

More recently the Scottish Executive Health Department issued *Delivering for Health*, as a response to the report from the group led by Professor David Kerr – *Building a Health Service Fit for the Future*. Both reports outlined future models of healthcare which move from acute based, episodic, reactive care to community-based, continuous, integrated and preventative care.

The new Scottish government launched *Better Health, Better Care* in December 2007 – this sets out a revised policy to continue the development of the NHS in Scotland. It is based on values of co-operation and collaboration and is aimed at tackling health inequalities, with patients at the centre of the NHS.

Fundamental Differences between England and Scotland

The main differences that exist between the operation of the NHS in Scotland and England are:

- NHSScotland reports to the Scottish Parliament rather than the UK Parliament
- There is no regional tier in Scotland between NHS boards and the Health Department
- There are no NHS trusts in Scotland
- There are very few non-NHS healthcare providers in Scotland.

Statutory Provisions

The following legislation is relevant to the operation of NHSScotland:

- *Public Finance and Accountability (Scotland) Act 2000* – this sets out the rules for the Parliament's budgetary process
- *Community Care and Health (Scotland) Act 2002* – this provides the legislative backing for improvements in care services
- *National Health Service Reform (Scotland) Act 2004* – this allowed for the dissolution of NHS trusts and the establishment of community health partnerships (CHPs); introduced a statutory duty for NHS boards to co-operate with each other with a view to enhancing the health of the nation (for example, through regional and national planning); established powers of intervention on behalf of Scottish ministers in case of service failure; and imposed on NHS boards duties to encourage public involvement and promote health improvement.

Following devolution in Scotland and the subsequent creation of the Scottish Parliament, NHSScotland became accountable to the Parliament, and not as previously to the Secretary of State for Scotland. The *Public Finance and Accountability (Scotland) Act 2000* has five main policy objectives, all of which relate to NHSScotland, concerning procedures for the approval of expenditure, use of resources, management of audit and scrutiny of the outputs obtained from that expenditure. They are:

- To ensure probity in the handling of the public funds under the Scottish Parliament's control
- To help maximise the cost effectiveness of the expenditure under the control of the Parliament
- To provide the information that the Parliament needs to make properly informed and timely decisions and to judge the probity and wider value of the actions of the Executive
- To provide the Scottish people with understandable, consistent, relevant and timely information
- To contain the overhead and compliance costs associated with the procedures.

Organisation of NHSScotland

The First Minister for Scotland has responsibility for NHSScotland and is assisted by the Cabinet Secretary for Health and Wellbeing. The Scottish Government Health and Community Care Directorate (SGHD) is responsible for NHSScotland and for the development and implementation of health and community care policy. NHSScotland comprises 14 territorial NHS boards responsible for the planning and delivery of all health services in their own area. In addition, there are eight special health boards in Scotland.

The fourteen NHS boards cover the whole of Scotland with population spans from 20,000 to 1,500,000 over widely differing areas. All NHS boards report to the chief executive of the SGHD. NHS boards are responsible for planning and commissioning hospital and community health services for their resident populations, as well as providing health services.

The roles of the different components of local NHS systems are as follows:

- NHS boards are responsible for strategic planning, governance and performance management

- Operating divisions are part of a single statutory organisation but have the ability to take operational decisions and manage the delivery of healthcare services within the governance framework of their NHS board. However, they must do so with continual reference to the central board of governance
- Community health partnerships (CHPs) are responsible for the planning and delivery of community services, and may report to the NHS board directly (through a CHP director) or via a community or primary care operating division
- Special health boards are national bodies which report directly to the SGHD and are responsible for particular business areas – for example, the Scottish Ambulance Service, National Waiting Times Centre, NHS 24 (similar to NHS Direct in England), NHS Education for Scotland and NHS Quality Improvement Scotland (again similar to NICE in England).

Operating divisions and CHPs have significant management authority at local level with those in the front line empowered to plan and deliver services within a framework of clear strategic direction and rigorous performance management. It is considered vital to the management arrangements that devolution of decision-making does not stop at the operating division level.

The key principles of NHS boards and operating divisions are as follows:

- NHS boards should retain their focus as boards of governance and take a corporate, inclusive approach to collective decision-making based on the principles of partnership working and devolution of powers to the front line of patient care
- NHS boards should support local leadership by delegating financial and management authority as far as possible and encouraging locally responsive approaches to service provision
- As integral parts of local NHS systems, well-defined operating divisions should have specific, delegated authority to act within a defined remit without constant reference to the NHS board, backed up by clear, formal schemes of accountability
- Organisations should recognise the complex interaction between clinicians and other staff who work directly with patients and common services which support them in that task
- Responsibility and decision-making should be devolved to staff who are directly involved in delivering healthcare
- The design and development of services should be grounded firmly in the patient's everyday experience of care at locality level
- NHS boards should continue to develop sustainable frameworks for patient focus and public involvement
- NHS boards should continue to develop CHPs and 'joint future' initiative (see later in this chapter) in a way that engages with community planning partners and maximises population alignment between CHPs and social care
- Health services should be delivered locally as far as possible, but always consistent with providing safe, sustainable and efficient services to patients
- To achieve this, NHS boards should promote, resource and actively manage the development of managed clinical networks and other clinical and care networks, both within and beyond their local boundaries.

Shared Services

NHSScotland has elected to develop a shared service approach for payroll and financial services through a number of NHS board consortia. The shared service consortia will supply these services to each of the NHSScotland organisations utilising a common chart of accounts and standard processes. It has provided a central service for practitioner services for several years.

Funding Flows

NHSScotland funding forms part of the Scotland vote, which competes in the public expenditure survey (PES) against UK votes such as defence, social security and the environment. The First Minister for Scotland has the task of dividing up the Scottish vote among the various services for which he is responsible including health, prisons, education and social services. Health is one of the major areas of expenditure and allocations tend to mirror the lead given by the Department of Health in England. However, differences in allocation do arise.

Barnett formula

The Barnett formula was introduced in 1978 and forms the basis of the additional changes to expenditure in Scotland (and Wales) and applies to only certain types of expenditure. There are two main components to Scottish public expenditure:

- The inherited expenditure base
- Incremental expenditure changes – this is the part determined by Barnett.

There are three components to the calculation:

- The change in planned spending in departments in England
- The extent to which the relevant English departmental programme is comparable with the services carried out by each devolved administration
- The population proportion of each country.

Spending review process

A bi-annual spending review process is undertaken by Scottish ministers to identify spending plans for the following three-year period. This is normally undertaken at the same time as other UK spending reviews.

The Scottish government finance department manages the process, scrutinising and challenging expenditure proposals and providing advice to departments and ministers.

Arbuthnott formula

The Arbuthnott review was the end product of the national review of resource allocation for NHSScotland. Entitled *Fair Shares for All*, its purpose was to review the methods for allocating funding between the fourteen NHS boards.

The key principles in developing the new formula were that it must:

- Be fair
- Be tailored to Scotland's needs and give everyone in Scotland equal access to healthcare
- Take account of the influence of deprivation on healthcare needs and support the aim of tackling inequalities in health
- Take account of the needs of people living in remote and rural areas as well as those in urban areas
- Be based on evidence
- Be clearly explained and open to scrutiny.

The formula recommended using information about population size and the characteristics of each of the fourteen NHS boards to determine the relative funding needs. Four key elements have to be taken into account in the formula:

- The share of the Scottish population living in each NHS board area
- The age/sex structure of the population
- Levels of deprivation
- The proportion of the population living in remote and rural areas.

A revised funding formula has been developed by the NHSScotland Resource Allocation Committee (NRAC). The NRAC was established to refine and extend Arbuthnott, in particular looking at evidence to determine healthcare need in different groups of people. The revised formula will be rolled out from April 2009.

Cash limited/non-cash limited

Funds allocated for hospital and community health services (HCHS) are distributed via a resource allocation. NHS boards are not allowed to overspend and are highly restricted in their ability to carry surpluses or deficits from one year into another. NHS boards are currently permitted to carry forward up to a theoretical 1% of their revenue resource allocations as a surplus into the following year. From 1 April 2004, general medical services (GMS) have also been included within the resource allocation with the introduction of the new GMS contract.

Funding for family health services (general dental services, general pharmaceutical services and general optical services) forms part of the Scottish government health allocation. Although this is subject to a cash limit nationally much of the expenditure is not subject to cash limits at NHS board level.

Resource accounting

In line with UK government policy, NHSScotland has moved to a resource-based system of public expenditure and control. The main change is the extension of an accruals based approach to accounting with the emphasis on outputs and achievements of aims and objectives rather than accounting on a cash target basis.

Capital planning process

NHS boards are now given an annual single capital allocation based on an agreed formula. This has introduced greater flexibility in capital planning programmes. The formula is based on two components:

- A core formula based on the Arbuthnott formula, adjusted for patients treated (as opposed to resident) within the NHS board area. This accounts for 90% of the capital allocation
- Recognition of specialist regional services to cover additional costs associated with treating patients outside the NHS board area. This forms the remaining 10% of the capital allocation.

One of the main features is the fact that each NHS board is notified of its capital allocation for the next three years on a rolling basis. Year one allocation is firm, with years two and three indicative.

A capital pool continues to be retained by the SGHD to provide limited funding for national priorities, new ministerial initiatives and to 'accelerate' specific projects.

Since April 2002, all non information management and technology (IM&T) projects with a value less than £5m have been approved at NHS board level. For IM&T this applies to schemes below £1.5m.

To ensure that capital investment is maximised NHS boards are also currently required to consider the use of public private partnerships (PPP) or private finance initiative (PFI) funding, where existing funding is not adequate to support investment or extension of services, subject to affordability and value for money. The new Scottish government is currently looking at alternative ways of providing additional capital funding without using the PPP/PFI approach.

Local and National NHS Plans

In Scotland planning is primarily the function of the NHS boards, although an overview is provided by the SGHD.

The role of the NHS board is to:

- Improve and protect the health of local people
- Improve health services for local people
- Focus clearly on health outcomes and people's experience of their local NHS system
- Promote integrated health and community planning by working closely with other local organisations
- Provide a single focus of accountability for the performance of the local NHS system.

The functions of the NHS board are:

- Strategic development through the local health plan

- Resource allocation and addressing local priorities
- Implementation of the local health plan (discharged through the operating divisions)
- Performance management of the local NHS system
- Preparation and implementation of the local health plan.

Each operational division is required to produce local operational plans to achieve the objectives of the local health plan. A performance and accountability framework has also been developed, which takes the reporting focus beyond purely finance-based performance indicators.

Joint Planning

The *NHS and Community Care Act 1990* introduced a fundamental change in the arrangements for encouraging people to be looked after in the community and preventing inappropriate accommodation in hospitals by assigning the lead responsibility for implementing policy to local authorities.

The old Scottish Executive created the 'joint future group' to look into the provision of community care in Scotland and identify practical ways of improving joint working. The main recommendation of this review was to introduce joint resourcing and management.

Since April 2002, NHS bodies and local authorities have been required to bring together all their available resources in the widest sense – including staff, money, equipment and property – under single management. Once the scope of the resources is known and has been agreed, each agency has the option of either aligning their budgets under existing arrangements or pooling them under the flexibility afforded by the *Community Care and Health (Scotland) Act 2002*.

The Scottish government has advocated a partnership approach to be taken by NHS bodies and local authorities. The partnership agreements should outline:

- Joint development priorities and targets for a three-year period, covering key community care client groups and carers
- Developments in joint service management and joint resourcing proposed to support the stated development priorities and targets
- The performance management framework to be used to monitor progress, evaluate impact, and guide corrective action, if necessary
- The governance and accountability framework for the partnership agreement, straddling a number of local agencies.

Joint Future is the name given to the joint planning, assessment and provision of services to ensure that users of the care system receive a coherent and integrated package of care and this is backed by legislation in the form of the *Community Care and Health (Scotland) Act 2002*. This Act identifies the practical arrangements for joint working covering:

- Payments by NHS bodies towards certain local authority expenditure

- Payments by local authorities towards expenditure by NHS bodies on prescribed functions
- Delegation between local authorities and NHS bodies
- Transfers of staff.

Costing and Pricing

Formally known as the *Scottish Health Service Costs Book*, the 'blue book' provides financial and related activity information in sets of published tables, with the information relating mainly to individual hospitals.

The *Costs Book* contains health board reports and hospital reports, the majority of which relate to hospitals. Hospital reports relate to hospital care and others relate to community care and National Services Scotland. Hospital reports are structured to provide two main dimensions of analysis, one being a care-type/patient-type analysis and the second a functional analysis. The care-type/patient-type analysis forms the bulk of the blue book.

Managers at all levels can use the information as an aid to decision-making, planning and control and it also provides a set of indicators of performance for comparison purposes.

The information contained within the reports is derived from financial and statistical information prepared as part of the annual accounts process. The majority of the information is derived from Scottish financial returns (SFRs). There are a range of these returns detailing costs down to specialty level.

HRG benchmarking service

Healthcare resource groups (HRGs) are a tool developed by the Department of Health in England as a means of categorising hospital patients. The National Services Scotland's information and statistics division (ISD) has used HRGs for several years as a casemix measure for inpatient and day-case datasets.

Costing of hospital patient activity is well established in England but is still under consideration in Scotland. ISD Scotland produces a benchmarking report for acute trusts, in which comparative cost information, taking account of casemix differences, is presented for inpatient and day case activity.

Tariffs

NHSScotland has introduced a tariff system for cross boundary activity flows. The tariff system has the potential to deliver improved benchmarking information and more accurate financial flows. It is expected that a move to a tariff-based system away from service level agreements will result in winners and losers amongst NHS boards; however work is ongoing to mitigate this effect. The tariffs continue to be developed, led by a group of representatives from the Scottish government and NHS boards. The aim is to maximise the benefits from the introduction of the tariffs, whilst improving the quality of the data used in its calculation.

Financial Accounting and Control

Revised financial framework

The financial framework of NHSScotland was historically complex, particularly from the perspective of trusts. As a result of the introduction of the *Scottish Health Plan* changes have been put in place to simplify the financial systems to allow for a patient focused and partnership approach.

This new approach is an integral part of the new accountability, governance and performance frameworks. The focus is intended to be on the whole system, which will, in turn, lead to improved planning and delivery of services.

Financial targets

To recognise the introduction of resource accounting and budgeting (RAB), the financial targets for NHS boards are to operate within their:

- Revenue resource limit
- Capital resource limit
- Cash requirement.

All NHS boards have a responsibility to control their finances throughout the year. Performance is monitored internally and externally. Also, on an annual basis audited accounts must be produced and various statements signed by the chief executive, including a statement on internal control. The annual accounts must be published and an extract made available publicly as part of the annual report. The SGHD determines the format of external reporting and the annual accounts so that consolidated accounts can be produced nationally. The principles of financial control and internal monitoring are set out in financial directions. It is left to local discretion to determine the exact nature of internal monitoring but it is sensible that this mirrors the external requirement. Internal financial control is ensured through the adoption of standing financial instructions, standard operating procedures and formal schemes of delegation.

NHS boards meet regularly with the SGHD to monitor and forecast progress against the statutory targets. Where an organisation is forecast not to meet a target, remedial action is expected so that the target can be achieved. In cases where an NHS board fails to operate within the revenue resource limit set, then an adjustment is made in the following year's financial allocation to reflect the amount by which the board has overspent as per RAB rules. The cumulative effect of successive years' failure to meet this target can be crippling for a board, as in the case of the NHS Argyll and Clyde Board, which the then Minister for Health took the decision to dissolve. The functions and services previously within Argyll and Clyde were subsumed within NHS Highland and NHS Greater Glasgow (now called NHS Greater Glasgow and Clyde).

Financial reporting

The revised structure of NHSScotland – namely, the introduction of RAB and NHS boards – has resulted in a new financial reporting system based on unified reporting within NHS board areas.

The introduction of resource accounting has led to changes in the prime financial statements used by NHS boards. Under resource accounting, NHS boards are subject to revenue and capital resource limits, and are no longer controlled by cash.

For monthly reporting purposes, the forms are as follows:

- Operating cost statement – this broadly follows the format of the statement of operating costs proposed by the resource accounting manual. It requires similar disclosure to the former income and expenditure account
- Revenue resource analysis – designed to provide the additional information required by the SGHD, this analysis must be completed by all NHS boards and special NHS boards
- Balance sheet – provides an analysis of total assets and liabilities held by each NHS board
- Statement of cash flows – designed to allow the SGHD to review the cash position of each NHS board and NHSScotland as a whole. NHS boards are required to complete their respective cash flows for each period and disclose forecasts for each month up until the year-end
- Capital resource analysis – this is used to monitor the flow of capital funds from source to application by NHS boards. Funds donated for the purchase of capital assets and those purchases should be excluded from the report
- Family health services (FHS) receipts and payments.

Corporate Governance and Audit

Audit Scotland

The audit of NHSScotland is the responsibility of the Auditor General for Scotland (AGS). The AGS is supported by Audit Scotland, which commissions audits from its own staff and commercial firms of auditors.

Audit Scotland is a statutory body set up in April 2000, under the *Public Finance and Accountability (Scotland) Act, 2000*. It provides services to the Accounts Commission and the AGS.

External and internal audit arrangements

NHS boards maintain an internal audit function to carry out more detailed work at local level. NHS boards may provide internal audit themselves, by means of a consortium arrangement with neighbouring boards, or contract out to private firms.

Counter fraud services

Counter Fraud Services (CFS) deters, detects and investigates frauds and other irregularities by FHS contractors and patients against NHS Scotland. CFS is hosted within the NHS National Services Scotland, and has links with every NHS board through partnership agreements and nominated fraud liaison officers. As partnership agreements develop, the role of CFS will extend to cover all aspects of boards' service delivery including acute hospitals and NHS staff.

Performance audits

Audit Scotland is responsible for carrying out performance audits (formerly known as value for money audits). The AGS also produces an annual overview of the performance of the NHS in Scotland, which provides information on a range of performance measures – clinical outcomes, waiting times, workforce issues and financial performance.

Risk assessment

Governance in NHSScotland has resulted in an emphasis on risk management.

The clinical negligence and other risks indemnity scheme (CNORIS) was launched in 2000 with mandatory membership for all health bodies. The scheme has two principal aims:

- Financial efficiency through cost effective risk pooling and claims management
- Effective risk management by encouraging a rigorous approach to the treatment of risk.

Endowment Funds

Legal arrangements

As with trust or charitable funds in England and Wales, endowment funds are derived from donations by individuals, legacies etc. The pre-1948 funds are still held centrally in Scotland under the Scottish Hospitals Trust, which distributes funds each year on a bed basis.

Scottish structure

Endowment funds are used for the purpose for which the original donation was given where that is known. Endowment funds are held and controlled by NHS boards whose members are ex officio appointed by the Cabinet Secretary.

Further information on endowment funds can be found in the HFMA Scotland publication *NHS Endowment Funds in Scotland.*

References and Further Reading

On line information from NHSScotland: www.show.scot.nhs.uk/

Introductory Guide to NHS Finance in Scotland, HFMA Scotland: www.hfma.org.uk/Branches/Scotland/

Partnership for Care – Scotland's Health White Paper, 2003: www.scotland.gov.uk/Publications/2003/02/16476/18730

Our National Health: A Plan for Action, a Plan for Change, 2000: www.scotland.gov.uk/Publications/2000/12/7770/File-1

Delivering for Health, 2005: www.scotland.gov.uk/Publications/2005/11/02102635/26356

Building a Health Service Fit for the Future, 2005:
www.scotland.gov.uk/Publications/2005/05/23141307/13104

Better Health, Better Care, 2007: www.scotland.gov.uk/Publications/2008/01/29152311/0

Public Finance and Accountability (Scotland) Act 2000:
www.opsi.gov.uk/legislation/scotland/acts2000/asp_20000001_en_1

Community Care and Health (Scotland) Act 2002:
www.oqps.gov.uk/legislation/acts/acts2002/asp_20020005_en_1

National Health Service Reform (Scotland) Act 2004:
www.opsi.gov.uk/legislation/scotland/acts2004/asp_20040007_en_1

Fair Shares for All, 2000: www.scotland.gov.uk/Publications/2005/10/19142752/27522

The NHS and Community Care Act 1990:
www.opsi.gov.uk/acts/acts1990/ukpga_19900019_en_1

Scottish Health Service Costs Book, Information Services Division:
www.isdscotland.org/isd/797.html

NHS National Services Scotland: www.nhsnss.org/

Audit Scotland: www.audit-scotland.gov.uk/

Clinical Negligence and other Risks Indemnity Scheme (CNORIS): www.cnoris.com/

NHS Endowment Funds in Scotland, HFMA Scotland: www.hfma.org.uk/Branches/Scotland/

19. The NHS in Wales

Introduction

The Welsh Assembly Government has responsibility for health and social care in Wales. It comprises a cabinet of Welsh ministers led by the First Minister who is appointed by the Crown. Cabinet responsibility for the NHS in Wales rests with the Minister for Health and Social Services.

The National Assembly for Wales consists of 60 elected Assembly Members. Its role is to scrutinise how Welsh ministers exercise their executive functions and the Welsh Assembly Government's budget. Detailed scrutiny of health matters is undertaken by the Assembly's Health, Wellbeing and Local Government Committee.

Under the *Government of Wales Act 2006*, the National Assembly is also able to seek powers from the UK Parliament to pass laws for Wales, called *Assembly Measures*, in the areas for which it has devolved responsibility, such as health.

While many of the principles underpinning NHS finance in Wales are similar to those in England this chapter looks at the key differences.

Health and Social Care Strategy in Wales

Designed for Life

Designed for Life was published in May 2005 as the Welsh Assembly Government's strategy for health and social care for Wales in the 21st century. It builds upon the 2001 NHS Plan – *Improving Health in Wales: a Plan for the NHS with its Partners* – and also frames the Assembly government's response to *Health Challenge Wales* and the *2003 Health and Social Care Review*, advised by Sir Derek Wanless.

The strategy sets out a vision for the kind of health and social care services the people of Wales can expect by 2015. It aims to:

- Improve health and reduce, and where possible eliminate, inequalities in health
- Support the role of citizens in promoting their health, individually and collectively
- Develop the role of local communities in creating and sustaining health
- Promote independence, service user involvement and clinical and professional leadership
- Re-cast the role of all elements of health and social care so that the citizen will be seen and treated by high quality staff at home or locally – or passed quickly to excellent specialist care where this is needed
- Provide quality assured clinical treatment and care appropriate to need, and based on evidence
- Strengthen accountability, developing a more corporate approach in NHS Wales so that organisations work together rather than separately
- Ensure full public engagement at both local and national levels.

The vision is planned to be delivered through a series of strategic frameworks, each covering three years. The first framework for 2005/2008 concentrates on redesigning the provision of healthcare, maximising the benefits from information and workforce developments and reducing waiting times in line with other parts of the UK.

Fulfilled Lives, Supportive Communities

Fulfilled Lives, Supportive Communities, is a complementary strategy for social care which was published in February 2007. It is a ten year strategy covering the period 2008 to 2018, and is a major programme of change to ensure that social services are:

- Strong, accessible and accountable
- Focused on citizen, family and community needs
- Focused on social inclusion and the rights of individuals
- Concerned with good outcomes
- Delivered in a joined up, flexible and efficient way to consistently high standards and in partnership with service users.

One Wales

One Wales is the Welsh Assembly Government's progressive agenda for the government of Wales, and forms the basis of the coalition government in the National Assembly for Wales. The commitment to health is covered in the chapter on 'a healthy future', and outlines a programme for government on health, including:

- Reviewing NHS reconfiguration
- Strengthening NHS finance and management
- Developing and improving Wales's health services
- Ensuring access to healthcare
- Improving patients' experience
- Supporting social care.

One Wales includes a commitment to publicly fund, own and manage health services, and to move purposefully to end the internal market.

Organisation of the NHS in Wales

The NHS in Wales currently comprises the Welsh Assembly Government's Department for Health and Social Services, 22 local health boards and Health Commission Wales (Specialist Services) and 14 NHS trusts. From April 2008, the number of trusts will reduce to 10. The *One Wales* commitment to end the internal market is likely to lead to further organisational change.

Welsh Assembly Government – Department for Health and Social Services

The Department for Health and Social Services of the Welsh Assembly Government is responsible for both policy development of health and social care services for Wales and performance management of NHS Wales organisations. The head of the department is the chief executive and accounting officer for NHS Wales as well as being a member of the Welsh

Assembly Government's management board. The Department comprises:

- Three regional offices headed by a regional director, located in North, Mid and West, and South East Wales, supporting and monitoring the performance of NHS trusts and local health boards, ensuring the delivery of the health agenda, supporting the health and social care interface and other relevant Assembly government initiatives
- Three policy divisions covering children and families; older people and long term care; and community, primary care and health services policy
- Three supporting divisions covering service delivery and performance; quality standards and improvements; and resources.

The Department interfaces with the Assembly's chief medical officer and chief nursing officer through the Department's management board.

Health Commission Wales (Specialist Services)

Health Commission Wales (Specialist Services) is an executive agency of the National Assembly for Wales and has responsibility for commissioning specialist services and certain all-Wales services, including NHS Direct and emergency ambulance services.

Health Commission Wales prepares an annual commissioning plan and is expected to operate within its resource limit.

Local health boards

The 22 local health boards[12] are coterminous with unitary local authority boundaries and have a statutory duty to work in partnership with local government. The boards are accountable for:

- Assessing the health needs of the people in their catchment area and, in conjunction with their local authority and other partners, developing health and well-being strategies
- Addressing those needs by sourcing and providing local primary healthcare services, community and intermediate care services and secondary care services.

In addition to these responsibilities, Powys Local Health Board provides community and intermediate care services.

Local health boards have a statutory duty to keep within their resource and capital limits. In addition they are expected to achieve a 95% compliance rate with the *Better Payment Practice Code*.

NHS trusts

There are currently 14 NHS trusts in Wales, which will reduce to ten 10 from April 2008. Twelve trusts (eight from April 2008) provide integrated secondary and community care on a

---

[12] As this guide went to press the Welsh Assembly Government issued a consultation paper that – inter alia – proposes a reduction in the number of local health boards from 22 to 8.

geographical basis. Velindre NHS Trust provides specialist cancer services for South Wales, as well as hosting several all-Wales services, including the National Public Health Service, the Welsh Blood Service, all-Wales screening services and the IT service, Health Solutions Wales. The Welsh Ambulance Services NHS Trust provides emergency and non-emergency ambulance services.

As with England, NHS trusts have a statutory duty to break-even, which is measured on an annual basis. They are also expected to keep within their external financing limits and achieve a 95% compliance rate with the *Better Payment Practice Code*. Unlike NHS trusts in England, trusts in Wales are not required to keep within capital resource limits.

The *Health and Social Care (Community Health and Standards) Act 2003* does not provide the Assembly with the delegated powers to introduce NHS foundation trusts in Wales, and there is currently no intention on the part of the Assembly to seek such powers.

Funding and Allocations

Funding

NHS Wales is funded by the Welsh Assembly Government, not the Department of Health. The Welsh Assembly Government receives funds voted by the UK Parliament via the Secretary of State for Wales.

Any changes to the funding provided to the Department for Health for the NHS in England will be matched by an increase in the Welsh Assembly Government's funding through the Barnett formula, but it is for the Welsh Assembly Government to determine how this funding is applied. This is done through an annual budget planning round which allocates funding to the sectors for which the Welsh Assembly Government has responsibility. The budget is formally presented to the National Assembly for approval in an annual budget motion.

Funding for the NHS in Wales is contained within the Assembly's health and social services main expenditure group, which is the largest expenditure group and comprises approximately 40% of the Assembly's total budget. The Department for Health and Social Services issues annual revenue allocations to local health boards and Health Commission Wales.

Revenue allocation process

Each local health board has a unified allocation that separately identifies funding for hospital and community health services, general medical services, prescribing, pharmacy and dental contracts. Health Commission Wales has an allocation for hospital and community services.

The revenue allocation includes a 'national finance agreement', which details the levels of baseline cost increases to be taken into account in financial planning and long-term agreement (LTA) negotiations. The Agreement details the attribution of financial risk for cost increases between local health boards, Health Commission Wales, and NHS trusts.

Progress is being made towards allocating funds to local health board areas using the direct needs formula, derived from Professor Townsend's 2001 report *Targeting Poor Health*. In October 2005, an NHS Resource Allocation Expert Group was established to advise on the development and maintenance of the direct needs formula. The group has undertaken a review of the data used in the formula, and is planning to consult on changes to the formula early in 2008.

The timescale for full implementation of the formula is determined by annual decisions made by the Minister for Health and Social Services. These decisions depend on the availability of growth funding which is allocated on a differential basis to those boards whose current allocations are furthest below target shares.

The flow of funds from local health boards and Health Commission Wales to provider NHS trusts is managed through LTAs. Unlike England, these agreements are currently based on locally agreed prices and not on a national tariff.

Financial flows review

The Department for Health and Social Services is undertaking a review of the financial mechanisms used to allocate funding to NHS Wales and to regulate the flow of funds from commissioners to providers. It will ensure that funding rewards efficient, effective and quality care, and will link funding to outcomes. The new mechanisms developed by the review will become operational from April 2009.

The success of the review is dependent on an improvement in the quality and consistency of NHS financial information. In December 2005 the then Department for Health and Social Care produced a *Financial Information Strategy*. A programme unit was established in April 2007 to take forward the objectives of the *Strategy* and to project manage the financial flows review.

Welsh NHS trusts are required to produce annual specialty cost returns and healthcare resource group (HRG) cost returns. An annual cost efficiency index of Welsh NHS trusts is published by the Department for Health and Social Services using the specialty cost and HRG cost returns. Local health boards and Health Commission Wales are required to analyse costs over the 23 programme budget categories, based on version 10 of the *International Classification of Diseases*.

Capital funding

NHS trusts are provided with a level of capital they can use for discretionary schemes below their delegated limit. £2m is the delegated limit for most trusts in Wales, but this can be increased to £8m for trusts with accredited capital planning processes.

Trusts are required to submit business cases for funding for major capital schemes above delegated limits using the *Five Case Model*. The Department for Health and Social Services has established an Investment Policy and Appraisal Group (IPAG) to provide support to trusts in the development of business cases, and also to scrutinise cases at all stages of their development. All major capital schemes are also required to undertake 'gateway reviews' using the process developed by the Office of Government Commerce.

Trusts are allowed to retain sale proceeds from the disposal of assets up to their delegated limit.

As with other parts of the public sector, the Welsh Assembly Government and NHS Wales are not able to vire funds between capital and revenue allocations.

As in England, the NHS in Wales is required to examine the possibility of using the private finance initiative (PFI) or public-private partnership schemes as an alternative source of capital for major schemes. However, the Welsh Assembly Government has imposed strict criteria on the categories of staff that can be transferred to private contractors in PFI deals. The current position is that most major capital investment in NHS Wales is being financed from public capital.

Strategic Planning and Performance Management

Local health boards are required to prepare three-year health, social care and well-being strategies in partnership with local authorities, NHS trusts and the voluntary sector. The strategies are based on an assessment of population needs. The current strategies cover the period from April 2005 to March 2008.

The Department of Health and Social Services issues an *Annual Operating Framework* for the NHS in Wales. This sets out the ministerial and other priorities that the NHS has to achieve in the year from within the revenue allocation. In response, health communities, comprising a geographically based partnership of local health boards and NHS trusts, are required to prepare an annual operating framework (AOF) for approval by the Assembly government's regional office. A health community or organisation that is unable to deliver a balanced financial plan is required to prepare a financial recovery plan for approval by the relevant regional office and the Department for Health and Social Services.

The performance management framework for NHS Wales is based on performance agreements derived from the AOF process, as well as the use of a balanced scorecard approach.

Lead responsibility for performance management of NHS organisations lies with the three regional offices. A delivery and support unit, hosted by Bro Morgannwg NHS Trust, has been established to provide direct intervention and support to organisations failing to achieve service and financial targets. Support to NHS organisations is also provided by the National Leadership and Innovation Agency in Healthcare.

Financial Accounting and Control

The format and presentation of statutory accounts for the NHS in Wales is similar to that for trusts and primary care trusts (PCTs) in England. The Welsh Assembly Government produces separate *Manuals for Accounts* for local health boards (similar to PCT accounts) and NHS trusts.

The individual accounts of local health boards and NHS trusts are summarised into two consolidated NHS accounts that are then subject to independent audit and scrutiny by the Wales Audit Office.

Each NHS organisation is also required to submit monthly monitoring statements reporting on actual financial performance and forecast outturn. This is supplemented by a detailed commentary from the director of finance detailing assumptions and risks behind the reported position. The overall position is monitored by the Department for Health and Social Services. The Minister will occasionally make a statement to the Assembly on the financial position of the NHS in Wales.

Corporate Governance and Audit

The external audit arrangements in Wales are different to England. The Wales Audit Office was created in April 2005 and the Auditor General for Wales is now responsible for auditing all public accounts and laying them before the Assembly.

Each NHS organisation is responsible for providing an effective internal audit service to meet NHS minimum audit standards. All NHS bodies are required to submit a statement on internal control as part of their annual accounts. Accountable officers (i.e. chief executives) are required to sign the statement on behalf of the board.

In May 2005, the Welsh Assembly Government published the *Healthcare Standards for Wales*. These provide a common framework to support the NHS and partner organisations in providing effective, timely and quality services across all healthcare settings. The standards are used by Healthcare Inspectorate Wales (HIW) as part of their processes for assessing the quality, safety and effectiveness of healthcare providers and commissioners across Wales. Existing Welsh risk management standards, which were developed by the Welsh Risk Pool, were incorporated into the self-assessment process for the *Healthcare Standards* during 2007.

Each NHS body must have an audit committee to oversee the governance and assurance processes for the organisation.

Capital Charging

Capital charging mechanisms operate in Wales along similar lines to those in England. The basis of valuation, determination of asset lives and the method of calculating capital charges are largely consistent between the two countries. Funding for NHS trusts' capital charges is included in the revenue allocations to local health boards and Health Commission Wales. The Welsh Assembly Government is undertaking a review of the capital charges regime during 2008/09.

Charitable Funds

Charitable funds are held by NHS trusts in Wales under the same legislative framework as exists in England. All funds are registered with the Charity Commission with the executive and non-executive directors of authorities and NHS trusts controlling the funds as trustees. Accounts must be submitted to the Charity Commission and individual bodies are responsible for compliance with the Commission's and charities accounting requirements.

References and Further Reading

Welsh Assembly Government Health web pages: http://new.wales.gov.uk/topics/health/?lang=en

Health of Wales Information Service: www.wales.nhs.uk

Government of Wales Act 2006: www.opsi.gov.uk/ACTS/acts2006/ukpga_20060032_en_1

Designed for Life – Creating World Class Health and Social Care in Wales for the 21st Century, Welsh Assembly Government, 2005: www.wales.nhs.uk/documents/designed-for-life-e.pdf

Improving Health in Wales: a Plan for the NHS with its Partners, Welsh Assembly Government, 2001: www.wales.nhs.uk/Publications/NHSStrategydoc.pdf

The Review of Health and Social Care in Wales (advised by Sir Derek Wanless): www.wales.nhs.uk/documents/wanless-review-e.pdf

Fulfilled Lives, Supportive Communities, Welsh Assembly Government, 2007: http://new.wales.gov.uk/consultations/closed/healandsoccarecloscons/952063/?lang=en

One Wales: http://wales.gov.uk/about/strategy/strategypublications/strategypubs/onewales/?lang=en

Health Commission (Specialist Services) Wales: http://new.wales.gov.uk/topics/health/hcw/?lang=en

Better Payment Practice Code: www.payontime.co.uk/

Health and Social Care (Community Health and Standards) Act 2003: www.opsi.gov.uk/Acts/acts2003/ukpga_20030043_en_1

Targeting Poor Health: Professor Townsend's Report of the Welsh Assembly's National Steering Group on the Allocation of NHS Resources, 2001: www.wales.nhs.uk/publications/TargetingPoorHealth_ENGLISH.pdf

Office of Government Commerce: www.ogc.gov.uk

Public Sector Business Cases using the Five Case Model: a toolkit, HFMA, 2007: www.hfma.org.uk

National Leadership and Innovation Agency in Healthcare: www.wales.nhs.uk/sites3/home.cfm?OrgID=484

Wales Audit Office: www.wao.gov.uk/

Healthcare Standards for Wales: www.wales.nhs.uk/sites3/home.cfm?OrgID=465

Charitable Funds: www.charity-commission.gov.uk

20. Health and Social Care in Northern Ireland

Introduction

The primary difference between the NHS in England and services in Northern Ireland is that in Northern Ireland health services and social care are integrated. The Department of Health, Social Services and Public Safety (DHSSPS) is one of the eleven government departments formed to administer the responsibilities devolved to the Northern Ireland Assembly which, after a period of suspension from October 2002, was restored in May 2007.

A *Review of Public Administration* (RPA), initiated by 'direct rule' ministers while the Northern Ireland Assembly was suspended, reached a conclusion in March 2006. It was a comprehensive examination of the arrangements for the administration and delivery of public services in Northern Ireland, covering over 150 bodies, including the 26 district councils, the health and social services boards and trusts, the five education and library boards and about 100 other public bodies. The Northern Ireland Assembly was restored while the results of the RPA were in the process of implementation, and a number of planned changes were deferred until Northern Ireland ministers had the opportunity to consider the proposals afresh.

Department of Health, Social Services and Public Safety

The DHSSPS was established by the *Departments (NI) Order 1999* and is the largest of all Northern Ireland Departments. In 2007/08 the Department's budget was £4bn – two fifths of the budget assigned to Northern Ireland. Of this, £3,451bn was budgeted for health and social care (including family health services).

The DHSSPS's current remit covers policy and legislation relating to:

- Health and social care (this includes hospitals, family practitioner services, community health and social services)
- Public health (to promote and protect the health and well-being of the population of Northern Ireland)
- Public safety (this includes the Fire Authority, food safety and emergency planning).

The DHSSPS's mission (as stated on its website) is to 'improve the health and social well-being of the people of Northern Ireland. It endeavours to do so by ensuring the provision of appropriate health and social care services, both in clinical settings, such as hospitals and GPs' surgeries, and in the community, through nursing, social work and other professional services. It also supports programmes of health promotion and education to encourage the community to adopt activities, behaviours and attitudes which will lead to better health and well-being'.

Health and social care (formerly referred to as HPSS or HSS) in Northern Ireland are the responsibility of the Minister for Health, Social Services and Public Safety.

The permanent secretary is also chief executive of the health and social care system, as well as principal accounting officer for all the Department's responsibilities. Within the Department, the key business groups are the Resources and Performance Management Group, the Healthcare Policy Group, the Social Policy Group and the Office of the Chief Medical Officer. The Department also has a Modernisation Directorate and a Human Resources Directorate. The Department has one executive agency, the Northern Ireland Health and Social Services Estate Agency (known as Health Estates). Additionally, until the necessary legislation is passed, the Health and Social Care Authority (designate) is located within the Department.

HSS Boards

Northern Ireland currently has four health and social services boards (HSS boards) – Eastern, Northern, Southern and Western. As agents of the DHSSPS, they assess needs, plan, commission and purchase health and social care services for their resident populations from a range of providers, including health and social care (HSC) trusts, voluntary agencies and private sector bodies. Following the report of the RPA, a regional Health and Social Care Authority (HSCA) designate was established, which was to supersede the four HSS Boards and incorporate some of the functions of the Department. Following the restoration of the Northern Ireland Assembly, these plans were reviewed afresh and final decisions are awaited as to what form the regional function may take. The four boards are expected to demise in 2009, their functions to be superseded by a regional organisation.

For each board area there is currently a Health and Social Services Council which is responsible for:

• Representing the public's views and interests
• Reviewing the work of health and social services
• Recommending any improvements needed.

These four bodies are to be replaced by a new Patient Client Council in 2008.

HSC Trusts

There are now six HSC trusts in Northern Ireland, offering a range of (acute and community services) services and a regional ambulance service. This resulted from a merger of trusts from April 2007 when 18 trusts became five, with the Ambulance Trust continuing as pre April 2007. The five merged trusts now comprise the Belfast, South Eastern, Southern, Western, and Northern HSC trusts. More information is available from the Department's website: www.healthandcareni.net/

HSS Agencies

A variety of specialist functions are carried out by HSS agencies on a Northern Ireland-wide basis. These agencies include:

• Northern Ireland Central Services Agency
• Northern Ireland Cancer Screening
• Northern Ireland Blood Transfusion Agency
• Northern Ireland Regional Medical Physics Agency

- Northern Ireland Guardian Ad Litem Agency
- Regulation and Quality Improvement Authority
- Health Promotion Agency.

These agencies establish service and budget agreements with the various boards and trusts for the delivery of specialist services to each HSC organisation. The future plans for the Central Services Agency are currently with the Minister for decision.

Local Commissioning

Local health and social care groups (LHSCGs) were established in April 2002, to coincide with the end of the previous GP fund holding scheme. There were 15 groups. Under the RPA these were replaced with effect from April 2007 by seven local commissioning groups (LCGs). These were planned to be committees of the HSCA with delegated power to commission services. LCGs are primary care led with 15 members, two of whom are lay people from the local community. The LCGs are to be the leaders and decision takers for commissioning, accountable to the HSCA board. These arrangements are also subject to fresh review and may be changed in due course (see the section on the commissioning process later in this chapter).

Funding and Allocations

The process through which resources are allocated to health and social care changed significantly following devolution of responsibilities to the Northern Ireland Assembly.

Overall public sector funding for Northern Ireland is provided via the Northern Ireland block vote, as part of the national spending reviews. Changes to the total provision for Northern Ireland are largely determined through the principle of comparability, whereby the Treasury adjusts the Northern Ireland block vote in line with comparable programmes in England.

The Northern Ireland Assembly has the discretion to allocate devolved resources within the Northern Ireland block across all departmental spending programmes. The DHSSPS sets its proposed allocations in the context of the Minister's overall priorities and objectives for the Department's public expenditure programme. Spending on HSC equates to approximately 40% of the total public expenditure within the control of the Northern Ireland Assembly.

The DHSSPS makes direct allocations to HSS boards for revenue for hospital and community health and social care services. Capital allocations are made directly to boards and agencies while trusts receive their capital allocation through the external financing limit (EFL) mechanism from the DHSSPS.

A weighted capitation revenue allocation formula is used to determine target allocations to HSS boards for hospital, community and personal social services on a programme of care basis. Separate allocations are given to boards for certain general medical services.

Substantial resources are also set aside for primary health services. These areas are subject to indicative budgets (particularly in the area of prescribing) and performance against budget is closely monitored.

The Commissioning Process

In Northern Ireland, service and budget agreements between commissioners and providers are broadly similar to those in other parts of the UK. At present, HSS boards commission the full range of health and social services from HSC trusts. The trusts, in turn, may contract with independent sector providers, principally for community care services. These latter arrangements are legal contracts rather than NHS service agreements.

The financial and governance regime is currently being reviewed in a project led by the Department. In February 2008, the Minister for Health announced his proposals for the reform of health and social care services, after a long period of consideration. The consultation paper (*Proposals for Health and Social Care Reform*) includes a proposal that a new Regional Health and Social Care Board will be established, answerable to the Minister. The new board's remit would be to focus on the following core areas:

- Commissioning – planning and resourcing of services from the five trusts and other organisations, to best meet the needs of the local population
- Financial management of the health and social care system
- Performance management and improvement – to ensure the delivery of targets, objectives and standards and improved safety and the creation and promotion of a culture of continuous development.

The consultation document also proposes:

- The establishment of five local commissioning groups to cover the same geographical areas as the five HSC trusts. These LCGs would operate as committees of the new Regional Board
- That the DHSSPS will be reduced in size and remit, with a focus on bringing forward legislation and policy development and advice
- The establishment of a 'shared services' organisation, designed to bring together services which are common, such as finance and recruitment of staff.

The consultation process ends in mid May 2008 and the intention is that the reforms will be implemented from April 2009.

Financial Accounting and Control

Currently HSS boards and HSC trusts prepare annual accounts in formats prescribed by the DHSSPS. For 2007/08 they are prepared using existing UK GAAP based accounting policies. From 2009/10 they will be produced using international financial reporting standards (IFRS).

The annual accounts are audited by the Northern Ireland Audit Office (NIAO), either by their own staff, or by contracting out to private sector firms of accountants and auditors. Each set of accounts is then formally laid before the Northern Ireland Assembly. The Assembly has a Public Accounts Committee (PAC) with a similar role to the committee of the House of Commons of similar title.

Under the 'faster closing' initiative, the deadlines for submission of accounts have been moved forward in the last two years, and will be further tightened for 2007/08.

The DHSSPS issues detailed *Manuals of Accounts* for boards and trusts, which are updated annually as required to reflect changes in reporting requirements.

Financial targets

HSS boards and trusts have different financial targets. HSS boards must stay within their resource allocation while trusts have four targets:

- Breaking even
- Remaining within their external financing limit (EFL)
- Achieving a 3.5% capital cost absorption rate on relevant net assets
- Staying within their capital resource limit (CRL).

Corporate Governance and Audit

The corporate governance regime is similar to that in place in the rest of the UK, including codes of conduct, accountability and openness, remuneration committees, audit committees, internal audit, external audit, board reports, annual accounts, annual report and annual public meetings.

External audit of the accounts of HSS boards and HSC trusts is the responsibility of the NIAO. A number of audits are contracted out to private sector accountancy and audit firms.

HSC bodies are required to have in place suitable internal audit arrangements. This service is provided on an in-service basis at present by four internal audit shared services. Internal audit must comply with HM Treasury's *Government Internal Audit Standards* issued in Northern Ireland in 2002, which are essentially the same as the *NHS Internal Audit Standards*. The adequacy of these arrangements is reviewed and reported on each year by the NIAO as part of their report to those charged with governance of each body.

Following the changes in HSC arrangements, it is proposed to merge internal audit services into one, strengthened, regional service.

Private Finance Initiative

The private finance initiative in HSC in Northern Ireland follows the same principles as in England with the underlying aim of achieving value for money and demonstrating a transfer of risk to the private sector. Treasury guidance must be adhered to.

Charitable Funds

Charitable funds are held by HSC trusts and boards in Northern Ireland and are derived, for example, from donations by individuals or legacies.

As in England and Wales these funds are used for the purpose for which the original donation was given, or bequest made, where that is known, unless the uses to which the funds can be put is unrestricted. Charitable funds are held and controlled by HSC trusts and boards as corporate trustees.

At present one of the main differences from the regime in England is that Northern Ireland does not have a Charities Commission. Legislation to establish a Charities Commission, inter alia (*The Charities (NI) Order 2007*), was in progress through Parliament in 2007 when the Assembly was restored.

References and Further Reading

Review of Public Administration: www.dhsspsni.gov.uk/index/hss/rpa-home.htm

Northern Ireland Agencies: www.n-i.nhs.uk/index.php?link=agencies

For details about current structures visit: www.dhsspsni.gov.uk

Health and Social Care in Northern Ireland: www.n-i.nhs.uk

Proposals for Health and Social Care Reform (consultation paper), 2008: www.dhsspsni.gov.uk/index/hss/rpa-home.htm

Northern Ireland Audit Office: www.niauditoffice.gov.uk

Northern Ireland Public Accounts Committee: www.niassembly.gov.uk/public/accounts.htm

Internal Audit Standards, 2002: www.dfpni.gov.uk/audit_standards.pdf

Charitable funds – via the Department for Social Development: www.dsdni.gov.uk

Tables

NHS Expenditure (estimated outturn), 2006/07 (England) £ million

Source: Department of Health Departmental Report, 2007 (table 9.1):
www.dh.gov.uk/en/Publicationsandstatistics/Publications/AnnualReports/DH_074767

	NHS Hospitals, Community Health, Family Health (discretionary) & Related Services & NHS Trusts	Family Health Services (non-discretionary)	Central Health and Misc. Services (including departmental admin)	NHS Total
	£m	£m	£m	£m
Current Expenditure				
Gross	79,427	1,411	1,653	82,492
Charges & receipts	−3,780	−409	−175	−4,363
Net	75,647	1,002	1,478	78,128
Capital Expenditure				
Gross	4,099	0	52	4,151
Charges & receipts	−606	0	0	−606
Net	3,492	0	52	3,544
Total				
Gross	83,532	1,411	1,705	86,642
Charges & receipts	−4,386	−409	−175	−4,970
Net	79,140	1,002	1,530	81,672

Hospital Activity Trends (England) in Finished Consultant Episodes (thousands): Inpatients

Source: Department of Health Departmental Report, 2007 (table 3.4):
www.dh.gov.uk/en/Publicationsandstatistics/Publications/AnnualReports/DH_074767

	2000/01	2001/02	2002/03	2003/04	2004/05	2005/06
General & acute – elective	5,045	5,080	5,308	5,492	5,607	5,732
General & acute – emergency & other	3,949	3,968	4,014	4,282	4,504	4,700
Geriatric	359	347	357	357	368	361
Maternity	896	877	924	970	1,000	1,038

Hospital Activity Trends (England) in Finished Consultant Episodes (thousands): New Outpatients

Source: Department of Health Departmental Report, 2007 (table 3.4):
www.dh.gov.uk/en/Publicationsandstatistics/Publications/AnnualReports/DH_074767

	2000/01	2001/02	2002/03	2003/04	2004/05	2005/06
General & acute	11,637	11,838	12,080	12,650	12,617	13,094
(of which, Geriatric)	114	115	115	125	122	131
Maternity	537	504	522	505	482	465
Mental illness	285	263	271	267	264	239
Learning disabilities	7	8	7	8	8	7
All specialties	12,466	12,613	12,879	13,431	13,370	13,805

Hospital Activity Trends (England) in Finished Consultant Episodes (thousands): New (i.e. first attenders) Accident and Emergency

Source: Department of Health Departmental Report, 2007 (table 3.4):
www.dh.gov.uk/en/Publicationsandstatistics/Publications/AnnualReports/DH_074767

Year	New Attendances
2000/01	12,953
2001/02	12,901
2002/03	13,253
2003/04	15,313
2004/05	16,712
2005/06	17,775

Extracts from NHS Staff by Occupation Code Staff Groups 1995–2005 (full time equivalents in thousands, rounded to 1 decimal place)

Source: The Information Centre's Bulletin: Staff in the NHS 1995–2005:
www.ic.nhs.uk/pubs/nhsstaff

	2000	2001	2002	2003	2004	2005
Professionally qualified clinical staff (includes doctors, ambulance staff, nursing staff, scientific, therapeutic & technical staff)	461.0	477.2	501.7	525.2	549.8	566.4
Support to clinical staff	234.7	249.2	262.7	277.2	284.4	291.7
NHS infrastructure support (includes managers, central functions, hotel, property and estates)	144.0	149.6	158.0	168.0	178.1	186.1

Net NHS Expenditure, 2006 and 2007 (England) £ million

Source: Department of Health Departmental Report, 2007 (table 9.2):
www.dh.gov.uk/en/Publicationsandstatistics/Publications/AnnualReports/DH_074767

	2006	2007
Hospital community & family health services – current	76,620	75,653
Hospital community & family health services – capital	5,180	3,492
Family health services (non-discretionary) – revenue	1,099	1,002
CHMS – revenue	1,180	1,200
CHMS – capital	23	28
Departmental administration – revenue	261	279
Departmental administration – capital	23	23
NHS Total	84,387	81,678

Family Health Services – Key Statistics on General Ophthalmic Services, England

Source: Department of Health Departmental Report, 2007 (table 3.6): www.dh.gov.uk/en/
Publicationsandstatistics/Publications/AnnualReports/DH_074767

	2001/02	2002/03	2003/04	2004/05	2005/06
Number of opticians	8,103	8,096	8,331	8,472	8,467
Number of NHS sight tests (thousands)	9,807	9,662	9,845	10,149	10,355
Number of optical vouchers (thousands)	3,607	3,472	3,520	3,624	3,678

Family Health Services – Key Statistics on General and Personal Dental Services, England

Source: Department of Health Departmental Report, 2007 (table 3.5):
www.dh.gov.uk/en/Publicationsandstatistics/Publications/AnnualReports/DH_074767

	2001/02	2002/03	2003/04	2004/05	2005/06
Number of general & personal dental practitioners	18,821	19,056	19,339	19,722	20,890
Number of patients registered (thousands)					
Adults	17,281	17,064	17,374	17,237	17,670
Children	6,982	6,841	6,964	6,891	7,044
Number of courses of treatment (thousands), adults	26,637	26,726	27,049	26,488	25,844
Number of courses of treatment (thousands), children	161	217	257	945	2,945

NHS General Medical Services: General Medical Practitioners (GPs) and Practice Staff Employed by GPs (full time equivalents rounded to 1 decimal place) as at 30th September

Source: The Information Centre's GP Bulletin: www.ic.nhs.uk/pubs/nhsstaff

	2000	2001	2002	2003	2004	2005
General practitioners (excludes GP retainers)	28.2	28.4	28.7	29.8	30.8	31.7
Practice staff						
Practice nurse	10.7	11.2	12.0	13.0	13.6	13.8
Direct patient care	1.9	2.1	2.5	3.0	3.6	4.1
Admin and clerical	49.5	51.4	51.4	52.2	53.3	53.6
Others	0.5	0.4	1.2	0.9	1.6	1.6

Abbreviations

AGS	Auditor General Scotland
AHPs	Allied Health Professionals
ALB	Arm's Length Body
ALE	Auditors' Local Evaluation
AME	Annually Managed Expenditure
AOF	Annual Operating Framework
ASB	Accounting Standards Board
CEDR	Centre for Effective Dispute Resolution
CFISSA	Centrally Funded Initiatives Services and Special Allocations
CFS	Counter Fraud Services
CFSMS	Counter Fraud and Security Management Service
CHAI	Commission for Healthcare Audit and Inspection (now the Healthcare Commission)
CHMS	Central Health and Miscellaneous Services
CHP	Community Health Partnership
CNORIS	Clinical Negligence and other Risks Indemnity Scheme
CNST	Clinical Negligence Scheme for Trusts
CPLNHS	Commissioning a Patient-led NHS
CRL	Capital Resource Limit
CSCI	Commission for Social Care Inspection
CSR	Comprehensive Spending Review
DBFO	Design, Build, Finance, Operate
DEL	Departmental Expenditure Limit
DFT	Distance from Target
DHSC	Directorate of Health and Social Care
DHSSPS	Department of Health, Social Services and Public Safety
DRG	Diagnosis Related Group
DV	District Valuer
EACA	Emergency Ambulance Cost Adjustment
EBITDA	Earnings before Interest, Taxes and Depreciation
EEA	European Economic Area
EFL	External Financing Limit
EFR	External Finance Requirement
ESF	Enhanced Services Floor
ETP	Electronic Transmission of Prescriptions
FBC	Full Business Case
FCE	Finished Consultant Episode
FCF	Free Cash Flow
FESC	The Framework for procuring External Support for Commissioners
FHS	Family Health Services
FIMS	Financial Information Management System
FRR	Financial Risk Rating
FRS	Financial Reporting Standard
FT	NHS Foundation Trust
FTFF	Foundation Trust Financing Facility
GAAP	Generally Accepted Accounting Practice

GDP	Gross Domestic Product
GDS (nGDS)	General Dental Services Contract
GMS	General Medical Services
GP	General Practitioner
HCAI	Healthcare Associated Infections
HCFHS	Hospital, Community and Family Health Services
HCHS	Hospital and Community Health Services
HCW	Health Commission Wales
HFMA	Healthcare Financial Management Association
HIW	Healthcare Inspectorate Wales
HPA	Health Protection Agency
HR	Human Resources
HRG	Healthcare Resource Group
HSC	Health Service Circular
HSCA	Health and Social Care Authority
HSS	Health and Social Services
IBD	Interest Bearing Debt
ICT	Information and Communications Technology
IFRS	International Financial Reporting Standards
IM&T	Information Management and Technology
IPAG	Investment Policy and Appraisal Group
ISD	Information and Statistics Division
ISTC	Independent Sector Treatment Centre
ITN	Invitation to Negotiate
JSNA	Joint Strategic Needs Assessment
LAA	Local Area Agreement
LCFS	Local Counter Fraud Specialist
LCG	Local Commissioning Group
LD	Learning Disabilities
LDP	Local Delivery Plan
LHB	Local Health Board
LHCC	Local Health Care Co-operative
LHSCG	Local Health and Social Care Group
LIFT	Local Improvement Finance Trust
LSP	Local Strategic Partnership
LTA	Long Term Agreement
MADEL	Medical and Dental Education Levy
MFF	Market Forces Factor
MPET	Multi Professional Education and Training
MPIG	Minimum Practice Income Guarantee
MUR	Medicine Use Review
NAO	National Audit Office
NDPB	Non Departmental Public Body
nGMS	New General Medical Services Contract
NHSLA	National Health Service Litigation Authority
NIAO	Northern Ireland Audit Office
NICE	National Institute for Health and Clinical Excellence

NMET	Non-Medical Education and Training
NPfIT	National Programme for IT
NPV	Net Present Value
NRAC	NHSScotland Resource Allocation Centre
NRCI	National Reference Cost Index
NSF	National Service Framework
NSRC	National Schedule of Reference Costs
OBC	Outline Business Case
OFR	Operating and Financial review
OGC	Office of Government Commerce
OJEU	Official Journal of the European Union
PAC	Public Accounts Committee
PASC	Public Administration Select Committee
PBC	Practice Based Commissioning
PBL	Prudential Borrowing Limit
PbR	Payment by Results
PCT	Primary Care Trust
PDC	Public Dividend Capital
PDS (nPDS)	Personal Dental Services Contract
PEC	Professional Executive Committee
PES	Public Expenditure Survey
PfH	Partnerships for Health
PFI	Private Finance Initiative
PFU	Private Finance Unit
PLICS	Patient Level Information and Costing Systems
PMS	Primary Medical Services
PPA	Prescription Pricing Authority
PPP	Public/Private Partnership
PSA	Public Service Agreement
PSS	Personal Social Services
PU	Prescribing Unit
PUK	Partnership UK
QOF	Quality and Outcomes Framework
RAB	Resource Accounting and Budgeting
RAfDS	Revenue Available for Debt Service
RATE	Regulatory Authority for Tissues and Embryos
RPA	Review of Public Administration
RRL	Revenue Resource Limit
RS	Reporting Standard
SaFF	Service and Financial Framework
SCG	Specialist Commissioning Group
SFIs	Standing Financial Instructions
SFR	Scottish Financial Return
SGHD	Scottish Government Health and Community Care Directorate
SHA	Strategic Health Authority
SI	Statutory Instrument
SIC	Statement on Internal Control

SIFT	Service Increment for Teaching
SLM	Service Line Management
SLR	Service Line Reporting
SO	Standing Orders
SOC	Strategic Outline Case
SOFA	Statement of Financial Activities
SOP	Standard Operating Practice
SORP	Statement of Recommended Practice
SPC	Special Purpose Company
SPV	Special Purpose Vehicle
SSAP	Statement of Standard Accounting Practice
SUS	Secondary Uses Service
TME	Total Managed Expenditure
TRU	Trust Financial Monitoring and Accounts Form
UDA	Unit of Dental Activity
VFM	Value for Money
WGA	Whole of Government Accounts

Glossary of Terms

Accruals
: An accounting concept. In addition to payments and receipts of cash (and similar), adjustment is made for outstanding payments, debts to be collected, and stock (items bought, paid for but not yet used). This means that the accounts show all the income and expenditure that relates to the financial year.

Amortisation
: The process of charging the cost of an intangible asset over its useful life as opposed to recording its cost as a single entry in the income and expenditure records – equivalent to depreciation for a tangible asset. Amortisation is an accounting charge so does not involve any cash outlay.

Assets
: An item that has a value in the future. For example, a debtor (someone who owes money) is an asset, as they will in future pay. A building is an asset, because it houses activity that will provide a future income stream.

Audit
: The process of validation of the accuracy, completeness and adequacy of disclosure of financial records.

Benchmarking
: The process of comparing performance against similar organisations with a view to identifying areas of potential improvement.

Break-even (duty)
: A financial target. Although the exact definition of the target is relatively complex, in its simplest form the break-even duty requires the NHS organisation to match income and expenditure, i.e. make neither a profit nor a loss.

Business cases
: A formal process (in written form) for identifying the financial and qualitative implications of options for changing services and/or investing in capital.

Business plan
: Also known as a service or operational plan, the business plan is the written end product of a process to identify the aims and objectives, and the resource requirements of an organisation over the next three to five year period. Generally business plans cover the forthcoming year in greater detail than those periods further in the future.

Capital
: In most businesses, capital refers either to shareholder investment funds, or buildings, land and equipment owned by a business that has the potential to earn income in the future. The NHS uses this second definition, but adds a further condition – that the cost of the building/ equipment must exceed £5,000. Capital is thus an asset (or group of functionally interdependent assets), with a useful life expectancy of greater than one year, whose cost exceeds £5,000.

Capital charges	Capital charges are a device for ensuring that the cost associated with owning capital is recognised in the accounts. A charge is made to the income and expenditure account on all capital assets except donated assets and those with a zero net book value. The capital charge comprises depreciation, and a return similar to debt interest. This rate of return is set by the Treasury and is currently 3.5%.
Capital cost absorption	The process whereby the cost of capital (see capital charges above) is taken account of fully ('absorbed') in an organisation's costs.
Capital resource limit (CRL)	An expenditure limit determined by the Department of Health for each NHS organisation limiting the amount that may be expended on capital purchases, as assessed on an accruals basis (i.e. after adjusting for debtors and creditors).
Comprehensive spending review (CSR)	A cyclical review undertaken by the Treasury to distribute public funding between the main governmental departments.
Cost centre	Rather than record every cost incurred separately costs are categorised into a number of distinct headings referred to as 'cost centres'. Usually cost centres are in line with an organisation's budget heads.
Cost improvement programme	The identification of schemes to reduce expenditure/increase efficiency.
Current assets	Debtors, stocks, cash or similar – i.e. assets that are, or can be converted into, cash within the next twelve months.
Depreciation	The process of charging the cost of an asset over its useful life as opposed to recording its cost as a single entry in the income and expenditure records. Depreciation is an accounting charge (i.e. it does not involve any cash outlay). Accumulated depreciation is the extent to which depreciation has been charged in successive years' income and expenditure accounts since the acquisition of the asset.
Direct costs	Direct costs are costs that can be directly attributed to a particular activity or output. For example, the cost of a radiographer is a direct cost to the radiology department, but an indirect cost to general surgery (as radiology serves several departments).
External financing limit (EFL)	A cash limit on net external financing set by the Department of Health. It is the difference between what a trust plans to spend on capital in a year and what it can generate internally from its own resources. The EFL is designed to control the cash expenditure of the NHS as a whole to the level agreed by Parliament in the public expenditure control totals.

Financial reporting standard (FRS)	Issued by the Accounting Standards Board, financial reporting standards govern the accounting treatment and accounting policies adopted by organisations. Generally these standards apply to NHS organisations.
Fixed assets	Land, buildings or equipment that are expected to generate income for a period exceeding one year.
Fixed cost	A cost which does not increase or decrease with changes in activity level.
General medical services	Medical services provided by general practitioners (as opposed to dental, ophthalmic and pharmaceutical services provided by other clinical professions).
Generic cost pressure	An increase in cost that is generally beyond the control of individual health organisations. These may also be referred to as 'national cost pressures', and include items such as national changes to the rate of employers' pension contributions.
Governance	Governance (or corporate governance) is the system by which organisations are directed and controlled. It is concerned with how an organisation is run – how it structures itself and how it is led. Governance should underpin all that an organisation does. In the NHS this means it must encompass clinical, financial and organisational aspects.
Gross domestic product (GDP)	A measure of the value of national economic activity.
Healthcare resource group (HRG)	HRGs are the 'currency' used to collate the costs of procedures/ diagnoses into common groupings to which tariffs can be applied. HRGs place these procedures and/or diagnoses into bands, which are 'resource homogenous', that is, clinically similar and consuming similar levels of resources.
Indexation	A process of adjusting the value, normally of fixed assets, to account for inflation.
Indirect costs	Indirect costs are costs that cannot be attributed directly to a particular activity or cost centre – see direct costs for an example.
Intangible asset	Goodwill, brand value or some other right, which although invisible is likely to generate financial benefit (income) for its owner in future, and for which you might be willing to pay.
Investment appraisal	The process that determines how an asset should be purchased – for example, using public capital funding, PFI or leasing.

Local cost pressure	An increase in cost that, although it may or may not be geographically widespread, is considered to be within the control of individual elements of the NHS.
Marginal cost	The increase/decrease in cost caused by the increase/decrease in activity by one unit.
Medical and dental education levy	The medical and dental levy is an income stream, or funding received from the deanery for the cost of providing the education element of junior medical staffing costs.
Net book value	The value of items (assets) as recorded in the balance sheet of an organisation. The net book value takes into consideration the replacement cost of an asset and the accumulated depreciation (i.e. the extent to which that asset has been 'consumed' by its use in productive processes).
Overheads	Overhead costs are those costs that contribute to the general running of the organisation but cannot be directly related to an activity or service. For example, the total heating costs of a hospital may be apportioned to individual departments using floor area or cubic capacity.
Prudential borrowing limit	The maximum cumulative borrowing that an NHS trust may have to fund additional capital investment.
Payment by results	A financial framework in which providers are paid according to the level of activity undertaken. Payment is based upon a national tariff system.
Private finance initiative	A form of public/private partnership designed to fund major capital investments without immediate recourse to public money. The public sector works with private sector partners who are contracted to design and build the assets needed.
Public dividend capital	This is a form of long-term government finance on which the NHS trust pays dividends to the Exchequer. It carries an expected return of 3.5% – this percentage figure is generally regarded as the long-term cost of capital in the public sector.
Public private partnership	See private finance initiative and chapter 10 of the guide.
Reference costs	NHS organisations are required to submit a schedule of costs of healthcare resource groups to allow direct comparison of the relative costs of different providers. The results are published each year in the National Schedule of Reference Costs.
Revenue	On-going or recurring costs or funding for the provision of services.

Semi-fixed cost	A cost whose magnitude is only partly affected by the level of activity – i.e. although there is a relationship between activity and expenditure, it is not directly proportional. Semi-fixed costs tend to stay the same until an activity increases above a certain level. They are sometimes referred to as 'step costs'.
Service increment for teaching	Payment from central resources to recognise the excess costs incurred in hospitals providing medical training.
Tangible asset	A sub-classification of fixed assets, to exclude invisible items such as goodwill and brand values. Tangible fixed assets include land, buildings, equipment, and fixtures and fittings.
Total absorption cost	A process whereby all the costs including fixed costs/overheads of an organisation are allocated to cost centres.
Variable cost	A cost that increases/decreases in line with changes in the level of activity.
Variance	The difference between budgeted and actual income and/or expenditure. Variances are an accounting tool used to analyse the cause of over/under spends with a view to proposing rectifying action.
Working capital	Working capital is the money and assets that an organisation can call upon to finance its day-to-day operations (it is the difference between current assets and liabilities and is reported in the balance sheet as net current assets (liabilities)). If working capital dips too low, organisations risk running out of cash and may need a working capital loan to smooth out the troughs.